THE DEBATE OVER
STABILIZATION POLICY

T0318915

RAFFAELE MATTIOLI FOUNDATION

Franco Modigliani

THE DEBATE OVER STABILIZATION POLICY

The right of th
University of Cambridge
to print and sell
all manner of books
was granted by
Henry VIII in 1534.
The University has printed
and published continuously
since 1584.

CAMBRIDGE UNIVERSITY PRESS

CAMBRIDGE

LONDON   NEW YORK   NEW ROCHELLE

MELBOURNE   SYDNEY

CAMBRIDGE UNIVERSITY PRESS
Cambridge, New York, Melbourne, Madrid, Cape Town,
Singapore, São Paulo, Delhi, Tokyo, Mexico City

Cambridge University Press
The Edinburgh Building, Cambridge CB2 8RU, UK

Published in the United States of America by Cambridge University Press, New York

www.cambridge.org
Information on this title: www.cambridge.org/9780521189705

First published 1986
First paperback edition 2011

A catalogue record for this publication is available from the British Library

Library of Congress Cataloguing in Publication data
Main entry under title:
The Debate over Stabilization Policy.
(Raffaele Mattioli Lectures)
At head of title: Raffaele Mattioli Foundation.
Bibliography: pp. 227-62
1. Economic stabilization – Addresses, essays, lectures.
2. Economic policy – Addresses, essays, lectures.
1. Modigliani, Franco. 11. Raffaele Mattioli Foundation. 111. Series.
HB3732.D43 1984 338.9 84–21366

ISBN 978-0-521-26790-8 Hardback
ISBN 978-0-521-18970-5 Paperback

RAFFAELE MATTIOLI LECTURES

In honour of the memory of Raffaele Mattioli, who was for many years its manager and chairman, Banca Commerciale Italiana has established the Mattioli Fund as a testimony to the continuing survival and influence of his deep interest in economics, the humanities and sciences.

As its first enterprise the Fund has established a series of annual lectures on the history of economic thought, to be called the Raffaele Mattioli Lectures.

In view of the long association between the Bocconi University and Raffaele Mattioli, who was an active scholar, adviser and member of the governing body of the University, it was decided that the lectures in honour of his memory should be delivered at the University, which together with Banca Commerciale Italiana, has undertaken the task of organising them.

Distinguished academics of all nationalities, researchers and others concerned with economic problems will be invited to take part in this enterprise, in the hope of linking pure historical research with a debate on economic theory and practical policy.

In creating a memorial to the cultural legacy left by Raffaele Mattioli, it is hoped above all that these lectures and the debates to which they give rise will prove a fruitful inspiration and starting point for the development of a tradition of research and academic studies like that already long established in other countries, and that this tradition will flourish thanks to the new partnership between the Bocconi University and Banca Commerciale Italiana.

CONTENTS

Function, pp. 127-8. 4. Implications for Propositions 2, 3 and 4, pp. 129-31. 5. Propositions 1 and 5 and the Role of Growth, pp. 132-9. 6. The Role of Bequests, pp. 140-2. 7. Proposition 6, pp. 143-5. 8. The Effect of Pension Funds on Saving, Private and National, pp. 146-62: i) The LCH Perspective, pp. 146-9; ii) Some empirical evidence, pp. 150-7; iii) Replacement versus induced retirement effects, pp. 157-60; iv) Some considerations on the Italian case, pp. 160-2.

CONTENTS

LIST OF FIGURES

LIST OF TABLES

FOREWORD

Today's world poses economic and social problems that can be tackled with some hopes of success only because of the awareness which stems from understanding history, the history of events and ideas. And history, in turn, acquires meaning and relevance from the issues and challenges of the present seen in the light of economic theory.

This complementary relationship between history of economic thought and the present, between culture and action – which was at the heart of Raffaele Mattioli's personality – represents the inspiring principle of these Lectures, which have been named after him. And it is in this light that we should see the significance of the partnership between a highly prestigious bank – which I wish to thank for its whole-hearted commitment to this enterprise – and our University.

Raffaele Mattioli was a great banker because he married the concrete responsibility of day-to-day decisions to the far-sightedness of his personal vision. His love for research, books and history was an integral part of his personality as an entrepreneur because it fostered his ability to take a long-term perspective and stimulated the innovative drive with which he was naturally endowed.

Because of his intellectual and human endowments, Raffaele Mattioli embodied the growth of the city of Milan, which proceeded hand in hand with the development of Lombardy's economic activities and cultural life, in all its different forms, including the foundation and growth of our Free University.

The issues examined in the present Lectures, as well as in the forthcoming ones, are not to be seen as over-sophisticated erudite reflections, on either a given period of the history of economic thought or certain economic theories, but rather as an invitation to ponder closely and directly linked to today's worrisome problems. It is as if Raffaele Mattioli were working here with us and we were discussing with him both as a scholar and as an experienced man of action.

The topic of the present series of Lectures – the problems associated with monetary theory and stabilization policies – fits well in the perspective sketched above. It is an issue where the analyses of economists and topical aspects of the political and institutional debate have always been intertwined: it will suffice to remind ourselves of Ricardo and of the debate in Great Britain throughout the first half of the nineteenth century. It is an issue that goes back a long way and is of great theoretical interest; yet, at the same time, it is essential for understanding and interpreting the history of political decisions and of the resulting responses and expectations. The topic of the present Lectures has given rise to a vast literature and to extensive debates which, especially in the last two decades, have become increasingly intense and a constant source of controversy, sometimes even excessive, but always stimulating.

In order to follow this line in the history of economic thought (which, in part, is very recent and, hence, not yet settled) and in order to survey the different theses, arguments and supporting evidence, we need an expert and safe guide. There can be no doubt that we have one such guide in Franco Modigliani who, in developing the theme of these Lectures, can give us a first-hand account of his experiences as one of the most prolific and original contributors to modern macroeconomics. Almost forty years ago, by undertaking a fundamental work of interpretation, he was among those who took up Keynes' legacy. Ever since he has untiringly pursued his research, always at the forefront of inquiry and knowledge. But Professor Modigliani's fame and scientific standing do not need further introduction; I would rather take this opportunity, on behalf of the Lectures' Scientific

Committee to thank him for having accepted our invitation and for having devoted his energy to the preparation of the Lectures.

Already in the very first Lecture, Professor Modigliani directly examines the debate between monetarists and Keynesians and the question of whether or not it is advisable that the authorities should take an "activist" stance when attempting to stabilize the economic cycle. This is a fascinating issue which, although dating back to debates preceding Keynes's own work, remains very topical. It is a diatribe which at times seems to subside or to take an altogether different tone, but then is rekindled with increased intensity, assuming once again a centre-stage position in the debate on economic policy.

As we all know, Professor Modigliani has never taken a neutral stand on this issue and here he will certainly not refrain from arguing his case. But only someone who, like him, has taken an active role in the debate, exploring all its complexities, can find an original way of summarizing the whole debate. And he will do so with clarity and balance, providing us with valuable insights which will enable us to follow the evolution of the debate itself.

Professor Modigliani's Lectures are structured in such a way that the theme of monetary theory and stabilization policies is examined not only from a wide general perspective, but also from specific analytic angles; the third and fourth Lectures, for example, deal respectively with the role of the structure of the financial system and with the problem of the formation of savings. The fact that Professor Modigliani himself has contributed to these areas of research lends his Lectures a special liveliness and interest, though the published version takes place a few years after their actual delivery.[1]

To conclude this brief introduction, I wish to express again the gratitude of the Bocconi University towards the Banca Commerciale Italiana which, through this venture, allows us to honour the memory of its former Chairman. I also wish to thank the many people attending the Lectures who turn this periodic meeting into a lively, wide-ranging and constructive debate. Their valu-

---

1. A number of changes have been made to the text of the Lectures delivered in 1977.

able contribution is witnessed by their comments on Professor Modigliani's Lectures, which are to be found at the end of his text together with his precise replies.

These Lectures represent the first stage of a dialogue which is going to reverberate not only throughout our University, enriching both our research and our teaching, but also in wider circles.

INNOCENZO GASPARINI
Rector
Luigi Bocconi University

FRANCO MODIGLIANI

THE DEBATE OVER
STABILIZATION POLICY

The four *Raffaele Mattioli Lectures* were delivered by Franco Modigliani at the
Luigi Bocconi University, in Milan, from 3rd to 7th October 1977.

FIRST LECTURE
Keynesianism, Monetarism, and the Case
for and against Active Stabilization Policies

*1. From the Keynesian Revolution to the Monetarist Counter-revolution. –
2. Where are the Real Differences between Monetarists and Non-Monetarists? –
3. Demand Shocks and Determinants of the Response of the System. – 4. Keynesian Assessment and Implications. – 5. The Initial Monetarist Attack. –
6. Empirical Evidence on the Critical Parameters. – 7. Wage-Price Behaviour
and the Phillips Curve. – 8. The Monetarist View of the Wage-Price Mechanism. – 9. The Macro Rational Expectations Salient. – 10. Criticism of the
Monetarist Paradigm. – 11. Sketch of an Alternative View of the Labour
Market and why it adjusts sluggishly. – 12. Implications of the Wage-Price
Mechanism for the Stability of the System. – 13. The Experience with Stabilization Policies. – 14. Concluding Remarks.*

1. From the Keynesian Revolution to the Monetarist Counter-revolution

I entered the world of economics in 1939 when John Maynard
Keynes' *General Theory*[1] was revolutionizing economics and the
economic profession was dividing into two schools. On one side
were those who espoused the "new gospel" and on the other
side those who appeared too old to change. For a substantial

NOTE: *Professor Modigliani introduced his Lectures with the following remarks:*

I should like to express my thanks for the honour bestowed on me by the invitation to inaugurate this series of Mattioli Lectures. It is an honour I have accepted
not without hesitation, being fully aware of the responsibility that goes with it.
My acceptance is above all my way of paying tribute to the memory of Raffaele
Mattioli. I only met him for the first time during the 1960s, the first of only two
meetings. However, I carry a vivid recollection of him from these meetings: a truly
unique personality from whom, in a few minutes, I learned more about the Italian
banking system as it was and as it should have been, than from all my reading. I
hope that these lectures will befit the occasion.

I must warn at the outset that I am not, by inclination, an historian of economic
thought. What I will be talking about is a very special kind of history of doctrines,
it is the history that I have lived through.

1. JOHN MAYNARD KEYNES, *The General Theory of Employment, Interest and Money*.
London: Macmillan, 1936 (see also RICHARD F. KAHN, *The Making of Keynes' General
Theory*, Raffaele Mattioli Lectures. Cambridge: Cambridge University Press, 1984).

3

period of time, virtually no one among the new generation had any doubt about the fundamental contribution of Keynes either to the theoretical or economic policy level.

However, it was not long before monetarists began a counter-attack for which the major credit, or perhaps responsibility, clearly lies with Milton Friedman. This counterattack was conducted in a masterly fashion and with some help from the oil crisis, it has, by now, put the Keynesian paradigm on the defensive, if not in retreat.

There is no doubt that monetarism is an important doctrine with both good and bad sides. On the good side it has called attention to many shortcomings of Keynesian orthodoxy and led to the re-examination of conclusions that were taken for granted. However, on the negative side it is threatening to sweep away many valid and vital contributions of the Keynesian revolution. This is partly the result of the appealing simplicity of its basic message: all our macroeconomic problems can be traced to a single cause – mismanagement of monetary policy – and they would fade away if only the growth of the money supply were controlled by a simple, mechanical rule. Naturally, sophisticated monetarists might not subscribe to that message without quali-fications. Yet, they seem to regard it as a useful simplification, for mass consumption, justified by the consideration that, even if a constant growth of money would not produce a perfect world, it would produce at least the best of all possible worlds.

The spread of "monetarism for the masses" has been signifi-cant, and in my view has had prevailingly undesirable effects on the conduct of monetary policy. I believe, for example, that it is largely responsible for the serious contraction that developed in the course of 1974 and that led to a peak unemployment of around 9 per cent in the spring of 1975. To a major extent, though not exclusively, that contraction was the result of the decision of the Federal Reserve Bank not to allow money to expand at a higher rate than the 6 to 7 per cent which it had established at the beginning of the year on the basis of monet-arist criteria. That same attitude has prevented a more rapid expansion during the first two years of the recovery. It has also interfered with a vigorous recovery of badly needed investment.

In order to accommodate rigid limits on money supply growth, stimulating fiscal policy has been relied upon time after time to support output instead of relying on a combination of tighter fiscal policy and easier monetary policy in order to encourage investment.

Thus the purpose of this lecture is to endeavour to clarify the basic differences that divide monetarists from Keynesians, or more generally from non-monetarist macroeconomists, both in terms of analysis and of practical policy prescriptions.

2. Where are the Real Differences between Monetarists and Non-Monetarists?

There is a commonly held view that the basic difference between the alternative schools is that Keynesians believe that money has little effect on aggregate demand and only government expenditure matters, whereas monetarists hold that what matters is money and only money. It is my contention that this difference is at best of secondary importance, a matter of emphasis rather than of principle. Neither of the schools denies – except for a few extremists – that, in principle, both monetary and fiscal policy have an effect on money and real income at least for some time. Similarly, monetarists and many non-monetarists largely agree that, in the long run, neither public expenditure nor the quantity of money will have a permanent effect on real income, and that, for a given initial impact, the long-run effect of money on money income will be larger than that of public expenditure.

What then are the true and essential differences between monetarists and non-monetarists that show themselves in the perennial, frequently sharp, differences in advice offered to policy makers, and which have greatly contributed to undermine the public confidence in the competence of the economic profession?

I have suggested elsewhere,[1] that the basic difference is that non-monetarists accept what I regard as the fundamental practical message of the *General Theory*, that a market economy is subject to fluctuations in aggregate output, unemployment and prices, which *need* to be corrected, *can* be corrected, and therefore *should* be corrected. Monetarists on the other hand hold that there is *no real need* to stabilize the economy as long as the growth of the money supply follows a simple predictable rule, that even if there were a need we *do not have* the ability to stabilize it, and that even if we could stabilize it we should *not trust* the authorities with the necessary discretionary power.

1. FRANCO MODIGLIANI, 'The Monetarist Controversy or, Should We Forsake Stabilization Policies?', Presidential Address delivered at the American Economic Association, 17th September 1976, *American Economic Review*, vol. 67 (2), March 1977, pp. 1-19; reprinted in MODIGLIANI, vol. 1, pp. 3-21.

It is my contention that these basic and overriding differences of attitude toward the need for stabilization policies and the proper role of government do not arise from *analytical* differences, but can be traced instead primarily both to differences in *empirical assessments* concerning the value of certain crucial parameters of the system and of their stability, and to no less a degree to differences in *social philosophy and attitudes*.

The different assessment of parameters leads, in the first place, to divergent judgements about the stability of the system in the absence of stabilization policies, both in terms of its disposition to disturbances and with respect to the magnitude and length of the response to such disturbances. In particular, for monetarists, the time required for the system, once disturbed, to return to its "long-run equilibrium" is measured in quarters if not in months. For non-monetarists, the long run is a matter of years not of months. In addition, monetarists believe the relevant parameters to be far from stable and hence question the possibility of predicting, with sufficient accuracy, the magnitude and timing of the response of the system to stabilization policies.

With respect to the differences in social philosophy, I suggest that monetarists on the whole are characterized by a profound mistrust for government and of government authority which permeates all of their views. Governments tend to be dishonest or, at least, self-serving and short-sighted and in any event are too inept to be trusted to use correctly discretionary power in the pursuit of difficult stabilization policies. Hence, they should not be entrusted with that responsibility or endowed with the necessary power.

In this first lecture I intend to examine both at the analytical and at the empirical level the issue of the need for, and the feasibility of, effective stabilization policies. However, my concern will be entirely with the problems created by demand shocks (to be defined presently). The problems posed by the so-called supply shocks will be dealt with in the second lecture.

On the basis of this evidence, I hope to establish that the monetarists' position must be rejected, even while acknowledging that much has been learned from their counterattack and that many of their reservations must be borne in mind.

7

3. Demand Shocks and Determinants of the Response of the System

It may be convenient to define a Keynesian demand shock along monetarist lines as any disturbance of the system that has the effect of changing significantly the level of aggregate nominal output consistent with any given money supply (or equivalently, the level of real output consistent with any real money supply). A shock can be described as positive if it increases aggregate output relative to the money supply. Clearly in monetarist terminology a positive demand shock is one that has the effect of increasing the velocity of circulation at the initial output level.

A simple example of a demand shock in this sense is provided by the case of a shift in the demand for money. In the United States, for instance, we have experienced in recent years a large and persistent decline in the demand for money as a result of changes in regulations as well as of financial innovations. Such a decline increases velocity and thus constitutes a positive demand shock. However, once we take into account liquidity preference (Keynes' great contribution to monetary theory), it must be acknowledged that demand shocks may also arise from disturbances to many real equations of the system. For example, a decrease in the propensity to invest, or a decrease in the propensity to consume and consequent increase in the propensity to save, constitutes a negative demand shock because it will tend to result in a fall in interest rates which, through liquidity preference, either raises the demand for money or lowers velocity, reducing the level of output consistent with a given real money supply. A change in exports, or in government expenditure, or in the propensity to import are other examples of demand shocks. In short, liquidity preference translates real disturbances into changes in velocity or demand shocks.

It should be acknowledged at this point that the mechanism that links real to monetary disturbances is not independent of the financial structure and monetary institutions of the economy. Liquidity preference may be regarded as the appropriate link in an economy like that of the United States which is characterized by complex financial markets and by stringent regulations on in-

8

terest on demand deposits. As will be shown in the third lecture, this formulation may not be equally appropriate in other economies. Nonetheless, it is generally the case that real disturbances will shift the relation between aggregate output and whatever the monetary authority controls in order to control aggregate money demand and output. For the moment, I will concentrate on the mechanism which is relevant to the United States and similar economies.

How will the system respond to a demand shock? The answer essentially depends on the response of wages and prices to positive or negative excess demand. If prices and wages are fully flexible, i.e., if they rise and fall quickly in response to positive or negative excess demand, or deviations from full employment, then demand shocks will not affect output and employment, except for a short time, as the change in wages and prices will produce the change in real money supply necessary to make it consistent with full-employment output and the new velocity.

Even in this case of high wage-price flexibility, liquidity preference has an important implication for the stabilization policy debate, for it implies that a passive monetary policy of the monetarist type could result in substantial instability in the price level. (A close examination of the social costs of unanticipated inflation, or deflation, will be undertaken in the Second Lecture). In the meantime, it suffices to recall that a modern economy relies heavily on long-term nominal contracts. Price-level instability makes it impossible to incorporate into such contracts a correct forecast of the course of prices over the life of the contract, which results in inequities and inefficiencies. Thus, with the occurrence of significant demand shocks and velocity changes, there is, in principle, a clear need for stabilization policies – monetary or, indeed, fiscal – even when wages and prices are quite responsive to positive as well as negative excess demand.

However, the effect of demand shocks is far more drastic in the presence of wage and price rigidities. Keynes himself[1] concentrated in particular on an extreme case, that is to say the

---

1. JOHN MAYNARD KEYNES, *The General Theory of Employment, Interest and Money.*

case in which wages are completely flexible in the face of excess demand, and absolutely rigid in the face of excess supply or unemployment. According to this assumption, positive supply shocks again have a limited and temporary effect on output as they lead quickly to the change in price levels required to produce the required decrease in the real money supply. Nonetheless in the case of negative demand shocks, rigidity of nominal wages implies that there is little scope, if any, for prices to adjust downwards and thus produce the increase in the real money supply required to accommodate the shock. Thus, a negative demand shock must result eventually in a contraction of output. Furthermore the lower output is permanent (Keynes' "permanent" unemployment) in the sense that there is no exogenous "mechanism" that could be relied on to produce the expansion of real money supply needed to re-establish full employment. In monetarist terminology the demand shock results in a fall in velocity and hence a decline in aggregate nominal expenditure – and in real income if prices are fixed.

It must be recognized, however, that the extent of contraction in output (or decline in velocity) resulting from a given demand shock depends on the value of certain crucial parameters of the system, a conclusion that can be readily established from the classic IS-LM paradigm of John R. Hicks.[1] Indeed because of the presence of amplifying and offsetting mechanisms, it could range from a fraction of the shock to a substantial multiple of it. There are three essential parameters:

i) The marginal propensity to save or its reciprocal, "the multiplier". The larger the multiplier, the larger will be the response of output to a given demand disturbance, and hence the more unstable the system.

ii) The elasticity of aggregate demand with respect to the interest rate or required rate of return on capital. The greater the elasticity of demand the larger the offset to the initial shock that will be produced by the fall in interest rates resulting from

---

1. JOHN R. HICKS, 'Mr. Keynes and the "Classics"; A Suggested Interpretation', *Econometrica*, vol. 5 (2), April 1937, pp. 147-59; reprinted in JOHN R. HICKS, *Critical Essays in Monetary Theory*. Oxford: Clarendon Press, 1967, pp. 126-42.

a given fall in income and velocity. Thus, a higher elasticity implies a smaller response of income to demand shocks.

iii) The elasticity of demand for money with respect to interest rates. If the elasticity is small, a decline in velocity will tend to be accompanied by a large change in interest rates which will increase demand and tend to offset the initial disturbance. An inelastic demand for money is thus also stabilizing.

The above applies to "real" demand shocks. The case of "money" demand shocks is quite different. Here a low elasticity of demand for money is destabilizing because to offset an exogenous decline in velocity a large increase in interest rates would be required, which in turn would adversely affect output. Similarly, a higher elasticity of demand with respect to interest rates is also destabilizing since the change in interest rates called for by a higher demand for money would give rise to a larger change in output.

The fundamental assertion of the *General Theory* was that these destabilizing effects of demand shocks could be readily offset by appropriate stabilization policies. These policies could generally take either one of two basic forms. First, monetary policy could be used to offset the effect of the shock by increasing the nominal, and hence the real, money supply to the extent necessary to accommodate full-employment output. Alternatively government expenditure could be expanded to the extent necessary to offset the decline in demand produced by the shock. Initially, attention tended to concentrate on one particular type of fiscal policy, that is to say government expenditure, but it was soon realized that demand could be equally increased by other types of fiscal policy such as tax reductions and tax incentives.

4. Keynesian Assessment and Implications

The early Keynesians, partly under the influence of the Great Depression, tended to share the view that the system was subject to large and capricious demand shocks, and that the value of the critical parameters were such to produce large responses to given shocks.

There was, in the first place, a commonly held view that the demand for money was highly interest-elastic. In fact the extremely low interest rates experienced in the late 1930s gave rise to a serious concern with the Keynesian liquidity trap, that is to say a situation in which the elasticity of demand for money is, essentially, indefinitely large. Thus, the velocity of circulation was regarded as very unstable and largely accommodating the fluctuations in output caused by demand shocks. At the same time, demand was not regarded as significantly affected in a systematic way by variations in the rate of interest. The extreme form of this view was the notion that investment was largely controlled by "animal spirits", rather than by rational calculations based on the cost of capital.

The situation with respect to the propensity to save is somewhat more complex because of a failure to distinguish between the long- and the short-run propensity. As a result, the long-run propensity was overestimated, justifying disquiet about oversaving and long-run stagnation, while at the same time the short-run propensity was conspicuously underestimated and, accordingly, the short-run multiplier was overestimated.

Given these views, it is not surprising that there was a rather general, if perhaps uncritical, acceptance of the view that the economy needed stabilizing and that this could be done with the instruments suggested by Keynes. Furthermore, just as the above assessment of the values of the relevant parameters implied a strong responsiveness of aggregate output to demand shocks, so it implied a strong responsiveness of demand to government expenditure (or more generally to fiscal policy actions) but only a weak and uncertain response to monetary policy. This is the origin of the popular generalization that in the Keynesian view output can be effectively controlled only through fiscal policy. A more accurate view is that the Keynesians tended to favour fiscal policy as a stabilization tool because they regarded it as more reliable.

5. The Initial Monetarist Attack

When monetarists began their counterattack, the dominant Keynesian orthodoxy had become so strong that their criticism tended to be viewed as an utterly absurd rejection of the whole Keynesian analysis. It is, however, more accurate and enlightening to view it as a criticism from within the same basic framework, perhaps because monetarists felt that they could be most effective by placing their theory within the dominant framework. Monetarists certainly rejected the idea that there was a clear need for stabilizing the system but this rejection can be seen as resting on a radically different assessment of the very same parameters on which the Keynesians based their case. (This, of course, does not rule out the possibility that the monetarist assessment of parameters was influenced by their *a priori* belief that the system had to be fairly stable).

Firstly, for the system to be stable with real demand shocks, the demand for money must be very inelastic. Indeed, Friedman, in a well-known paper,[1] proceeded to establish, by means of rather unusual techniques, that the effect of interest rates on the demand for money which he had acknowledged, in principle, in another famous contribution,[2] was in practice so negligible that it could not be detected.

Secondly, they contended that aggregate demand was in fact quite sensitive to interest rates. To support this conclusion they pointed not only to components of demand generally acknowledged as sensitive to interest rates, such as plant and equipment, but also to many other components, including even consumption. Moreover they maintained that the transmission occurs in part through interest rates other than those measured explicitly in financial markets.

The combination of interest-insensitive velocity and interest-sensitive real demand ensured that real demand shocks would

1. MILTON FRIEDMAN, 'The Demand for Money: Some Theoretical and Empirical Results', *Journal of Political Economy*, vol. 67 (4), August 1959, pp. 327-51.

2. MILTON FRIEDMAN, 'The Quantity Theory of Money: A Restatement', in MILTON FRIEDMAN (ed.), *Studies in the Quantity Theory of Money*. Chicago: University of Chicago Press, 1956, pp. 3-21.

have very limited effects on output. In addition, monetarists rejected the view that the economy was subject to large and capricious shocks. Even the traumatic experience of the Great Depression was no evidence of the ruinous effects of momentous shocks, because it could be readily accounted for as the consequence of costly errors of the monetary authority in permitting the money supply to shrink greatly and for an extended period. Furthermore erroneous money supply management could be largerly blamed even for the smaller post-war fluctuations.

Certainly a combination of low elasticity of demand for money and high elasticity of demand for output with respect to interest rates implies that the system is unstable with respect to shocks in the demand for money. However, this was of little consequence because, in the monetarist assessment, the demand for money is held to be quite stable.

These assessments imply that the effects of fiscal policy, like any other real shock, are small and temporary, whereas the effects of changes in money are large and permanent. However, this implication was not emphasized by monetarists who were mainly interested in promoting the view that there was no need to use *any* stabilization tools, rather than in finding the most effective instruments for stabilizing the economy. From their point of view the essential implication of their empirical assessment was that the velocity of circulation was quite stable. This conclusion established the basis for the monetarist contention that, provided only the money supply was kept on a steady course, output could be relied on not to stray far from full employment. The only additional appropriate role for government policy was to bring about some simple *structural* reforms which would have resulted in shifting parameters in a stabilizing direction – the so-called built-in stabilizers. Beyond that there was little *need* for discretionary stabilization policies. Moreover, such policies were unworkable. In fact there was enough instability in the critical parameters and in particular in the lag structure to make it impossible to assess the magnitude and timing of response of the system to the "shocks" of stabilization policies with the accuracy necessary to offset exogenous disturbances successfully. Furthermore the problem of variable lags could be exacerbated even further by variable "inside lags", i.e., the recognition lag between occurrence of the shock and the realization of a need to counteract it, and the lag between recognition and policy action. Under these conditions discretionary policy was more likely to increase than to reduce the instability of the system.

6. Empirical Evidence on the Critical Parameters

Over the last two decades a substantial amount of evidence has been accumulating, partly through econometric models, which permits some tentative conclusions to be drawn as to where the truth lies between the contrasting assessments. In so doing, I will rely in part on the MPS model (MIT-Penn-Social Science Research Council), which has been conceived and estimated with my participation. I propose to show that this evidence unmistakably supports the monetarist position – but only up to a point. The estimated values of the parameters imply a far less unstable economy than assumed by the early Keynesians, but still not a very stable one.

Firstly, with respect to the multiplier, extensive analysis of the consumption function has established that the short-run or cyclical propensity to consume tends to be very much lower than the long-run one. This can be deduced from an empirically validated model such as the "ratchet" effect of the Duesenberry[1] and Modigliani[2] consumption function or from models resting on firmer microeconomic foundations such as the permanent income hypothesis of Milton Friedman[3] or the Life Cycle Model of Modigliani-Brumberg-Ando.[4] With current consumption determined by expected resources over life, short-run variations in income, caused in particular by shocks, will be largely absorbed

1. James S. Duesenberry, *Income, Saving, and the Theory of Consumer Behavior.* Cambridge, Mass.: Harvard University Press, 1949.
2. Franco Modigliani, 'Fluctuations in the Saving-Income Ratio: A Problem in Economic Forecasting' (Paper prepared in connection with a Research Project of the Institute of World Affairs and presented at the Conference on Research in Income and Wealth); in *Studies in Income and Wealth,* vol. xi. New York: National Bureau of Economic Research, 1949, pp. 371-443; Sections i-vii (pp. 371-402) and xiii (pp. 427-31) reprinted in Modigliani, vol. 2, pp. 3-40.
3. Milton Friedman, *A Theory of the Consumption Function.* Princeton, N. J.: Princeton University Press, 1957.
4. Franco Modigliani and Albert Ando, 'The Relative Stability of Monetary Velocity and the Investment Multiplier', *American Economic Review,* vol. 55 (4), September 1965, pp. 693-728; Franco Modigliani, 'The life cycle hypothesis of saving twenty years later', in Michael Parkin and A. Robert Nobay (eds.), *Contemporary Issues in Economics.* Manchester: Manchester University Press, 1975, pp. 2-36; reprinted in Modigliani, vol. 2, pp. 41-75 (especially Sections 5 and 8).

into saving. When further allowances are made for the high marginal income tax rate prevailing in the United States as well as in many other countries, and for the propensity to import it is found that, even for a relatively closed economy like the United States', the relevant short-run marginal propensity to consume is below one half, implying a multiplier of less than two.

Secondly, with respect to the demand for money, a series of theoretical contributions by Baumol,[1] Tobin[2] and Miller-Orr[3] has suggested that the elasticity of demand with respect to (short-term) interest rates should be somewhere between one half and one third, and this conclusion is supported by a considerable amount of empirical evidence. This is not a large elasticity, though it still allows for substantial variation in velocity, given the variability of short-term rates. Finally, there is ample evidence to support the monetarists' contention that interest rates have a marked and pervasive effect on demand. In the MPS model, for example, this effect extends well beyond the traditional area of plant, equipment and residential housing to reach almost every component of demand. In particular, interest rates affect the market value of consumers' net worth, through the capitalization of the return from assets and, through this process, an expansion of the money supply tends to have a significant direct expansionary impact on consumption.

However, while these estimates of the parameters are inconsistent with the view that the economy is highly unstable, nevertheless they turn out to imply that the response to shocks is far from negligible. According to the MPS, for example, a persistent $ 1,000m exogenous demand shock – a decline in exports or government expenditure – has a substantial and permanent effect on output, even though the money supply is kept constant. The initial effect is moderate, in the same order of magnitude

1. WILLIAM J. BAUMOL, 'The Transactions Demand for Cash: An Inventory Theoretic Approach', *Quarterly Journal of Economics*, vol. 66 (4), November 1952, pp. 545-56.

2. JAMES TOBIN, *Essays in Economics. Volume 1: Macroeconomics*. Amsterdam: North-Holland, 1971.

3. MERTON H. MILLER and DANIEL ORR, 'A Model of Demand for Money by Firms', *Quarterly Journal of Economics*, vol. 80 (3), August 1966, pp. 413-35.

as the shock itself. However, the effect grows larger for a while, partly because of gradual responses and partly through acceleration effects, reaching a peak of about two by the second year. It then declines slowly toward a "permanent" effect of approximately $ 1,500m. However, in an economy which was very open these figures might be expected to be smaller because of "leakages" through foreign trade.

7. Wage-Price Behaviour and the Phillips Curve

Until the late 1950s both the analysis and the empirical results cited above had maintained the Keynesian hypothesis of complete or, at any rate, extreme downward wage rigidity. This view, however, soon gave way to new empirical evidence such as that set forth in the influential article by Phillips[1] suggesting that nominal wages did, after all, respond to excess demand as measured by the rate of unemployment. These results, which soon came to be labelled "the Phillips Curve", gained ready acceptance because they were compatible with the standard assumption of dynamic analysis that excess demand results in price increases. Yet they had fairly dramatic implications for the strict Keynesian paradigm, even though probably these implications had not been fully appreciated in the beginning.

In the first place acceptance of the Phillips Curve implied that the notion of a well defined "full employment and associated 'equilibrium unemployment'" had to be abandoned. The policy makers could now choose their preferred rate of "permanent" unemployment out of a selection represented by all points on the Phillips Curve provided, of course, they were also prepared to accept the associated permanent rate of inflation (and were prepared to accommodate it by an appropriate rate of monetary expansion). When shortly thereafter Lipsey[2] generalized the Phillips Curve by showing that the rate of change of wages responded also to the received rate of inflation, the notion of a trade-off between unemployment and inflation became more complex. A distinction now had to be made between a more "favourable" short-run and a steeper long-run trade-off which reflected the feedback of wages on prices as well as of prices on wages.

1. ALBAN W. PHILLIPS, 'The Relation between Unemployment and the Rate of Change of Money Wage Rates in the United Kingdom, 1861-1957', *Economica*, vol. 25 (100), November 1958, pp. 283-99.

2. RICHARD G. LIPSEY, 'The Relation between Unemployment and the Rate of Change of Money Wage Rates in the United Kingdom, 1861-1957: A Further Analysis', *Economica*, vol. 27 (105), February 1960, pp. 1-31.

Acceptance of the Phillips-Lipsey Curve also meant abandoning the Keynesian notion that a negative demand shock would cause a "permanent" rise in unemployment. Certainly, starting from a given unemployment rate and associated growth of the money supply, a negative demand shock could initially increase unemployment; yet, provided the money supply growth was maintained, the unemployment was bound to return to the initial level. For, as long as unemployment remained above that level, wages and prices would be rising more slowly than money (adjusted if necessary for productivity trend) causing a rise in the real money supply and thereby a reduction of unemployment, until the shock had been fully accommodated.

However, despite these theoretical implications, the Phillips-Lipsey Curve did not appreciably weaken the case for active stabilization policies. Indeed, even though the Phillips Curve mechanism might eventually re-establish full employment, there was no reason to wait for this to happen. If anything, the scope for stabilization policies seemed to expand, for, as noted earlier, in choosing an employment target, policy makers seemed no longer constrained by a unique full-employment rate beyond which lay hidden an unsustainable price explosion.

8. The Monetarist View of the Wage-Price Mechanism

The monetarist view of the wage-price mechanism reached its full development in the second half of the 1960s in connection with an all-out attack on the Phillips Curve and in particular on its implication of a wide discretion for policy makers in the choice of employment targets. Once again the attack was led by Milton Friedman[1] though similar ideas were set forth simultaneously by Edmund S. Phelps.[2]

Friedman rejects completely the hypothesis of rigidity or even sluggishness of nominal wages and the associated notion of "involuntary" unemployment, and supports his claim by a brilliant re-interpretation of the Phillips-Lipsey evidence aimed at showing that this evidence is in reality perfectly consistent with wage flexibility.

According to his classical paradigm of competition the labour market can be described by: i) a classical demand function for labour which is a decreasing function of the current real wage, defined as the ratio of the nominal wage rate to the price level, and ii) a supply of labour which is an increasing function of the "perceived" real wage defined as the ratio of the currently offered nominal wage to the "expected" price level. The labour market always clears in the sense that the nominal wage, employment and prices are determined by the intersection of these demand and supply functions, in conjunction with a third function, the monetarist-Keynesian aggregate demand function relating aggregate nominal demand to the money supply. Naturally, for a given money supply the short-run equilibrium level of wages and prices so determined is an increasing function, and the level of employment a *decreasing* function, of price expectations. In terms of this construct, a "long-run" equilibrium level of employment can be identified as the level which would be generated by the market if and when the expectation of the

1. MILTON FRIEDMAN, 'The Role of Monetary Policy', *American Economic Review*, vol. 58 (1), March 1968, pp. 1-17.

2. EDMUND S. PHELPS, 'Money-Wage Dynamics and Labor-Market Equilibrium', *Journal of Political Economy*, vol. 76 (4, Part II), July-August 1968, pp. 678-711.

price level on which the supply of labour was based coincided with the actual price level, i.e., when there were no errors of expectations. This unique equilibrium level of employment – and the associated unemployment rate – is Friedman's famous "natural rate", a concept which in the final analysis broadly coincides with Keynes' "full employment".

It is obvious that in this world of Friedman, actual employment can differ from full employment, but only because of errors of expectations. In particular, suppose that, starting from full employment, there occurs a negative demand shock requiring for the maintenance of full employment a rise in the real money supply and hence an appropriate fall in prices, expected prices and nominal wages. The shock initially would lower prices and wages, but because initially the decline in prices could not be reflected in price expectations, it would generate a decline in the perceived real wage and a rise in the effective real wage which would result in a fall of employment. Thus aggregate nominal demand, prices and employment would be observed all falling together. A positive demand shock would produce the symmetrical opposite reaction. Friedman argues that it is this kind of association that is recorded by the Phillips Curve. Indeed, if the reasonable assumption is made that expected inflation is largely determined by recent inflation, then the Friedman-Phelps model can readily account for the Lipsey-type association between the current rate of change of prices, the past rate of change and the rate of employment. However, the previously accepted interpretation is turned upside down; it is not that excessive labour demand and employment causes inflation – it is rather that (unexpected) inflation causes excessive employment.

This reinterpretation has wide-ranging policy implications. It implies that policy makers could not hope to make use of the Phillips Curve trade-off which is merely a statistical illusion. For employment could be kept away from the natural rate only by indefinitely maintained expectational errors – a conclusion which would not be desirable or even possible. In particular, if the expectations of inflation are largely shaped by past inflation, then a policy-induced expansion of aggregate demand could raise initially employment above the natural rate, at the cost of some initial inflation, by deceiving workers into working more, in the belief that they were offered higher real wages. However, if inflation was kept constant at that level, expected inflation would soon rise toward that level causing employment to move back to the natural rate. Thus the deviation of employment from equilibrium depends not on the rate of inflation but on the (unexpected) *increase* in the rate of inflation – the so called accelerationist hypothesis. Following from this, as long as aggregate demand and prices rise at a *constant* rate, no matter how high, employment must tend toward the natural rate – the so-called long-run vertical Phillips Curve.

This last conclusion in turn provides a powerful addition to the earlier monetarist conclusion that stabilization policies are not needed or, in fact, possible. In view of the stability of velocity a stable growth of the money supply insures a stable growth of nominal demand and hence a stable and predictable rate of inflation. Therefore, with little opportunity for expectational errors, employment can be relied upon not to deviate widely or for long from the natural rate. Furthermore, the variations in employment around the natural rate, though undesirable because they result from errors, should not be viewed with excessive concern because they do not reflect the availability of jobs. They only reflect voluntary variations in the labour supply in response to actual or perceived movements of the real wage.

On the other hand attempts by policy makers to stabilize the economy at any particular level (or path) of output and employment would only bring disaster; for the only target consistent with a stable rate of inflation (zero or otherwise) is the natural rate. However, the natural rate is a "knife-edge", and is subject to variations over time, and attempts at enforcing any other target could only result in cumulative inflation or deflation.

9. The Macro Rational Expectations Salient

The argument outlined above has recently provided the basis for a "palace revolution" within the monetarist camp that may be labelled the "Macro Rational Expectations" (MRE) movement.[1] It adheres to the basic monetarist tenet that stabilization policies are unnecessary but goes well beyond monetarism in so far as it asserts that such policies, and monetary policy in particular, are impotent if they are fully anticipated, in the sense that they are altogether incapable of affecting output – a conclusion which, understandably, even mainstream monetarists find difficult to support.

These surprising conclusions are established by adding to the monetarist belief that deviation of employment from the natural rate can only be caused by expectational errors the further assumption that expectations are *rational* in the sense developed by John Muth.[2]

Muth's contribution was a very fundamental one. He criticized earlier theorizing which assumed an optimizing response of economic agents to given expectations but then relied on naive or *ad hoc* assumptions with respect to the formation of these expectations. He argued that rational behaviour must extend to the formation of expectations, and essentially defined rational expectations as forecasts representing the best possible statistical inference that economic agents could derive from all the available information. Muth proceeded to make interesting use of his hypothesis for individual commodity markets and his approach has found many further useful applications to highly organized auction markets, such as certain financial markets. However, the MRE school makes an unqualified extension of this scheme to

1. ROBERT E. LUCAS JR., 'Expectations and the Neutrality of Money', *Journal of Economic Theory*, vol. 4 (2), April 1972, pp. 103-24; THOMAS J. SARGENT and NEIL WALLACE, ' "Rational" Expectations, the Optimal Monetary Instrument, and the Optimal Money Supply Rule', *Journal of Political Economy*, vol. 83 (2), April 1975, pp. 241-54; THOMAS J. SARGENT, 'A Classical Macroeconometric Model for the United States', *Journal of Political Economy*, vol. 84 (2), April 1976, pp. 207-38.
2. JOHN F. MUTH, 'Rational Expectations and the Theory of Price Movements', *Econometrica*, vol. 29 (3), July 1961, pp. 315-35.

the expectations of *macroeconomic* variables, such as the price level, without taking into account the extremely imperfect and highly heterogeneous nature of the labour market. Acceptance of this postulate does not rule out deviations of employment from the "natural" rate, because rational forecasts can still be erroneous, but does imply that such deviations must be short-lived and self-correcting because rational expectation errors cannot be systematically autocorrelated.

The proposition that fully anticipated monetary policy is powerless is also derived by adding to the rational expectation postulate one further assumption, namely that the classical quantity theory of money holds instantaneously (except for expectational errors) and is therefore also incorporated into the macroeconomic model used by the public to form rational expectations. As a result, an announced change in the money supply results in an equi-proportional increase in the expected price level, with the result that the price level itself must rise by the same proportion, leaving output unchanged irrespective of however far output might deviate from the natural rate. With respect to unanticipated changes in money supply, they can have an impact on output, but only by deceiving the public. Accordingly, they could be stabilizing only if the government forecasts of shocks and their implications were superior to those of the economy, which is impossible by the very nature of rational expectations. Thus while unanticipated monetary policy will have an effect on output this effect is more likely to result in destabilizing shocks to the economy.

Clearly the MRE construction is highly ingenious and this perhaps explains why it seems to assert such a power of attraction for the younger generation of macroeconomists even though its assumptions and conclusions are so outrageously counterfactual.

It may be noted first that if the basic contention that anticipated monetary policy cannot affect output were to be accepted, then the conclusion would also have to be made that money supply management is very powerful in affecting prices and hence should be used to stabilize the price level in the face of shocks. However, the basic contention is untenable since the quantity theory of money cannot hold instantaneously in an economy characterized by explicit and implicit long-term (i.e., non-instantaneous) contracts and by many kinds of lags, and even rational expectations must take this into account. These considerations help to explain why the empirical evidence is highly inconsistent with the MRE implication that observed fluctuations in unemployment should be short-lived and random. Some MRE authors have rejected this inference by pointing out that because of technological constraints, uncorrelated expectational errors are not inconsistent with some viscosity in the employment series. However, the variations in employment that MRE (as well as the parent monetarist model) can account for are voluntary changes in labour supply, i.e. simultaneous movements in *employment* and *labour force*, and not variations in unemployment, which can only reflect errors and hence should be uncorrelated. Nonetheless, as is well known, the movements of unemployment are characterized by a high degree of persistence, just like the movements of employment of which they are basically the mirror image. Indeed, if unemployment were but a fleeting phenomenon there would be no cause for debate about stabilization policies nor, for that matter, would Keynes have written the *General Theory*.

A way has been suggested for salvaging the MRE construction, but in my view it amounts to declaring its bankruptcy – namely hypothesizing that the serially correlated movement in actual unemployment reflects slow-motion changes of the natural rate.[1] This is tantamount to hypothesizing that cyclical fluctuations (including the Great Depression) reflect the free choice of the community, and that an effort to eliminate or reduce them is an unwarranted interference with the preferences of society.

It may be concluded that the MRE school is making a useful contribution by calling attention to the role of rationality also in the formation of macroeconomic expectations. However, many counterfactual and unacceptable assumptions lie between this useful notion and the outrageous claims that monetary policy

1. THOMAS J. SARGENT, *Macroeconomic Theory*. New York: Academic Press, 1979, Chapter 16.

is powerless to affect output or that it works only by deceiving the public. While there is no doubt that sometimes it can be used to deceive the public it can also be used to relieve them from past commitments which have become unsuited under the new circumstances.

10. Criticism of the Monetarist Paradigm

In evaluating the mainstream monetarist paradigm a distinction has to be made between the model itself and one specific implication of that model, namely the non-existence of a "long-run trade-off" between inflation and unemployment. The latter proposition can be seen as a rehabilitation of Keynes' notion of a unique upper bound to sustainable employment or, from a different perspective, of the traditional view that in the longest run the stock of money – or its time derivative of any order – must be "neutral". This view, which was briefly lost in the burst of enthusiasm over the Phillips Curve, is at present broadly accepted by macroeconomists of most persuasions, at least as implying an upper bound to employment in the Keynesian sense. This acceptance has no doubt contributed not only to monetarist theorizing but also to the substantial amount of supporting evidence that has been produced in recent years. However, this acceptance does not imply complete support of the monetarist paradigm since a long-run "vertical" Phillips Curve is equally consistent with a variety of other models; nor does it settle the debate over stabilization policies, in part because of the same old question: how long and tortuous is the path to the long run?

The basic objection to the monetarist paradigm is its endeavour to place fluctuations of employment in an equilibrium context. Markets always clear given the expectations, no matter what the resulting level of employment. However, the theory cannot provide a convincing explanation of fluctuations in employment and even less of the cyclical behaviour of unemployment. For movements in employment are supposed to arise from a positive association between the labour supply and the perceived real wage. Yet there is no *a priori* reason why the labour supply schedule should be significantly upward sloping, and no clear empirical evidence to support this hypothesis. Furthermore the theory cannot account for the crucial fact that variations in employment are accompanied at most by moderate variations in labour supply or labour force and instead go together with changes in unemployment. Nor can it account for many other well established phenomena such as the fact that resignations tend to vary with employment instead of inversely, or because of the role of lay-offs and recalls. Similarly the negative association between simultaneous real wages and employment changes, implied by the assumption of atomistic competition in the output market, receives little, if any, support from the data.

11. Sketch of an Alternative View of the Labour Market and why it adjusts sluggishly.

Many alternative paradigms have been suggested in part because the most suitable model depends on country-specific institutions such as the strength of trade unions and the extent of synchronization in wage bargaining, and in part on account of other features like the openness of the economy. In the case of the United States in particular, where trade unions are not a dominant force and oligopolistic market structures predominate, the empirical observations mentioned earlier can be accounted for by an alternative paradigm. In this alternative view, the monetarist labour demand function is replaced by an oligopolistic mark-up model of the Bain and Sylos Labini type,[1] while the behaviour of employment and unemployment is modelled through aggregate demand and a job search model. Finally the response of nominal wage is accounted for through labour market pressures generated by the rate of unemployment and vacancies in concomitant perceptions of the warranted real wage and expected prices.

It is not possible to pursue here the details of this model, which, incidentally, is broadly consistent with the price-wage-employment sector of the MPS model. However, a few major implications must be emphasized because they are relevant to the conclusion of this analysis. Firstly, in this model all unemployment is somehow a frictional phenomenon: the pool of unemployed is fed by the flow of separations from jobs (redundancies and resignations) and by new entrants, and drained by the filling of vacancies and withdrawals, two flows that balance at any given constant level of unemployment. The size of the unemployed pool is controlled by the magnitude of the above flows and the average length of job search, or permanence

---

1. JOE S. BAIN, *Barriers to New Competition*. Cambridge, Mass.: Harvard University Press, 1956; PAOLO SYLOS LABINI, *Oligopolio e Progresso Tecnico*. Milan: Giuffré, 1957; revised edition: *Oligopoly and Technical Progress*. Cambridge, Mass.: Harvard University Press, 1969; see also FRANCO MODIGLIANI, 'New Developments on the Oligopoly Front', *Journal of Political Economy*, vol. 66 (3), June 1958, pp. 215-33; reprinted in MODIGLIANI, vol. 1, pp. 400-18.

in the pool. However, while the flows do not seem to be greatly affected by cyclical variations in aggregate demand, the length of job search is, because one of its major determinants is the number of vacancies which in turn depend on the relation between the labour force on the one hand and the number of jobs on the other.

If aggregate real demand generates a number of jobs which results, for example, in an abnormally high level of vacancies and correspondingly low rate of unemployment, the model implies a tendency for inflation to increase through the combined behaviour of the demanders and the suppliers of labour. Firms will endeavour to outbid each other in order to receive the benefits of eliminating excess vacancies, and expect to pass the higher cost onto higher prices. Therefore labour, taking advantage of the tight market, can endeavour to wait for a higher real wage, i.e., for a rise in nominal wages relative to expected prices. In reality both firms and labour are bound on the whole to be disappointed. With a constant mark-up, in fact, workers cannot achieve a higher real wage, as the higher labour cost is passed on to higher prices. Similarly the higher nominal wage offered by firms cannot *per se* increase labour supply except to the minor and temporary extent that it may speed up the acceptance of job offers because it is misinterpreted as a rise in real wages. In the final analysis the higher wages can fill vacancies only insofar as they bring about a reduction in aggregate demand and jobs, which will happen only to the extent that monetary and fiscal policies succeed in curbing the growth of nominal income below that of wages and prices. In this case vacancies and unemployment will drift back toward a natural rate where, as in the monetarist model, inflation should have no systematic tendency to rise or fall and which I have elsewhere labelled the "Non-Inflationary Rate of Unemployment" (NIRU).[1]

However, it should be noted that while returning to the NIRU region implies a stable rate of inflation, it does not imply that the

1. FRANCO MODIGLIANI and LUCAS D. PAPADEMOS, 'Targets for Monetary Policy in the Coming Year', *Brookings Papers on Economic Activity*, 1975 (1), pp. 141-63; reprinted in MODIGLIANI, vol. 1, pp. 419-41.

stable rate coincides with the long-run target. If it is too high, policy makers will be faced with the "cruel dilemma" of bearing the cost of excess inflation or accepting the cost of deliberately creating a period of demand slack and excess unemployment – a dilemma that is examined more closely in the second lecture. The excess supply pressure will set in motion a process analogous to that generated by excess demand, but leading this time to declining inflation. However, the process may not be entirely symmetrical and may not converge to the same NIRU. This is because the restraint of nominal wages relative to other wages and price expectations tends to be seen by all participants as an encroachment on the real wage, even if in the end the average real wage may not be much affected. This will be resisted by the employed and relied upon reluctantly even by the employers concerned with resignations and the maintenance of good labour relations.

Among the factors that will contribute to slowing down the process is the existence of explicit and implicit long-term contracts.[1] These imply, in the first place, that unemployment can exercise pressure only on those wages which are being currently negotiated while the behaviour of other wages will continue to reflect past circumstances. They further imply that, even when price expectations are "rational", those who currently accept a lower nominal wage will in fact, at least temporarily, suffer a lower real wage because, even with a constant mark-up, the price level, at least initially, can respond only partially to their wage behaviour.

---

1. STANLEY FISCHER, 'Long-Term Contracts, Rational Expectations, and the Optimal Money Supply Rule', *Journal of Political Economy*, vol. 85 (1), February 1977, pp. 191-206.

12. Implications of the Wage-Price Mechanism for the Stability of the System

The conclusion of the above analysis is that, even without accepting the monetarist paradigm, one can agree with their view that the wage-price mechanism may, in principle, be expected to contribute to the self-equilibrating properties of the system. That is to say, even in the absence of any stabilization policies, deviations from the natural rate would set in motion a mechanism tending to bring about the required adjustment in the real money supply. However, the relevance of this conclusion for the stabilization debate depends, as already noted, on how effectively and quickly that mechanism works. Unfortunately the evidence, at least for the United States, suggests that it is painfully slow. Estimates by a number of different authors cited by Okun[1] suggest that maintaining unemployment at one per cent above the "natural" rate for a year might reduce the rate of inflation by only one third to one half of one percentage point, an insignificant reward for the huge social cost (about $ 50,000m of lost output, at current rates). These econometric estimates are certainly consistent with a cursory perusal of the historical record. In the United States there was persistent excess demand from 1965 to the mid-1970s and during the entire period inflation grew only from 1.5 to 5.5 per cent. Furthermore the response to excess supply pressure in the years following 1974 was equally disappointing.

Therefore this mechanism cannot be expected to make a significant contribution in offsetting quickly the effect of demand shocks. This expectation is confirmed by a simulation of the effect of a demand shock carried out on the MPS, but this time allowing for the response of wages and prices. However, apparently because of this slow response, the wage-price mechanism has no significant effect in the first year, so that both the real and the nominal multiplier remain around unity, as in the case of fixed wages. Thereafter, the mechanism does become in-

---

1. ARTHUR M. OKUN, 'Efficient Disinflationary Policies', *American Economic Review*, vol. 68 (2), May 1978, pp. 348-52.

creasingly effective causing the real income multiplier to reach a peak not much above two in the second year and to decline thereafter until the effect of the shock on employment and output has completely faded out, though only by the end of the third year. As might be expected, the nominal income multiplier peaks at a higher level than with fixed wages (2.5 versus 2) and takes longer to reach it, and eventually tends towards a *positive* value because a maintained real positive demand shock leads to high interest rates and hence, through liquidity preference, to a higher velocity.

We must conclude that the monetarists have a good case in calling attention to a number of factors and mechanisms which ensure that the economic system has a fair amount of resiliency against demand shocks. However, their case falls far short of establishing that, as a result, there is therefore no need for stabilization policies. The theory and evidence reviewed in this lecture point unmistakably in the opposite direction and this conclusion is supported by the post-war record of six recessions. We must therefore proceed to their last argument: the authorities are not able to stabilize the economy and any attempt to do so would only increase the instability of the system.

13. The Experience with Stabilization Policies

As mentioned earlier, Friedman has endeavoured to establish this last conclusion as a logical implication of his "natural rate" analysis.[1] He argues that stabilization policies aim for a specific employment target. If the target differs from the natural rate the effect is explosive inflation or deflation. However, because the target is a "razor edge", shifting over time, the probability of coincidence is "a set of measure zero", and therefore the probability that stabilization policies will prove unstabilizing equals one. If, on the other hand, money follows a stable growth path, then the system will automatically "home" on the natural rate.

The trouble with this reasoning is that, on the one hand, it says nothing as to how long it will take for the system to "home" on its own, and, on the other hand, it assumes that stabilization will aim for a specific target and will stick to it whatever the consequences. In reality, of course, stabilization will aim for an approximate target and moderate deviations from the natural rate will have small and gradual undesirable effects, and evidence of these, together with other information, can be used to monitor the target. Thus, the only relevant issue is whether the system left by itself will have a smaller average distance (and perhaps a smaller variability of distance) from "home" than the policy-stabilized system. However, this is clearly an empirical not a logical issue.

Unfortunately an attempt at settling this issue from the record of stabilization policies runs into formidable difficulties. The monetarists have repeatedly claimed that instability in money growth, fostered by misguided attempts at stabilization, bears a major responsibility for economic fluctuations. However, while this claim may be plausible in connection with the Great Depression,[2] which preceded Keynesian stabilization policies, there is no convincing evidence to substantiate this proposition for the post-war period, at least not before the oil crisis.

1. Milton Friedman, 'The Role of Monetary Policy'.
2. Milton Friedman and Anna J. Schwartz, *A Monetary History of the United States: 1867-1960*. Princeton, N.J.: Princeton University Press, 1963.

36

In an earlier paper,[1] I have reviewed various attempts at developing rigorous tests of whether variations of the money supply have on balance been stabilizing or destabilizing, but concluded that none could be counted upon to provide a reliable answer. I have also reported some tests relating the stability of the economy to the stability in the growth of monetary aggregates such as the money supply. I have shown that two periods of relatively stable monetary growth – from 1953 to 1957 and from 1971 to 1974 – correspond to the two most unstable periods of the relevant post-war era, especially if one allows for a one-year lag. Each of these periods is characterized by two recessions and the instability extends, to some extent, even to prices. It has recently been brought to my attention that there exists a similar period of comparable monetary stability in the early 1960s, and this period, from the slow gradual recovery after the 1961 recession to the outbreak of the Vietnam War, turns out, by contrast, to be one of the most stable on record. Clearly the only inference that can be drawn from this evidence is that a stable growth of money is neither sufficient nor necessary for a stable development of the economy.

There is however another type of evidence which, though difficult to quantify and unsuitable for formal statistical tests of significance, is nonetheless highly relevant and impressive. It rests on an analysis of the overall historical record of economic fluctuations. According to the leading business cycle analyst, Arthur Burns, this analysis shows that since 1937 the United States economy has become distinctly more stable as is shown in particular by shorter and milder depressions.[2]

Very similar conclusions have been reported for other industrialized countries, in particular in the proceedings of a conference held in 1967 under the suggestive title, *Is the Business Cycle Obsolete?*.[3] On the whole, the question was answered in

---

1. FRANCO MODIGLIANI, 'The Monetarist Controversy or, Should We Forsake Stabilization Policies?'.

2. ARTHUR F. BURNS, 'Progress Towards Economic Stability', *American Economic Review*, vol. 50 (1), March 1960, pp. 1-19.

3. MARTIN R. BRONFENBRENNER (ed.), *Is the Business Cycle Obsolete?*. New York: Wiley-Interscience, 1969.

the negative, but this reflected in part the readiness to make up for the dearth of actual contractions in output by redefining recessions not as an actual decline in economic activity but merely as a sustained decline in the rate of growth ("growth recession"). This evidence, though not in the nature of a controlled experiment, is inconsistent with monetarist claims that stabilization policies are bound to be destabilizing on balance. On the contrary the prevailing view among participants in the conference was that the greater stability reflected at least in part successful stabilization policies.

14. Concluding Remarks

The conclusions that seem to me to emerge from this review of the history of the debate over the stability of the system and the role of stabilization policies can be summarized in three points. Firstly, there is *need* for stabilization policies, though the relevant parameters of the system suggest that the instability with respect to demand shocks is substantially less than might have appeared forty or thirty or even twenty years ago. Secondly, fairly successful stabilization policies are *possible*, although again the danger of poor timing and parameter uncertainty is sufficiently serious to counsel against attempts at "fine tuning". Thirdly, under these circumstances whether or not one should trust the government with the required discretionary power is a question that I personally would, unhesitatingly, answer in the affirmative, at least with reference to existing United States institutions. However, I will not try to defend this conclusion because it is a value judgement, not a matter of economic analysis.

SECOND LECTURE
Aggregate Demand and the Control of the Inflationary Process

1. Introduction

The first lecture dealt with the problems posed by demand shocks and concluded that it was both desirable and feasible to stabilize the economy against such shocks, and that a great deal of progress had been made in this respect.

This lecture deals with the problem of inflation and, more specifically, with the question of how aggregate demand policy can be utilized to bring under control and eventually liquidate an on-going inflationary process. Unfortunately, our conclusion will have to be far less optimistic than in the case of demand shocks. While these policies do offer a solution to the problem, it will be shown that this solution can hardly be described as a satisfactory one.

2. *The Nature of Inflation*

What causes an inflationary process? The traditional answer, which still seems to find credence even among certain economists, is that inflation, in all circumstances, times and places, is caused by "too much money chasing too few goods". To put this formulation in more operational terms, inflation occurs because the money supply is growing faster than the volume of goods that the economy is able to produce.

This explanation is appealing for its simplicity and also because it suggests that curing inflation is a simple matter. All that needs to be done is to ensure that the growth of the money supply is kept in line with the economy's capacity to produce.

That this explanation is a totally inadequate explanation of the type of inflation that, at the present time, afflicts most of the world, including the industrial countries, can be seen clearly from the fact that in most, if not all, countries inflation is accompanied today by a substantial rate of unemployment and under-utilized capacity. In other words, what is being observed is not merely inflation but stagflation – the simultaneous presence of inflation and excess unemployment. Clearly, as long as inflation is accompanied by excess unemployment it cannot be the result of an excess of nominal demand – whether from over-expansion of money supply or from any other cause – over the country's capacity to produce.

Another popular opinion is that inflation is fed by government deficits. This view is encouraged by the observation that, in many countries which are in the midst of stagflation, there are, in fact, substantial government deficits. This view, too, must be rejected unconditionally as an explanation of the current inflation in Western countries. Indeed, situations can be conceived of where the government is unable to cover its needs through taxation, or by drawing on savings through debt issues, and is forced to rely on the "printing press". This may happen for instance in the course of a major war effort or in a country with a primitive financial structure. However, these circumstances clearly do not apply to the current inflation in most Western countries. For these countries there is no necessary connection between government deficits and money creation. Deficits can be covered either with the creation of money or through the sale of debt instruments to the public. If the monetary authority chooses to cover some portion of the deficit through money creation, it is because it wants to create money, not because of the deficit as such. Paradoxical as this may seem, for many countries the large deficits prevailing at present may well be regarded as a consequence rather than a cause of inflation. This inverse causation arises from the fact that the tax and transfer structure in the more advanced countries is designed to produce a counter-cyclical behaviour of the government deficit – the so-called built-in flexibility – combined with the fact that the restrictive policies adopted to fight inflation have produced excess unemployment and cyclically depressed levels of output. In addition, inflation fuels expenditure thus raising interest rates.

An inflationary process can, of course, find its origin in demand disturbances and, more precisely, in a period of sustained excess demand, whether the result of monetary or fiscal over-expansion. The American inflation, for instance, began with a period of substantial excess demand between 1966 and 1969, resulting from the Vietnam War and the method by which it was financed. However, it can also have its origin in a large "supply shock", which can be defined as an exogenous event which requires a substantial change in relative prices. Examples of such supply shocks are the large changes in wages which occurred in many European countries in the late 1960s and early 1970s, and, of course, the enormous increase in the price of oil which occurred in 1974. The change in relative prices first manifests itself with the actual rise in some prices. This rise directly lifts the overall price level since there is, realistically, no mechanism that would cause the other prices to decline in the absence of slack. The initial rise in prices causes other prices, notably those of close substitutes, to rise; and also causes wages to rise in an attempt to maintain their purchasing power – that is, in effect, to prevent the change in relative price from occurring. The higher wages in turn lead to higher prices which lead to higher wages. Thus, the inflationary process continues, fed by its own momentum, at least as long as monetary policy accommodates the rising prices. However, it should be noted that in "accommodating", the monetary policy is following and not leading the inflationary process.

The process can be slowed down and presumably finally brought to an end through either a non-accommodating monetary policy or other restrictive aggregate demand policies. However, this can be accomplished only through the economically wasteful, and socially costly, process of an extended period of unemployment of men and productive capacity. When this 'cure' is applied, as it has been in most countries, and since it works slowly, as will be shown later, it results in a period of "stagflation". Nonetheless it should be clear from this description that it is not accurate to think of stagflation as a disease for which economists have no remedy. The point is that the unemployment component of stagflation is not an independent disease. It is instead brought about intentionally – or at least tolerated – as a *cure* for the disease, which is inflation.

To give an analogy, consider a man who is overweight and is persuaded by his doctor to go on a very strict diet. While the cure is going on, he will be both overweight and hungry. Hunger is not an independent illness that the doctor is unable to treat, but a symptom of the cure for the disease.

3. The Italian Inflation – a special case

It should be noted at this point that the mechanism of the inflationary process set out above does not account adequately for the experience of Italy, and, at least in part, of a few other countries. The Italian inflation, as is well known, began with a supply shock – the huge increases in wages following the "hot autumn" of 1969. However, as I have tried to show in an article with Padoa-Schioppa[1] what has kept inflation going at a sometimes higher, sometimes lower rate, has been primarily the excessively high real wages which the unions were able to impose and which were perpetuated through escalator clauses, providing protection against cost of living changes, not far from 100 per cent, at least at the outset. The real wage was excessively high in the sense that it made the objectives of full employment and balance of payment equilibrium mutually inconsistent. That is, given the rate of productivity, the real labour cost was such that the Italian demand for foreign goods could come into reasonable balance with the foreign demand for Italian goods only at levels of income clearly below the full-employment level. Thus, demand policies aimed at expanding domestic demand so as to ensure full employment were bound to create unsustainable deficits in the foreign account, which sooner or later would result in the devaluation of the exchange rate. The devaluation in turn would directly lead to rising prices, which in turn drove up wages through escalator clauses, pushing prices still higher, though at a decreasing rate as long as the exchange was kept fixed at the new level. This process tended to re-establish the initial real wage and price structure in terms of foreign prices, removing any initial gain in the balance of trade from the devaluation. It would thus set the stage for a new devaluation and a new inflationary spiral, which could only be avoided or slowed down

1. Franco Modigliani and Tommaso Padoa-Schioppa, 'La politica economica in una economia con salari indicizzati al 100 o più', *Moneta e Credito*, vol. 30 (117), March 1977, pp. 3-53; translated in 'The Management of an Open Economy with "100% Plus' Wage Indexation"', *Essays in International Finance*, no. 130, Princeton, N. J.: Princeton University Press, December 1978, pp. 1-39; reprinted in Modigliani, vol. 3, pp. 220-59.

by a policy of holding down domestic demand and employment. Over time the situation could improve, but only to the extent that productivity increased relative to real wages, or, within limits, through other measures designed to decrease real unit labour costs such as reduction of social security levies (the so-called fiscalization of social security).

It is apparent that this Italian-style inflation differs in one fundamental respect from the momentum inflation described earlier. In both types of inflation, unemployment can be relied upon in order to produce a gradual reduction in inflation. However, in the case of "momentum inflation", the cure so achieved should be "permanent" — once inflation has abated it should be possible to return gradually to full employment without rekindling inflation. In the Italian case of excessive real wages, on the other hand, unemployment must be relied upon not only to bring down inflation, but also to keep it low. The inflationary spiral would tend to start again if employment was moved back toward the full employment level.

In the article cited, we have surveyed what measures might be taken in the Italian-type of inflation so as to reduce the inconsistency between price stability and full employment and have shown that the choices are extremely limited. However, in what follows I will concentrate on the question of how to deal with momentum inflation.

4. The Issues involved in the Choice of a Stabilization Path

As has been shown, the basic method by which aggregate demand management can deal with momentum inflation is by creating enough slack in the economy, for a long enough period of time. The presence of slack tends to produce a reduction in the on-going rate of inflation, and the cumulated reduction can eventually wipe out the initial inflation. The policy problem is, then, that of deciding how quickly inflation should be eliminated, or, equivalently, how best to distribute the slack, or unemployment over time. For instance, a very quick reduction in the rate of inflation might be chosen, but that would entail a large amount of unemployment, concentrated in a relatively short period of time. Alternatively one might choose a very gradual elimination which would call for a relatively small level of excess unemployment, but persisting over a long span of time. There are in other words alternative paths of inflation and unemployment that could be followed in trying to return the system to a final target of full employment and price stability.

The choice of an optimum path has been at the centre of the stabilization policy discussions in recent years both at the national and the international level. In the United States, for instance, one can observe a division between a group, predominantly of conservative beliefs, which favours a drastic and rapid cure, and a group, more "liberally" minded, which tends to favour a more gradual approach. Discussion carries over to the international level, as is illustrated by the OECD-commissioned report of the McCracken group,[1] for the reason that the ability of any given country to choose a certain path is strongly conditioned by the path chosen by other countries. Especially for a small open country, an attempt to pursue a path different from, and in particular appreciably less deflationary than, that of its major trading partners, would create substantial problems and might

[1]. ORGANISATION FOR ECONOMIC CO-OPERATION AND DEVELOPMENT (OECD), *Towards Full Employment and Price Stability*. A report to the OECD by a Group of independent experts (Paul McCracken, Guido Carli, Herbert Giersch, Attila Karaosmanoglu, Ryutaro Komiya, Assar Lindbeck, Robert Marjolin, Robin Matthews). Paris: OECD, June 1977.

even prove infeasible because of balance-of-payments constraints. These considerations have been prominent in the debate over the so-called "locomotives" approach to world-wide stabilization.

Any given plan can be characterized by the cumulated amount of (excess) unemployment which it calls for, and by the cumulated amount of inflation which will result before the price level is stabilized. A choice between the alternative plans thus will typically involve a trade-off between cumulated unemployment and aggregate inflation. A rational choice must depend on an assessment of the economic and social costs of the disease to be cured, inflation, and of the cure to be applied, unemployment. Those who in the current debate express strong preference for the fast or the slow alternative, must at least implicitly make such assessments. The quality of the debate could be considerably raised by a careful attempt at understanding and, as far as possible, quantifying the costs involved. An attempt to do so will be made below.

5. *The Economic and Social Cost of Unemployment*

Consider first the cost of unemployment which is the more transparent of the two and more readily quantifiable, at least in part. The most tangible cost is clearly the loss of output to the community as a whole. This loss is appreciably larger than the rate of excess unemployment itself. In the United States, for example, it has been estimated that a one percent increase in unemployment above the "natural rate" leads to a loss of aggregate output of about $2\frac{1}{2}$ per cent (the so-called Okun's law). This multiplier of 2.5 occurs because the increase in unemployment tends to be accompanied by a contraction in the labour force as well as by a reduction in the number of hours effectively worked by those that remain employed (less overtime, a shorter working week and more slack). In countries where the dismissal of excess labour is more difficult than in the United States (e.g., Italy and Spain) the trade-off between unemployment and output is likely to be even less favourable.

However, the loss of income represents only a portion of the total cost of unemployment. Further costs must be deemed to arise from the very uneven way in which the loss of income is distributed. Most of it falls on the unemployed who tend to come from the poorest strata of the society; those less endowed with human capital tend in fact to be the first to lose their job and the last to be rehired. Today it is generally acknowledged that taking away one dollar from the poor will have a larger social cost than if the same dollar were taken away from higher income groups.

The loss suffered by those unable to find a job goes well beyond the loss of income. This is particularly true at present, as the burden of unemployment has tended recently to fall disproportionately on new entrants to the labour force and hence in particular on young people. They have been excluded from employment despite an adequate education (or even an excessive one, according to some observers) largely because the pressure of organized labour, sometimes reinforced by legislation, has made it increasingly hard for firms to dismiss workers. As a reaction, firms have tended, understandably, to be slow to take on new

49

recruits. Youth unemployment is likely to involve significant social costs, both because it fosters alienation in all its forms, and because it delays the formation of human capital with consequences that may extend over a substantial span of the life cycle.

The other sections of the population that tend to bear the brunt of the reduction of income are the entrepreneurs and equity holders; indeed, because of the short-run rigidity of most elements of costs, when output falls short of capacity, profits tend to fall, proportionately much more than output. It is generally supposed that entrepreneurs come from the upper strata of the income distribution and, to this extent, their loss might not be deemed as significant, from the social point of view, as that of the unemployed. However, this conclusion must be qualified in the extent that equity is also held directly, or through pension funds, by retired people whose income may not be particularly high. The fall in profit also tends to have an unfavourable effect on investment and, hence, on productivity growth, but this effect need not be given much independent weight since it could always be counteracted by an appropriate mix of monetary policy and of fiscal policy and incentives.

On the whole, the above considerations suggest that the cost of one per cent excess unemployment may be estimated (at least in the United States) at no less than 3 per cent of income, and possibly considerably more.

6. The Cost of Inflation

i) *An area of great controversy*

Another, much more difficult problem is how to measure the cost of inflation. This is an area which, at least until recently, has been characterized by sharp disagreements. The public at large, journalists and opinion leaders, including politicians, have tended to take a catastrophic view of the consequences of inflation, referring to it as a scourge, as well as a horrible sin, sapping the very roots of society; and this judgement has even been shared by some outstanding economists, like Irving Fisher.[1] A widespread attitude among economists has been to regard the above view as resulting from "nominal fallacies", born out of economic illiteracy; in contrast to popular belief, it is held, inflation cannot truly be a significant source of economic costs.

In my view, this attitude arises from the application of a perfectly valid proposition in the wrong context. The valid proposition, which may be regarded as one of the central concepts of economics, is that money is "but a veil", or in other words, that the quantity of money and the absolute level of prices have no effect on the real economy. An economy would, in all real respects, be the same if the quantity of money and the level of all prices were ten times larger. To paraphrase Shakespeare, an absolute price is but a name, and, "a rose by any other name would smell as sweet". However, from the justified proposition that the level of money and prices is neutral in the long run, one cannot go straight to the conclusion that *changes* in money and the level of prices cannot produce real effects over extended periods of time. This would ignore some essential facts of life, such as the existence of nominal contracts, of "nominal" institutions, and of nominal habits of thinking and carrying out economic calculations.

1. IRVING FISHER, 'Stabilizing the Dollar in Purchasing Power', in ELISHA FRIEDMAN (ed.), *American Problems of Reconstruction*. New York: E. P. Dutton & Co., 1918, pp. 361-90; see also IRVING FISHER, *Stabilizing The Dollar*. New York: Macmillan, 1920 and IRVING FISHER, *The Money Illusion*. New York: Adelphi Company, 1928 (also London: Allen & Unwin, 1928); especially Chapters 4 and 5, pp. 105-6.

ii) *The mythical fully indexed economy*

One could certainly conceive a mythical economy in which all contracts were "indexed", all institutions "inflation proof", and in which economic agents had learned to see through the veil of nominal fallacies. In such an economy, the real effects and costs of inflation would be insignificant. The main real effect would probably arise from the infeasibility of indexing currency or paying a nominal interest rate on it. As a result, the cost of holding currency, measured by the loss of purchasing power incurred while holding it, would grow with the rate of inflation. This would lead the public to economize on currency – a costly and wasteful activity since, at least according to Professor Friedman,[1] the provision of currency has no significant social costs.

However, if the private cost of this economizing could be estimated, it would turn out to be fairly trivial. In addition, this estimate certainly overstates the true social cost (if it exists at all). This is because the cost borne by the private sector represents an income for the government that is supplying the currency – the so-called inflation tax – and that income can be used to reduce other taxes or, at the very least, to provide additional services. Moreover, if the ratio of wealth to income is constant – as implied, for instance, by the life-cycle hypothesis of saving discussed in the last of these lectures – then the reduction in the real amount of currency held would tend to be accompanied by an expansion in the stock of productive capital, which would in turn produce additional income. In other words, the social cost of holding currency is not zero but is equal to the marginal productivity of capital.

In short, in a fully indexed economy, inflation would have few real effects, and even the effect that has attracted the attention of many economists – the economizing on currency – would produce a cost which is, at worst, small, and might even be negative.

In reality, however, today's economies are very different from

---

1. MILTON FRIEDMAN, 'The Optimum Quantity of Money', in MILTON FRIEDMAN, *The Optimum Quantity of Money and Other Essays*. Chicago: Aldine Press, 1969, pp. 1-50; also London: Macmillan, 1969.

the mythical inflation-proof economy described above, and for this reason inflation produces a large array of real effects, many of which have significant costs.

iii) *Effects of inflation apart from errors in expectations and other errors*

a) *The effect of a "nominal" tax system*

A first important set of real consequences derives from the fact that government institutions, and in particular those pertaining to taxation, are drawn up in nominal terms. Where there is a progressive income-tax system, the brackets are defined in nominal terms. Thus, when inflation increases nominal income, real tax liabilities tend to rise or, equivalently, the total tax revenue becomes a larger share of income. This problem can of course be remedied by raising the income brackets accordingly, as has been done repeatedly in many countries. Nonetheless real effects will still occur in between revisions and also because the revisions seldom take the form of mechanically adjusting all income brackets in accordance with the change in a general price index. Thus the real effects could be avoided efficiently only by indexing the brackets, a procedure which has been seldom followed, in part perhaps because governments and legislators prefer a system which yields rising revenue without new taxes and may give the opportunity to claim the credit for tax rebates.

More pervasive and serious effects arise from the nominal definition of income for tax purposes. The aspect that has received most attention is that related to the required use of historical costs, for both inventory valuation and plant and equipment depreciation, in the computation of taxable income. The resulting taxation of fictitious income produces two consequences in turn: it tends to reduce after-tax profits with further consequences on the valuation of stocks, to be discussed later, and it also tends to increase the cost of capital, other things equal, with consequences on investments.

However, a more serious, though less widely recognized, distortion arises from the treatment of interest income and payments. If inflation were "neutral", in a world without taxes the interest

53

rate on nominal loans would be expected to increase by an inflation premium equal to the rate of inflation – a proposition known as Fisher's Law. Thus, if the interest rate in the absence of inflation were 5 per cent, with a 20 per cent inflation one would expect the interest rate to rise to 25 per cent. However, of this 25 per cent, the 20 per cent representing the inflation premium is not really an income to the receiver nor a cost to the payer. It represents in reality a partial return of principal, since it merely makes up for the loss of value of the principal in real terms. Yet our nominal tax system treats the whole 25 per cent as income to the recipient and a cost to the debtor. The result is that inflation can drastically reduce after-tax real return. If Fisher's Law holds, the decline equals the (marginal) tax rate times the rate of inflation. Thus, if we assume a 40 per cent marginal tax rate, then a 20 per cent rate of inflation will reduce the real after-tax return by 40 per cent of 20 per cent – or 8 per cent. In our illustration, while before inflation the real interest was 60 per cent of 5 per cent, or 3 per cent, with a 20 per cent inflation and a 25 per cent nominal rate, the after-tax real rate is reduced by 8 per cent to a negative 5 per cent. A corresponding reduction occurs in the cost to the borrower, insofar as he is allowed to deduct interest expenses from his gross income in computing net income for tax purposes.

The resulting distortions may be expected to have profound effects throughout the financial markets, especially when tax payers pay different marginal tax rates (and some transactors may pay no tax at all), and when various types of debt may also receive a differential tax treatment. In general, if Fisher's Law holds approximately, the negative real after-tax return and cost on nominal assets and debts would be expected to provide a strong incentive to shift portfolios in the direction of holding physical assets, and to encourage the flight into commodities, discussed below; for, even if the real return on these real assets is zero or negligible at least the inflation-induced nominal appreciation is, typically, untaxed.

In principle, the shift from nominal to real assets should tend to cause a rise in the nominal interest rate beyond what is called for by Fisher's Law. For instance, in order to preserve unchanged the real after-tax rate, the nominal rate would have to rise not just by the rate of inflation but rather by that rate divided by one minus the tax rate. In our illustration, a 20 per cent rate of inflation should drive the nominal tax rate up, not by 20 percentage points but by 33, i.e., from 5 per cent to 38 per cent. One of the surprising features of the recent world-wide inflation is that, even in countries with well-working and relatively free capital markets, nominal interest rates have, on the whole, tended to rise less, and not more, than the rate of inflation. For some possible explanations for this phenomenon examined later, the role of counterbalancing distortive real effects must be looked at.

b) *The role of private nominal institutions*

With respect to the effect of private nominal institutions two such institutions stand out because of their widespread impact on the economy: the mortgage contract and the pension contract. Both are characterized by the fact that they involve the exchange of a capital sum for a constant nominal stream of payments. Of course, with a reasonably stable purchasing power of money, the constant nominal stream implies a stream of constant purchasing power, which is what the contract was really designed to achieve. However, in the presence of inflation, a constant nominal stream means a declining real stream. For example with a 25-year contract, and a 20 per cent rate of inflation, the extent of unevenness is extreme. If Fisher's Law holds, the present value of the total stream of real payments will be unaffected by inflation, but its time profile is profoundly affected: the higher the inflation the higher will be its starting value, and the lower its terminal value. For instance, if the nominal interest rate rises from 5 to 25 per cent because of 20 per cent inflation, the initial rate of payment will rise by a a factor which quickly approaches 5 as the life of the mortgage contract is extended. This high starting payment rate is, of course, made up by the fact that in the latter part of the life of the mortgage the real payments will become quite small. However, the high "front load", and the implied very fast accumulation of equity in the house, causes enormous, sometimes insurmountable, difficulties for many types

55

of buyers, in particular those in the early phase of their life cycle, who having no other accumulated assets to fall upon, and bearing a large family burden, are unable, through current saving, to build up equity at the rate required by the contract.

This problem has caused profound disruptions in the housing market in many countries, especially because it took some time for the would-be borrowers to understand that the high interest rates and huge initial payments, though they posed a cash flow problem, did not change the overall real cost and return of holding a house. In many countries, the initial response has been to provide interest subsidies to certain classes of borrowers, thus failing to appreciate that a rational solution would have called for changes in the contract itself.

Recently a good deal of work has been done on redesigning mortgage instruments for an inflationary world, including some carried out by the author in collaboration with a number of colleagues.[1] However, the adoption of reforms in house financing has been painfully slow, partly because of resistence related to inflation illusion and partly because of nominal taxation and legal institutions. Nevertheless, there has been a tendency for the problem to become less serious, thanks also to a greater appreciation by the public of the return potential from investment in houses, favoured by the tax treatment of the interest payments mentioned above, and by the poor performance of other forms of investment.

In the case of the pension contract, the pensioner receives a constant flow of nominal payments and, therefore, he finds that this income steadily decreases in terms of purchasing power. Again, if Fisher's Law holds, the total amount of payment he receives over his retirement period (at least before tax), need not be different in real terms from what would have happened in the absence of inflation in the case of so-called "defined contribution" plans. But the problem arises from the fact that the streams of receipts decrease in time and the recipient may not realize the need to redistribute in time the flow of receipts in order to

---

1. FRANCO MODIGLIANI and DONALD LESSARD (eds), *New Mortgage Designs for an Inflationary Environment*, Conference Series No. 14, 1975, Federal Reserve Bank of Boston.

stabilize his consumption, or may not have the ability and foresight to do so. Furthermore, even if he tried to do that, his carry-over would not benefit from the insurance protection against the "risk of life", which is one of the major purposes that the pension contract is designed to achieve.

In addition, of course, when the inflation first erupts, pensioners may suffer from the re-distributional effect resulting from unanticipated inflation, mentioned below. In the case of social security and related state schemes, the "pension problem" has by now been largely solved, in most countries, by explicit indexation – one of the few instances where nominal public institutions have been recast in real terms. This has greatly helped to reduce the hardships of inflation as state pensions are, in many countries, by far the most important source of income for the retired "poor". However for private pensions, a solution of the problem poses complex questions as to how to allocate the uncertainty of future real interest rates, questions which are only beginning to receive attention.

iv) *The effects of errors in expectations*

a) *Long-term nominal contracts and unanticipated inflation*

All the real effects discussed so far are largely independent of whether inflation was predicted or predictable, or even whether it was stable or variable over time (except possibly in so far as a stable rate of inflation might have made it easier for people to recognize certain mistakes). We come now to a set of real effects which depend not on the rate of inflation as such but on its being unpredicted or unpredictable.

These effects, which are better known and understood than those examined earlier, all derive from the fact that in the absence of inflation, there are important advantages and extensive inducements to entering into long-term nominal contracts. These are contracts involving the exchange of tangible or intangible commodities or services for future sums of money. By far the most important type of long-term nominal contract in our economy appears to be the loan contract (and related ones, such as long-term leases). When the price level is fixed, or fully predict-

57

able, such contracts have the unique property of creating certainty for at least one of the parties in the bargain, even in a world full of uncertainty. However, if the price level at the payment date (or dates) deviates from that anticipated in the contract, there is an "uncontracted for" transfer of wealth between the payee and the payer.

In assessing the importance of transfer effects, the level of aggregation is crucial. First, consider the broadest aggregate, namely the whole national economy. If the economy were closed, *net* transfer would clearly be zero, as the loss of the creditors is offset by the gain of the debtors. Even in an open economy the net transfer would presumably be small, being limited to net domestic claims on the rest of the world denominated in domestic currency. This cancelling-out effect is undoubtedly one of the reasons why economists may play down the costs of inflation.

However, clearly the *net* gains or losses by no means exhaust the real effects which emerge by looking at sub-aggregates. Thus, when we move from the economy as a whole to its most important sub-aggregate, the household sector, and even allowing for indirect ownership of firms through equities, we typically find that there is a sizable net loss because the private sector is a net creditor of the public sector. From this consideration it is frequently concluded that inflation "benefits" the government at the expense of the private sector. Some, with an unkindly disposition toward governments, have even suggested that governments consciously foster inflation for this reason. What is interesting about this "cynical" view of governments is that anyone could take it seriously, at least in a democratic system where the government does not owe personally the debt, and where inflation is highly unpopular among voters. In reality, in a democratic system, the government is only an agent of the community, not an entity in itself that can get richer while *all* the people get poorer. Closer examination will show that the reduction of the real national debt is really a transfer between generations. It benefits future generations, who will have less taxes to pay to service the debt, at the expense of the current generation that loses wealth and is forced to consume less over the rest of its life (though it should be remembered that any member of the current generation is also a member of future generations to the extent of his life expectancy). Note also that the lower government interest *received* by future generations will not result in less income from capital, for, as I have argued in an earlier paper,[1] the reduced consumption of the current generation can be expected to result in additional capital formation, the return from which will replace the lower interest on the national debt.

The redistributional effects are far larger if we move down to the maximum level of disaggregation, that of individual households. Clearly an unanticipated (i.e. not contracted for) *permanent* increase in the price level by one per cent, in a given period, will tend to cause a windfall loss of wealth to all creditors, amounting in aggregate to one per cent of the outstanding money fixed claims maturing thereafter. The magnitude of this loss can be better appreciated by relating it to the annual rate of income flow through the ratio of outstanding nominal claims to income. In the United States, for instance, the sum total of money fixed claims held by households has amounted in recent years to about $1\frac{1}{2}$ times aggregate income, implying a transfer of $1\frac{1}{2}$ per cent of income per one percentage point of unanticipated inflation – a rather considerable effect.

This measure no doubt overstates the magnitude of the transfer since many households are simultaneously debtors and creditors, and for these households the transfer is partly cancelled out. Unfortunately no estimate of the aggregate net loss of the net loser is presently available. On the other hand, to assess the full implications of the transfer loss one must also take into account who are typically the losing creditors. The common or simplistic view is of course that the debtors are the poor and the rich are creditors. If so, the transfer effect might be deemed less serious since it would be redistributing from the rich to the poor. However, closer scrutiny, as well as statistical evidence, at least for the United States, suggests that this "romantic" view is quite wrong. Nor is this surprising since the really poor are hardly credit-

1. FRANCO MODIGLIANI, 'Long-Run Implications of Alternative Fiscal Policies and the Burden of National Debt', *Economic Journal*, vol. 71 (284), December 1961, pp. 730-56; reprinted in MODIGLIANI, vol. 2, pp. 415-41.

worthy – it is much easier to be in debt if one owns a house or a business. On the other hand, everybody, rich or poor, tends to have some nominal assets. Consistent with these considerations, the evidence for the United States suggests that while income is not a major determinant of portfolio composition, the lowest third of income recipients are, to a modest extent, net creditors, and all the others are moderately net debtors, except for the very highest class (representing 0.4 per cent).[1] Hence, inflation would seem to redistribute from the lower end and the very top to the middle, but to a rather moderate extent.

The life-cycle theory suggests that a more important determinant of portfolio composition should be age, and the United States the evidence fully supports this inference. The households in the lower third of the age distribution tend to have little net worth since they had little opportunity to accumulate. However, because they need physical assets, they must turn to borrowing, relying on the collateral of the assets as well as of human capital; their net debt turns out to be some 70 to 80 per cent of net worth. In middle life net worth is accumulated and debts are repaid, nominal assets grow to a certain extent, but households still remain net debtors. When the oldest third is reached (i.e. the group aged 55 and above), wealth stops rising or even declines, debts dwindle while nominal assets rise sharply. Thus, the oldest group turns out to be society's creditor. It can be inferred that one important systematic real effect of unanticipated inflation is to transfer wealth from the old to the young.

b) *The effect of price-level uncertainty*

Further real consequences arise from the uncertainty of future inflation. When the future price level is uncertain, society loses the important benefit of a contract which permits the carry-over of resources with an assured outcome, even over a long span of time. Similarly, long-term borrowing also becomes riskier. Since inflation is typically accompanied by uncertainty of future price levels, it tends to disrupt long-term debt markets. In

---

1. GEORGE L. BACH and JAMES B. STEPHENSON, 'Inflation and the Redistribution of Wealth', *Review of Economics and Statistics*, vol. 56 (1), February 1974, pp. 1-14.

particular, new issues of long-term instruments tend to dry up, as is evidenced by the experience of many countries.

The risk resulting from price-level uncertainty can be reduced by falling back on a sequence of short-term loans – generally a costly and risky procedure, at least for the borrower – or by issuing long-term loans whose rate floats with short-term rates. Recent experience suggests that either method would reduce the risk of the ex post real rate because, on average, short-term real rates have been relatively stable. Nonetheless even these devices do not provide lenders and borrowers with a way of ensuring a fixed real long-term rate.

Only formal indexation of the principal, i.e., denominating the principal in "commodity baskets", could achieve this result. However in fact, indexed loans have had very limited development, except in a few countries. This failure appears to be attributable to general antipathy, borne of misunderstanding, and to inflation illusion, as well as to unfavourable tax treatment and "nominal" legal institutions.

v) *Other inflation-induced errors and their effect*

a) *Inflation illusion and financial markets*

I come now to an aspect of the real effect of inflation that is generating a good deal of controversy.

In my view, some of the most serious disruptive effects of inflation arise from what may be termed "inflation illusion" – the inability of economic agents to make correct rational calculations in the presence of unfamiliar inflation. The task of distinguishing between real and nominal quantities, and in particular between real and nominal rates, seems to be a difficult one, except possibly for a few economists who have devoted themselves to that task; and in my experience even for the "expert" it is easy to fall into traps.

All accounting is carried out in nominal terms, and, in most countries including the United States, corporate profits are still reported on nominal standards – that is, on original rather than replacement costs basis – and without including the gain from the depreciation of corporate net indebtedness. Even the national

61

income accounts of the United States, which are generally fairly sophisticated, have gone as far as correcting corporate income for inventory valuation and for replacement costs depreciation; however, in calculating profits they subtract the whole nominal interest bill without adding back the gain from the devaluation of the debt and subtracting that same devaluation from reported income from interest.

Inflation also makes it extremely difficult to estimate the cost of capital and the cash flow relevant to the calculation of the net worth of an investment. In the absence of inflation, the cost of capital should presumably be estimated as an appropriate average of an earning-price ratio (corrected for true growth potential) and the interest rate (duly tax-adjusted). However, with inflation, this procedure is no longer appropriate since the earning-price ratio is a real rate, while the interest rate is a nominal one. A choice has to be made from two options: i) recast the earning-price ratio on a nominal base by adding back expected inflation, before averaging it with the nominal rate, and compare the resulting *"nominal* required return" with an estimated *nominal* cash flow; or ii) convert the nominal interest rate to a real basis before averaging with the earning-price ratio and perform all calculations in real terms. If the nominal approach is chosen, there should be consistency between the rate of inflation built into the nominal rates and that which is assumed implicitly in the nominal cash flows. Calculations in real terms would seem to be less susceptible to pitfalls, but there is little evidence that this procedure is generally followed. In addition, proper allowance must be made for the tax treatment of interest. Very little seems to be known at this time on just how firms have managed to make rational profitability calculations during the period of rising and variable inflation. It would be surprising indeed if serious distortions had not crept in.

Similar difficulties arise with respect to the valuation of intangibles, such as corporate equities. In a paper with Richard Cohn[1] we have advanced, and found strong empirical support for,

1. Franco Modigliani and Richard A. Cohn, 'Inflation, Rational Valuation and the Market', *Financial Analysts Journal*, vol. 35 (2), March-April 1979, pp. 24-44.

the hypothesis that inflation-induced errors in the valuation of equity are largely responsible for the depressed state of the equity markets in the United States (and probably elsewhere). We provide evidence for two kinds of market errors. Firstly, there is a failure to make proper correction for the gain from the devaluation of net debt. The error resulting from this source depends of course both on the extent of the indebtedness, or leverage, of firms and on the magnitude of the inflation. In the United States where both inflation and leverage are moderate, this error in recent years has amounted to perhaps 30-40 per cent of profits. However, in a country like Italy, where leverage is far greater and the rate of inflation has been much higher, the error can be much more substantial, and indeed exceed 100 per cent – that is, accounting profits may well show a negative figure, even when true profits are positive.

A second source of undervaluation can be traced to the market tendency to price shares in relation to earnings so as to secure an earning-price ratio which follows the nominal rate, and therefore rises with inflation. This is, of course, a serious valuation error. The earning-price ratio should be a *real* rate, unaffected by the rate of inflation, since equity is a claim to a real asset, whose value should grow at the rate of inflation – at least as long as inflation does not have an adverse long-run effect on real profits. Thus, while holders of money-fixed claims need to be compensated for inflation by a higher nominal rate, the equity owner should obtain that compensation through the rise in equity prices, which would occur as profits rise with inflation, while the earning-price ratio is unchanged.

It may well be wondered how such a valuation error could have persisted after so many years of inflation – a question which has been forcefully raised by some of our critics. Without attempting a full answer here, we may point to the fact that, in periods of prevailingly rising inflation and interest rates, the error to which we call attention tends to be self-fulfilling. It is not difficult to believe that the rise in interest rates, which accompanied the initial burst of inflation, could have resulted in a rising earning-price ratio, since this response was appropriate prior to inflation. However since initially this response prevents the price of equities from rising with the general price level, it encourages the view that the price of equities behaved more like that of a nominal instrument, and that therefore the cash return has to increase with inflation to compensate for the real depreciation in the value of the stock.

We have estimated that, as of 1978–79, equity values in the United States were approximately one half of what they should be under rational valuation. Given the importance of equities in total net worth – approximately one million million dollars (10^{12}) and around one quarter of household net worth – this error could be the source of an enormous destruction of wealth and well-being.

It may be noted, in passing, that several of the real effects just reviewed may help to explain why, at least in the United States, the nominal rate has failed to rise appreciably more than the rate of inflation, as might have been expected. The point is that this rise should have occurred as the result of an endeavour to shift from nominal to real assets, or to borrow in order to increase the holding of real assets. In reality, the poor performance of equities has made them unattractive. As for housing, the main traditional form of tangible investment, returns have tended to remain satisfactory, except where held down by actual or threatened rent controls. However housing is not a good substitute for conventional nominal assets and equities because of illiquidity and indivisibility. Furthermore, the cash flow difficulties connected with the mortgage contract have limited its accessibility.

One consequence is that, at least in the United States during the recent inflationary periods, the real after-tax returns on most traditional forms of investment have tended to be low, if not negative, and otherwise unattractive. For low-income brackets, whose real return from lending was not much affected by taxes, the before-tax yield has tended to be equally poor because of ceilings imposed by regulation on the typical "poor man's assets" such as savings accounts. As already noted, the unattractiveness of traditional instruments in turn has tended to encourage the flight into unconventional forms of investment, for example the hoarding of gold, land and collectables, the results of which will be looked at later.

b) *The inflation discomfort syndrome*

There is much evidence, supported by public opinion surveys, that inflation produces a widespread discomfort in the population. This would seem consistent with the result of our analysis except for one puzzling aspect: the discomfort is not easily related to the various real effects which we have mentioned. For instance, an analysis of data collected by the Survey Research Center at the University of Michigan measuring attitudes toward comparative costs of unemployment and inflation[1] fails to provide evidence that older and/or poorer respondents were more concerned with inflation and less with unemployment, than the younger and/or richer people.

There is reason to believe that some of the widespread resentment against inflation may stem from "inflation illusion". Even when take-home pay keeps up with inflation, people may not link the rising nominal income with the inflation. They may look instead on the rise in nominal income as intended to award them a higher real income, and regard inflation as robbing them of this deserved increase. This attitude tends to be reinforced by the fact that inflation frequently turns up at times of serious economic disruptions and impoverishment. Even in the current period, peak inflation rates have corresponded to the dramatic rise in oil prices (and in agricultural prices) which corresponded to an overall impoverishment of the majority of citizens. Of course, inflation was a concomitant, an expression of the impoverishment, and not the cause, but it was easy to misinterpret the causal relation. Politicians for the most part have done their best to reinforce this misconception, and economists seem to have had little success in correcting it.

vi) *Inflation and saving*

One further effect of inflation that has received some attention is that on the rate of saving. According to conventional wisdom,

1. STANLEY FISCHER and JOHN HUIZINGA, 'Inflation, Unemployment, and Public Opinion Polls', *Journal of Money, Credit and Banking*, vol. 14 (1), February 1982, pp. 1-19.

inflation will tend to reduce saving in favour of consumption, both because of the decline in the after-tax return on most assets examined earlier, and because of the greater uncertainty of returns mentioned above.

There is, however, a diametrically opposite view, favoured by psychologists like Katona,[1] according to which inflation would increase saving because it increases uncertainty in general, not merely uncertainty of return, and thus leads to "retrenchment". A related view is that saving will increase because inflation reduces household wealth, creating the need for larger accumulation. This reasoning is appealing but the effects of inflation on wealth must be put in proper perspective. In the first place the relevant decline in the real wealth of the household sector is that arising from its *net* holding of nominal assets., i.e., basically from its net nominal claim against the government. Secondly, what matters is only the loss resulting from *unanticipated* inflation. To the extent that inflation is anticipated, higher nominal rates would be expected to compensate for the loss. On the other hand, the effect via nominal assets may be reinforced by the inflation-induced undervaluation of equities, which could be substantial.

There is also a very different mechanism through which inflation could tend to depress saving, namely by inducing people to channel their savings into the acquisition of assets, traditionally regarded as "inflation hedges". Since these assets typically have zero or very low elasticity of supply, additional demand does not result in additional output. Instead it will bid up prices, fuelling inflation as well as increasing wealth. In turn the increased wealth – notably of those reaping capital gains – will cause an increase in consumption. Through this mechanism – which is consistent with the life-cycle model of saving discussed in the last lecture – a portion of intended saving ends up by raising consumption instead of financing investment.

In conclusion, it is difficult to say *a priori* whether inflation

---

1. GEORGE KATONA, *Essays on Behavioral Economics* (with a contribution by JAMES N. MORGAN). Ann Arbor, Mich.: Survey Research Center, Institute for Social Research, University of Michigan, 1980.

should, on balance, increase or decrease saving. The empirical evidence, by and large, appears to suggest that the former effect dominates.[1] However this evidence is suspect because it is based on an incorrect measure of both income and saving, namely, the conventional measure. This measure includes in income the entire nominal flow of interest received, without allowing for the fact that part of that interest offsets the real depreciation of the debt and is therefore in the nature of a return of capital. Similarly for the same reason, the measure of saving obtained by subtracting consumption from the wrong income treats as saving what is really reinvestment of principal. No clear evidence is available at present on the behaviour of savings correctly measured.

vii) *The cost of inflation – an overview*

The conclusion can be drawn from this analysis of the consequences of inflation that inflation does have widespread real effects. However, to quantify the cost of these effects is an altogether different matter. In particular, inflation, unlike unemployment, does not result *per se* in a reduction of output. Even if some of the real effects might tend to reduce aggregate demand, in principle they could be offset by an appropriate aggregate demand policy. These considerations may help to explain why many economists have tended to minimize the importance of the cost of inflation. However, to identify social costs with a loss of aggregate output is to take a peculiarly myopic point of view. It may perhaps reflect an understandable bias of those who have devoted their life to the task, quite worthy in itself, of maximizing gross national product. Clearly our analysis indicates that even if it does not affect aggregate output, inflation does have severely disruptive effects on the allocation of resources, the functioning of markets, and the welfare of large strata of society.

This conclusion is particularly true of the redistributional effects, even though by their own nature these effects produce no

---

1. ANGUS DEATON, 'Involuntary Saving through Unanticipated Inflation', *American Economic Review*, vol. 67 (5), December 1977, pp. 899-910.

net pecuniary loss to society. However, because of their arbitrary and capricious nature they must be regarded as a costly evil, much as the damage suffered through robberies is regarded as a social loss, even if it is offset by an equal gain secured by the robber. If the social loss were assessed as equal to the aggregate loss borne by all creditors, then it could be concluded that just through this channel each additional point of (unanticipated) inflation permitted in the course of the stabilization path would produce a cost which for the United States could amount to approximately around one percentage point of income – an order of magnitude similar to our estimate of the cost of one additional percentage point of unemployment for one year.

This assessment might be viewed as an obvious overstatement since it neglects the benefits obtained by the gainers. However, the additional cost arising from the incidence of transfer losses must also be taken into account. As has been shown, inflation tends to redistribute systematically from the old to the young. There are good reasons to argue that a given windfall loss produces more hardship the older the person that bears it, for the simple reason that an older person has less opportunity to make it up or to spread it over the remainder of life. On the whole, therefore, I would be prepared to argue that, even if the transfer gain has some positive social value, it is overwhelmed by the social cost of the transfer loss.

There seems no way at this time to assign to all other real effects of inflation, specific costs commensurate to those assignable to unemployment or the redistributional effect. This is notably true of the state of unhappiness and anxiety that inflation appears to generate in the public, insofar as it results from misunderstanding of its real effects.

7. The Relative Costs of Excess Unemployment and Inflation over the Re-entry Path

On the whole, even if our analysis has succeeded in uncovering and providing some understanding of the major economic and social effects of inflation and of a cure relying on economic slack and unemployment, it must still be recognized as inadequate to provide a solid base to place objective cost tags on either phenomena. Yet some conclusions do stand out which, as will be presently shown, can provide some guidance in the choice between alternative paths.

The first and safest conclusion is that extreme positions, asserting that either the cost of unemployment or the cost of inflation is minor or overwhelmed by the other, can be safely rejected. Both inflation and unemployment have awesome economic and social costs; to be forced to choose between them is indeed a "cruel dilemma".

A second conclusion that I would be willing to advance, though admittedly on much less secure grounds, pertains to the nature of social costs associated with a given path of inflation and unemployment. Firstly the case of unemployment; an examination of its real effects suggests that the resulting costs can be taken as roughly proportional to the sum (or cumulant) of excess unemployment over the path and independent of other characteristics of the path. For example, suppose that one path called for three per cent excess unemployment in the first year, and one per cent in the second, while another called for two per cent for three consecutive years. Then the second path would have a cumulated unemployment of six per cent and by the proposed criterion would be one and one half times as costly as the second path, calling for cumulated unemployment of only four per cent (even though the second path called for a higher peak rate). Secondly, with respect to inflation it would seem that the same "cumulant" nature of cost should tend to hold at least with respect to transfer effects. However, many other major effects – aside from those related to price-level uncertainty – would appear to share similar characteristics, at least approximately. One qualification is worth mentioning in regard to the cost of inflation. Insofar as a stabilization plan implies an explicit projection of the future course of inflation, a good case might be made for assessing the cost of the inflation path as proportional to an appropriately *discounted* sum of inflation (rather than to the simple sum). The discounting is suggested by the consideration that the cost of inflation should tend to be smaller the earlier it is anticipated. This point will be considered further below.

With respect to those effects that depend on uncertainty, the main implication of our analysis is to strengthen the case for a stabilization policy which explicitly sets out the course of inflation over the re-entry path and endeavours to keep to it.

These results are clearly meagre. Yet research undertaken in collaboration with Lucas Papademos[1] leads to the conclusion that even this limited information of the nature of costs permits some useful inferences to be drawn about the broad characteristics of an optimal stabilization path.

1. FRANCO MODIGLIANI and LUCAS D. PAPADEMOS, 'Optimal Demand Policies against Stagflation'. *Weltwirtschaftliches Archiv*, vol. 114 (4), December 1978, pp. 736-81.

8. The Nature of the Optimal Stabilization Path

i) Feasible paths – the Phillips Curve

In order to establish the nature of the optimal path, the results concerning the social cost, or "objective" function, summarized above, must be combined with a "budget constraint" expressing the relation between any given unemployment path and the corresponding inflation path. This relation is essentially the Phillips Curve already discussed in the first lecture.

For present purposes, it is useful to think of the Phillips Curve as expressing a relation between the change in inflation (or acceleration in the price level) over some interval of time and the rate of unemployment; the lower the rate of unemployment the larger (algebraically) the increase in inflation. According to the

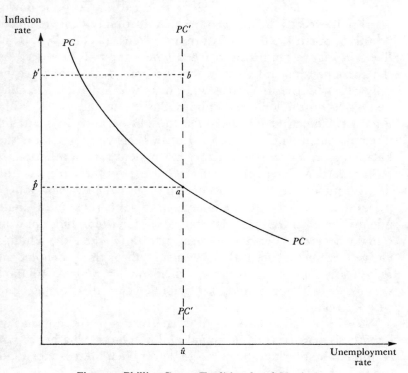

Figure I. Phillips Curve, Traditional and Vertical.

71

"traditional" view of the Phillips Curve, the change in inflation would also depend (inversely) on the received rate of inflation: it is precisely this dependence that ensures a long-run or "permanent" trade-off between unemployment and inflation. This point is illustrated in Figure 1.

Suppose the economy starts out at some point like b, with unemployment $\hat{u}$ and inflation p'. If unemployment were kept at $\hat{u}$, the ensuing change in inflation – i.e. whether point b would tend to move up or down – would depend on the balance of two opposing forces. There is on the one hand an upward thrust reflecting demand pressure which is stronger the lower the rate of unemployment. However, according to the traditional view, this push is countered on the other hand by a downward pull, reflecting a tendency for inflation to decay spontaneously, other things being equal, and this pull is stronger the higher the initial rate of inflation. In our graph it is assumed that at b the downward pull exceeds the upward push. Accordingly b moves down. As this happens the downward pull weakens. Eventually a point like a in Figure 1 must be reached where the pull produced by the corresponding inflation, $\hat{p}$, has become weak enough to be fully offset by the upward push. Thus, at a, inflation is stable, i.e., a falls on the long-run Phillips Curve denoted by PC-PC in Figure 1. The curve falls from left to right because for a smaller unemployment rate, the upward push is stronger and thus the balancing must occur at a higher permanent rate of inflation.

The vertical long-run Phillips Curve hypothesis rejects the decay component of this mechanism. Thus the acceleration of prices depends only on unemployment and there is but a single unemployment rate – the natural rate – for which inflation can remain constant. Let this natural rate be $\hat{u}$, then the Phillips Curve becomes a vertical line passing through $\hat{u}$, denoted as PC'-PC' in Figure 1. For values of u smaller than $\hat{u}$, inflation would rise without bound, while for lower u it would decline without bound.

We will postpone entering into the merits of the alternative hypothesis because the traditional Phillips Curve, whether or not is empirically relevant, turns out to be very helpful to understand the nature of the optimal path.

ii) *Optimal policy with a long-run trade-off*

The nature of the optimal path is illustrated in Figure 2, adapted from our paper.[1] The curve *PC-PC* is again the long-run traditional Phillips Curve. The curve *WW* is a representation

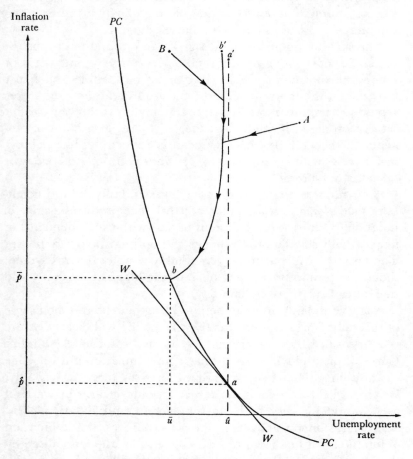

Figure 2. Illustration of the Turnpike Property of the Optimal
Unemployment Path for Alternative Initial States.

1. Franco Modigliani and Lucas D. Papademos, 'Optimal Demand Policies against Stagflation'.

of the relative costs assigned by the social preference function to unemployment and inflation respectively. More precisely it is a social isocost curve: the locus of combinations of u and p which have the same social cost. Our conjecture that social cost can be approximated by a linear function of cumulated inflation and unemployment implies that WW is a straight line. Its slope reflects the cost of inflation *relative* to that of unemployment: the greater the relative cost of inflation the flatter the line.

The starting point for the design of an optimal path must be the choice of the long-term target, or "re-entry" point. Let it be represented by point a. Clearly it must be feasible and hence must lie on the long-run Phillips Curve. In addition, the target should presumably represent an optimal point within the feasible set. Accordingly, it might be expected to fall at a point of tangency of the Phillips Curve with an isocost curve, like point a, in Figure 2, with coordinates $(\hat{u}, \hat{p})$. That point can therefore be taken as our target.

Now suppose that the economy was initially in the neighbourhood of a, and some sudden disturbance produces a spurt of inflation, pushing it up to a point like B (with excess demand) or like A (with stagflation). What is the optimal policy response? The answer turns out to be remarkably simple: unemployment should be promptly brought back to the long-run target $\hat{u}$, and thereafter kept there indefinitely.

A few considerations may help to bring out the common sense of this policy prescription. Firstly, this policy will clearly ensure re-entry, since by the very nature of the "traditional" Phillips Curve, if unemployment is kept at $\hat{u}$, then inflation must decline steadily along the path $a'a$ toward the long-run target a. Secondly, keeping u below the long-run target $\hat{u}$ would clearly be wasteful as it would increase both unemployment and inflation costs. Thirdly, keeping it above $\hat{u}$ in order to speed up the liquidation of inflation can be shown to be inefficient, for the loss caused by the cumulated excess unemployment outweighs the gain from lesser cumulated inflation. In short, the optimal policy for the case under consideration calls for maintaining at all times unemployment as close as possible to the long-run target, and letting price level disturbances work themselves out.

74

iii) *"Long-run costs" versus "stabilization costs". The "turnpike" solution.*

Nonetheless it must be recognized that while the long-run target must lie on the Phillips Curve, it really need not lie at a point of tangency with the isocost *WW*, like point *a*. It might instead fall on the Phillips Curve to the left of *a*. This proposition rests on the consideration that the social cost function relevant to the choice of a long-run unemployment inflation *target* might well be systematically different from the "stabilization cost function" which is relevant to the choice of a stabilization path, and which we have been examining so far. The reason is that several of the costs of inflation which enter the stabilization cost are associated with *unanticipated* inflation. However, the inflation component of the *long-run target* should presumably be regarded as fully *anticipated*. If so, the "target cost function" should assign a lower cost to inflation than that embodied in the stabilization cost function.

On the other hand the cost of unemployment should not be very different whether anticipated or not. If so, the isocost of the "target cost function" should be steeper than those of the "stabilization function", resulting in a point of tangency with the Phillips Curve at some point to the left of *a*, like point *b*, with coordinates $(\bar{u}, \bar{p})$.

In this case, which might well be deemed more general, optimal stabilization policy is slightly more complex and is described by the path *b'b* marked by arrows. It calls for an immediate restraint on demand so as to raise the unemployment rate above the long-run target $\bar{u}$ to, or close to, an "intermediate target" $\hat{u}$ which is defined by *the point of tangency, a, of the long-run Phillips Curve with the isocost of the "stabilization cost function"*. The restraint should not be significantly relaxed until inflation has declined to a level close to the long-run target, $\bar{p}$. Only at that point is unemployment returned to its long-run target $\bar{u}$.

This solution has a number of interesting features – some intuitively appealing and some less obvious. In the first place, it calls for the highest restraint at the very beginning and not for gradually rising restraint as would tend to occur, for instance, if a policy of "non-accommodation" were pursued by maintaining the historical growth of the monetary aggregates. In this respect, optimal policy is closer to a "frontal attack" than to gradualism. At the same time, it has a gradualist nature in that it does not call for stamping out inflation at once by enforcing a degree of initial restraint commensurate to the size of the initial shock. It calls instead for a limited degree of restraint in the sense that the appropriate unemployment target never exceeds the upper bound $\hat{u}$, no matter how large the initial shock. Thus, the optimal response to a larger shock is not to increase appreciably the initial restraint but rather to allow more time for its liquidation. This aspect of the solution can be traced to the non-linearity of the relation between the rate of change in inflation and unemployment. Both *a priori* considerations and empirical evidence suggest that, though inflation will tend to decline faster the higher the unemployment level, successive increments in unemployment will produce a smaller and smaller incremental response, and these considerations are reflected in the specifications of most empirical studies. It is for this reason that there is an upper bound $\hat{u}$ to the initial amount of slack that it pays to create, no matter how high the initial inflation. If unemployment is pushed beyond $\hat{u}$, what is gained in terms of faster reductions of inflation cannot make up for the additional unemployment cost.

Finally, it is worth noting that the optimal path we have derived has the nature of a so-called "turnpike solution". The terminology can best be understood by reference to Figure 2. Suppose that an exogenous shock has landed the system at point B, directly above the target b, where inflation is excessive, but unemployment is at the long-run target $\bar{u}$. One possible path would be to keep u at $\bar{u}$, and let inflation decline, moving gradually the economy from B to b. But this is not the optimal solution; it is best instead to move to the neighbourhood of the intermediate target $\hat{u}$ and descend along, or close to, the path $a'a$ because that path corresponds to the most cost-efficient way of reducing inflation. Only when the final inflation target is close at hand is the path abandoned in order to reach $\bar{u}$. The solution is analogous to that chosen by a person wishing to travel between two centres not served by a turnpike, who finds it advantageous not to take the shorter route but instead to make a detour in order to reach an appropriate turnpike, and to abandon it only at a point where the turnpike is close to his final destination.

The turnpike character of the solution has interesting implications with respect to the accuracy of forecasting needed to determine the optimum path. It should be noted in fact that in selecting the path, the policy makers need to take into account not only the initial rate of inflation but also the effect of any later shocks anticipated over the re-entry horizon. Insofar as the optimal response is the same for a wide range of possible disturbances, forecast errors will not compromise appreciably the optimality of the chosen path, but will impinge only on the forecasted re-entry time.

iv) *The empirical relevance of a non-vertical long-run Phillips Curve*

To what extent is the case of the non-vertical Phillips Curve relevant? Here we must distinguish between short- and long-run verticality and between *a priori* considerations and empirical evidence. The hypothesis that the Phillips Curve is vertical even in the short run as asserted by the Macro Rational Expectations School,[1] can be quickly dismissed. It has neither empirical support nor *a priori* credibility except possibly in a world of auction markets which has no empirical relevance. On the other hand the hypothesis of a long-run vertical Phillips Curve has considerable theoretical appeal (especially in the modified version mentioned below). The empirical evidence both for the United States and for other countries seems inadequate to discriminate between a truly vertical and a fairly steep but non-vertical long-run Phillips Curve. For the United States in particular, and using annual data, our best estimate of the effect of received inflation in reducing the rate of inflation was -0.18 rather than zero as would be implied by a truly "vertical" Phillips Curve. At the same time it should be recognized that the difference between -0.18 and zero is not large, and, in fact, statistically is

---

1. ROBERT E. LUCAS JR., 'Expectations and the Neutrality of Money', *Journal of Economic Theory*, vol. 4 (2), April 1972, pp. 103-124.

not very significant, when an allowance is made for imprecision of estimation.

However, there is one further consideration that points to the empirical relevance of the analysis of the non-vertical case. The proponents of a vertical Phillips Curve have made a strong case for the existence of a "natural" rate of unemployment determined exclusively by *real* forces such as turnover rates, entry to and exit from the labour force (and including, possibly, "structural" factors), and largely independent of nominal variables, at least in the long run. Accordingly unemployment could deviate from the natural rate only transiently because of errors in expectations, long-term contracts, etc. However, it could not be maintained permanently below or above the natural rate, except possibly at the cost of ever-rising or ever-falling inflation.

This view seems quite convincing with respect to the feasibility and consequences of keeping unemployment *below* the natural rate. It is much more questionable with respect to the implications of unemployment above the natural rate. Taking into account the asymmetry between upward and downward rigidity, implied by the dominant role of those already employed in the determination of wages and the tendency for employers' and employees' interest to converge in the face of excess demand but not in the presence of excess supply, it seems questionable that excess unemployment, even if maintained for a long time, would ever lead to inflation becoming increasingly negative. On the basis of these considerations it was suggested in a joint paper with Papademos[1] that the notion of a natural rate should be replaced by that of a Non-Inflationary Rate of Unemployment (NIRU) on the left of which the long-run Phillips Curve would be vertical, while on the right it would have the traditional properties. For the United States we estimated the value of NIRU at slightly below 6 per cent. If this hypothesis provides an acceptable description of the economy, as we believe, then the solution to the optimal stabilization path coincides with that which is appropriate in the case of the traditional Phillips

1. Franco Modigliani and Lucas D. Papademos, 'Optimal Demand Policies against Stagflation'.

Curve, for the obvious reason that the optimal solution will call for unemployment rates never lower than NIRU, and therefore falling on the non-vertical side of the Phillips Curve.

9. *Optimal Stabilization Policies for the United States – an illustration*

i) *The non-vertical case*

To illustrate the implication for our approach, we have calculated the optimal stabilization path for the United States using the estimate of the Phillips Curve mentioned above. This estimate, it will be recalled, implies some long-run trade-off, at least on the high side of NIRU, but rather limited in scope. It also implies a rather slow response of the change of inflation to excess unemployment. In our exercise, we also assume that the long-run inflation target is 2 per cent, which is consistent with the experience of the United States in the 1960s. Given the current rather un-favourable composition of the labour force, this target turns out to imply, at present, a target unemployment rate of slightly below 6 per cent. This corresponds to our measure of NIRU, and is consistent with estimates obtained by others.

As noted earlier, the essential characteristics of the optimal path, when the Phillips Curve is non-vertical above NIRU, is the "intermediate target" or "turnpike" rate of unemployment, which controls the appropriate initial degree of demand restraint. That intermediate target depends, of course, not only on the Phillips Curve but also on the relative cost assigned in the (stabilization) social cost function to unemployment and inflation respectively. It is this relative cost which controls the slope of the isocosts WW. Even though we have no solid basis for assign-ing a specific cost, we can explore the implications of alternative "plausible" assumptions.

Suppose first that the cost of an additional one per cent excess unemployment for one year is rated higher than that of one per cent additional inflation – specifically, twice as high. It turns out that with this assessment the optimal solution corresponds to the extreme case in which the intermediate unemployment target coincides with the long-run target. In this case the optimal policy would consist in keeping unemployment around 6 per cent des-pite any inflationary shocks.

Suppose next that unemployment and inflation were rated equally costly. Then, the optimal policy would call for initially raising unemployment toward an intermediate target of just below 8 per cent – an appreciable but not drastic response. On the other hand if inflation were assessed to be twice as costly as unemployment, then the intermediate target would become much higher, in excess of 10 per cent, reflecting the steepness of the Phillips Curve. Unfortunately, even with a non-vertical Phillips Curve the choice of an optimal policy is affected substantially by the assessment of relative costs, an area in which consensus may be difficult to achieve.

ii) *The case of a long-run vertical Phillips Curve*

Our approach can be applied also to the case of a truly vertical Phillips Curve, and the nature of optimal path turns out to be fairly similar to that described above. Firstly, the optimal response consists again in using aggregate demand policy to bring unemployment initially to some appropriate target level above the natural rate. There is a difference though: that target no longer has an upper bound, but is higher the greater the initial inflation. Yet the difference is more one of form than of substance in so far as, for large shocks, the target is found to be rather insensitive to the shock. Furthermore, it turns out that if in the cost function we allow for time discounting of future inflation, then, even the formal difference disappears: with time discounting the initial target again has an upper bound.

However, in assessing how sensitive the optimal path is to the "verticality" of the Phillips Curve two further considerations pointing in opposite directions must be taken into account. On the one hand, the upper bound in the vertical case turns out to be large and hence to be operational only for quite high rates of inflation. In the range more likely to be relevant, the initial unemployment target does depend on the magnitude of the initial shock and on forecasts of future disturbances, making the choice of the path more complex and more sensitive to forecasting errors. On the other hand, we have found that the optimal path for the United States, assuming a vertical Phillips Curve, was not different from that generated by our non-vertical Phillips Curve, as long as the same cost assessment was used. (For this purpose an estimate of the vertical Phillips Curve was obtained from the non-vertical Phillips Curve by setting the coefficient of past inflation at zero. The natural rate implied by this estimate roughly coincides with our estimate of NIRU (or just below 6 per cent). For instance, if the cost of unemployment and inflation are assumed equal and inflation is discounted at a rate of 10 per cent (as suggested by various considerations) the difference between the optimal unemployment path corresponding respectively to the vertical and non-vertical Phillips Curve ranges within a band of two percentage points, and becomes even smaller if unemployment is assigned a higher relative cost.

10. The Role of Aggregate Demand Policy to control Inflation: An Overview and Critique

At this point we may attempt to summarize our analysis of how aggregate demand policy can be utilized to bring under control an on-going inflationary process, highlighting both its potential and its shortcomings.

We have endeavoured to show that aggregate demand policy can be used effectively to eliminate inflation gradually, but that since the elimination can only be gradual, the question of choosing an optimal path must be faced. To design an optimal path, a realistic estimate of the Phillips Curve is needed as well as an explicit assessment of the costs of excess unemployment and incremental inflation. If our assumption that these costs are roughly proportional to the cumulated excess unemployment and inflation over the chosen path is accepted, then the optimal policy will call for responding to the initial shock by implementing restrictive demand policies which would raise unemployment to some initial target which is relatively insensitive to the magnitude of the shock. The slack is to be maintained, or reduced only marginally, until inflation has returned close to the target level. Only then unemployment should be returned, gradually, to the target level.

The choice of the initial target is of crucial importance, and in turn depends on the nature of the cost function (the social preference) and of the Phillips Curve (the opportunity set). With respect to the Phillips Curve, the crucial characteristics appear to be: i) the responsiveness of the change in inflation to unemployment and ii) the steepness of the long-run trade-off. Whether or not the Phillips Curve is vertical in the long run – an issue which has generated much controversy – does not seem to be crucial. We have found that as long as the Phillips Curve is steep – and all the evidence seems to point in that direction – it does not make any difference qualitatively whether it is truly vertical or not.

With respect to the cost function the crucial parameter is the relative cost of unemployment and inflation. It is at this point that it can be appreciated why demand management is bound to run into far greater problems when endeavouring to control

83

inflation than in stabilizing the system against demand shocks. When a demand shock has produced or threatens to produce a shortfall of output and employment below the warranted level, in a non-inflationary environment, everybody can agree that the appropriate target is to re-establish full employment, as this will contribute both to income and to price stability. There may be disagreement on how best to achieve that target, but not on the target itself. However, in the case of anti-inflationary policy, a choice has to be made between two evils. There are bound to be different opinions in assessing the two evils, especially when the benefits of the painful cure are delayed in time. Accordingly, anti-inflationary aggregate demand policy is unlikely to be timely or consistent. Even successful policies will never earn economists the acclaim they obtained during the 1950s and 1960s when the crucial problem was stabilizing aggregate demand.

However, the use of aggregate demand policies to fight inflation suffers from another and even greater shortcoming – namely cost-ineffectiveness. To see this point let us raise an embarrassing question: suppose that we were to rely on the optimal path mentioned above for the United States to get back to target – how much excess unemployment and how much additional inflation would it call for? This question is embarrassing because the honest answer appears to be the following, at least in the United States: a horrifying amount of unemployment over an unbearably long period of time. The point is that according to the estimate of the Phillips Curve used above, an additional percentage point of unemployment for a year reduces the annual rate of inflation by approximately 0.3 percentage points. Other recent estimates have been a little more encouraging, but the estimate of the trade-off seldom exceeds half a percentage point. Assuming that it were 0.5, then, to reduce the inflation rate from the current rate, say 7 to 8 per cent to a long-run target approximating the traditional rate of between 2 and 3 per cent, it would require at least 10 per cent excess unemployment years. According to our assessment this amount of excess unemployment would result in a loss amounting to approximately 30 per cent of the national product, or well over $500,000 millions (0.5×10^{12}) at 1978 prices. To this alarming figure we would still have to add the cost of approximately 12 per cent cumulated extra inflation over the five years that would be required, assuming that the initial unemployment target was 8 per cent. In comparison with these awesome costs, the direct burden of the explosion of oil prices that largely triggered the current inflationary process pales into insignificance.

In view of these costs, it would be difficult to escape the conclusion that, even though aggregate demand management is a possible answer – and not everyone would support this view – it cannot be accepted as *the* answer. There must be less painful cures. Developing alternatives and selling them to the politicians is in my judgement a major, if not *the* major, challenge that faces economists at present.

A number of alternatives have received consideration. However, the only ones that have been seriously tried out so far have been along the lines of income policies and price controls, an approach whose results have been far from encouraging. Certainly the experience of the United States in 1971–73 must be regarded as a conspicuous failure, and even in other countries it would be difficult to find examples of success.

In my view there remains a number of alternatives to be pursued, notably approaches based on the imaginative uses of the tax system. These include, in particular, the use of direct taxes as a deterrent and/or an incentive to moderate the wage-price spiral – the so-called "carrot and stick" approach – and reliance on indirect taxes as a component of cost, to affect directly the course of prices. Needless to say, these devices should not be thought of as an alternative to, but rather as complementary to, aggregate demand management, with a view to increasing its cost-effectiveness. Nor should one disregard opportunities for institutional changes which would relieve some of the most painful consequence of inflation.

This is not the proper place to pursue this topic. In conclusion, however, I am prepared to state my conviction that despite their problems and shortcomings, these alternatives will have some role to play in the years to come in managing inflation, especially if we continue to be exposed to large and capricious shocks at the hands of oil producers.

85

THIRD LECTURE
The Monetary Mechanism Revisited and its Relation with the Financial Structure

1. Introduction

The purpose of this third lecture is to take a new look at the "monetary mechanism", that is, the mechanism through which the Monetary Authority manages to control (more or less tightly) aggregate nominal income. I propose to argue that the traditional view that puts the money supply in the forefront and encompasses both the monetarist and the Keynes-Hicks formulations, far from being a general one, is really focusing on a rather special case; that there are aggregates other than the monetary liabilities of the banking system whose control ensures control of nominal income; correspondingly, there exist paradigms other than those based on the money supply that are useful in describing the working of the monetary mechanism; and finally, that the effectiveness of alternative aggregate targets and the usefulness of alternative paradigms depend critically on the financial structure of the economy.

At present the two broadly accepted views of the monetary mechanism are the "monetarist" and the "Keynesian" views. These two views, though different in some important respects, share the basic notion that the Monetary Authority controls money income through its control of the supply of money – the medium of exchange – interacting with a well-defined and stable demand for money. The difference between the two schools relates to differences of views concerning the arguments of the demand for money – or at least their empirical importance: and these differences in turn have implications for the working of the monetary mechanism.

The monetarist school can be regarded as a generalization of the classical "quantity theory of money" – a theory that has been in existence for at least a couple of centuries and possibly even longer. (According to an account which I have been unable to verify, the theory was enunciated in China several thousand years ago). Although it has had many formulations, including most recently the Cambridge cash-balance approach and the Fisher Equation of exchange, its essence consists in the proposition that the "real demand for money", i.e., the demand for money expressed in terms of purchasing power over commodities, is a "real" phenomenon, i.e., independent of the nominal quantity of money or the price level. Together with the classical view that the volume and composition of real output is also a real variable independent of the money supply, it leads to the conclusion that the price level, and hence money output, is proportional to the stock of money – at least once money demand has fully adjusted to money supply, which is supposed to happen quite quickly. It should be noted that this theory does not assume, or require, that the proportionality factor be constant in time. On the contrary, it may be expected to change in response to both changes in real factors and financial structure. What is essential is that the real demand for money is independent of the nominal quantity of money. The modern monetarist version retains the hypothesis that the demand for money is proportional to money output, but accepts the Keynesian view that, in the short run, prices may not be perfectly flexible. Accordingly, while nominal output is still seen as determined by the interaction of money demand with the money supply, the change in money income arising from a change in the stock of money may result in part from a change in output rather than exclusively from a change in the general price level.[1]

1. MILTON FRIEDMAN, 'A Theoretical Framework for Monetary Analysis', *Journal of Political Economy*, vol. 78(2), March-April 1970, pp. 193-238; reprinted in ROBERT

The main difference between this monetarist formulation and the Keynesian one is that the latter stresses that the demand for money depends not only on money output but also, in an essential way, on the opportunity cost of carrying money. This cost can be measured by the spread between the short-term market rate of interest and the rate, if any, paid on money or its components (such as demand deposits). This "liquidity preference" effect,[1] that causes the demand for money to depend on market interest rates, may, in principle, be acknowledged also by monetarists but it is then disregarded as empirically insignificant. Keynesians, on the other hand, consider this dependence to be not only empirically important but also of major conceptual significance. In their view it provides the means for understanding the mechanism by which expansion or contraction of the money supply, brought about by Central Bank policy, succeeds in producing variations in aggregate money output. This mechanism is very unclear in the elementary monetarist formulation which disregards liquidity preference. Certainly it might be argued that, when the money supply first expands, the public will find itself with more money than it wants to hold, given its initial income, and hence will respond by spending that money on goods – the extra money "burns holes in their pockets", as Professor Samuelson has expressed the argument. The additional expenditure in turn raises income and the demand for money until it matches the new supply. However, this simplistic view ignores the fact that, in an advanced financial system, the money supply typically expands through the "monetization of debt", i.e., through the acquisition by the banking system (including the Central Bank) of debt from the private sector, against newly created money. Clearly, this transaction does not change in any way the wealth of the private sector (or its income, at least to a first approximation). Furthermore, since the acquisition of the additional money by the public occurred as a result of an entirely voluntary transaction, it cannot be argued that the public holds more

J. GORDON (ed.), *Milton Friedman's Monetary Framework: A Debate with His Critics.* Chicago: University of Chicago Press, 1974, pp. 1-62.

1. JOHN MAYNARD KEYNES, *The General Theory of Employment, Interest and Money.* London: Macmillan, 1936.

money than it wants to or that it has any inducement to dispose of it by buying commodities.

How then does an increase in the money supply lead to a rise in aggregate nominal output? The mechanism, as interpreted by the Keynesians, can be described along the following lines. Firstly, to induce the public to exchange debt instruments for money, the banking system must initially bid down the interest rate (or, equivalently, bid up the price of the debt instruments). Secondly, the fall in market rates, though it might initially concentrate on short-term instruments which are the closest substitutes for money, will eventually spread, as the public endeavours to shift to longer-term bonds whose yield has become more attractive relative to shorter-term bonds. The fall in the interest rate structure will eventually make it profitable to exchange money-fixed assets, including newly created debt, for physical assets or equities. The first operation increases the demand for investment goods directly. The second, by bidding up the value of shares, makes it attractive for firms to acquire capital goods whose market valuation rises relative to the acquisition cost. Finally, the decline in the market rate should lead banks to lower their loan rate, inducing an expansion of borrowing. The expansion may be expected to contribute directly to nominal demand as the sellers of the newly created debt are likely to spend the proceeds mainly on goods and services rather than to add significantly to their cash balances.

2. A Formulation of the Traditional Model

This traditional view of the monetary mechanism is formalized in a very concise fashion in the model set forth in Part A of Table 1 (see overleaf).[1] The first four equations are essentially the standard equation of the Keynesian reformulation of the classical Quantity Theory as formalized by Hicks.[2] The first equation is the demand for money: the real demand for money (nominal demand deflated by the price level P) is proportional to real income (nominal income Y, deflated) but with the proportionality factor depending on another real variable, the interest rate, r. Equations (2) and (3) are the saving and the investment functions respectively, while equation (4) is the market clearing or equilibrium condition in the commodity market. Equation (2) could be written in a more general form, including the interest rate on the right hand side and, similarly, (3) could include Y; but this would not make much difference since, in any event, the three equations (2) to (4) contain four unknowns (after both sides of (4) are deflated by P) and can therefore be solved for Y/P in terms of r, yielding the Hicksian IS curve (for P given). It is also important that the slope of this relation be negative. This condition is necessarily satisfied in our formulation, but will hold also in the more general version provided the coefficients of r in (2) and of Y in (3) are "well behaved".

Equation (5) is less usual. It is intended to formalize the "price mechanism" by relating the price level to nominal, and hence also real, income. Equations (5a) and (5b) formalize two well-known special cases of this mechanism. The first corresponds to the case of complete price flexibility – irrespective of the value of nominal income, the price level always adjusts so to ensure the maintenance of full-employment output, denoted by $\bar{X}$. It corresponds to the "classical" assumption and also to long-run equilibrium in more general models in which prices adjust but require time to do so. Equation (5b) formalizes the diametrically

1. For ease of reference, Table 1 is reproduced in the pull-out page at the end of the volume.

2. John R. Hicks, 'Mr. Keynes and the "Classics"; A Suggested Interpretation', *Econometrica*, vol. 5 (2), April 1937, pp. 147-59; reprinted in John R. Hicks, *Critical Essays in Monetary Theory*. Oxford: Clarendon Press, 1967.

Part A – Conventional Model

(1)	$M = k(r)\,Y$	Demand for money	M	= Money demand
			r	= Interest rate
			Y	= Nominal income
(2)	$\dfrac{S}{P} = S\left(\dfrac{Y}{P}\right)$	Saving function	S	= Nominal saving
			P	= Price level
(3)	$\dfrac{I}{P} = I(r)$	Investment function	I	= Nominal rate of investment
(4)	$I = S$	Commodity market clearing		
(5)	$\Phi(P,Y) = 0$	"Price" equation		
(5a)	$\dfrac{Y}{P} = \bar{X}$	Perfect price flexibility	$\bar{X}$	= "Full-employment" output
(5b)	$P = \bar{P}$	Absolute price rigidity	$\bar{P}$	= "Received" price level
(6)	$M = M^s$	Money market clearing	M^s	= Money supply
(P.1)	$M = \bar{M}$	Monetary policy equation	$\bar{M}$	= Exogenously set money supply

Part B – Financial Structure

(1a)	$m = k(r)\,Y - M(-1)$		$m = M - M(-1)$ increment in money holdings	
(7)	$I = E + B$	Source and use of funds for firms' sector	E	= Equity sources
			B	= Credit sources
(8)	$B = \beta(r,\,Y)$ $\beta_r < 0$ $\beta_Y < 0$	Determinants of borrowing		
(9)	$S = m + da + E$	Source-and-use statement for household sector	da	= Increase in deposit accounts balances
(10)	$m + da = L^b$	Source-and-use statement for banking sector	L^b	= Flow of bank credit
(11)	$B = L^b$	Loan market clearing		
(P.2)	$L^b = \dfrac{\bar{M}\,\bar{B}^b}{\lambda} = \bar{L}^b$			

Table 1. The Monetary Mechanism

opposite case of complete price rigidity. This assumption has been shown above to be close to Keynes' original hypothesis but it can also be usefully regarded as a short-run approximation to an economy in which the adjustment of prices to excess capacity is slow – at least as long as output is below full employment. Finally, equation (6) is the equilibrium condition in the money market.

It is seen from the table that the system (1) to (6) consists of six equations but contains seven unknowns – it is therefore not closed or sufficient to determine uniquely all the variables. In fact in the case of price flexibility, equation (5a) and equations (2) to (5) can be seen to form a closed sub-system, determining all the real variables, including output $\bar{X}$ and the interest rate (the classical dichotomy). However, the remaining equations (1) and (6) contain three unknowns, M, M^s and the price level P, and are therefore insufficient to determine these variables. In the case of price rigidity, there is no dichotomy and, in general, no variable, real or nominal, is determined.

The traditional way of closing the system is to introduce a Monetary Authority (M.A.) having the power of fixing "exogenously" the nominal money supply. There exist many techniques by which this may be achieved; however, there is no need to elaborate at this point. For our purposes the M.A.'s power can be formalized through the "policy" equation (P. 1) which provides the missing equation. Under price flexibility, that equation fixes the price level; under price rigidity it fixes all the variables including nominal income, and hence real income, since P is given.

It should be acknowledged at this point that (P. 1) is not the only recognized way of closing the system and making income determinate: at least under price rigidity the M.A. could alternatively fix the interest rate. This would directly determine investment equation (3) and income equations (2) and (4). Equation (1) would then determine the money demand which the M.A. would have to be prepared to supply (by putting the banking system in the position to do so). In that case (P. 1) would be formally replaced by (P. 1') $r = \bar{r}$.

This alternative approach has at times been favoured by

Keynesians, though recently it has tended to lose favour because of the problems created by inflation. However, there is no need to elaborate on this point any further as it is not essential to the argument.

In fact, the choice between M and r as the control instrument would not be a significant issue if the relevant equations of the system held precisely and the monetary authority had a reliable estimate of them. The point is that, even though in principle the M.A. can set either M or r at will, in practice it must be presumed to do so in order to achieve a desirable, or target, level of income, $\hat{Y}$. However, the system (1) to (6) in conjunction with (P. 1) implies that to any given $\hat{Y}$ corresponds a unique target value of M and r, $\hat{M}$ and $\hat{r}$. The M.A. could therefore indifferently set either variable at its target level and the other would also achieve the target value – indeed, it would be impossible to know which target was being enforced.

In reality, the M.A.'s knowledge of the relevant behaviour relation is subject to "stochastic" errors. In this case, it can still calculate the $\hat{M}$ and $\hat{r}$ that correspond to $\hat{Y}$ in the absence of errors, but the value of Y which would actually obtain would, in general, be different and would depend on whether it chooses $\hat{M}$ or $\hat{r}$ as the "intermediate target" to be enforced. Under these conditions the M.A. faces the problem of which target to choose, and the choice will presumably depend on which targets may be expected to be more accurate in the long run. This problem has been analyzed in a well-known article by William Poole.[1] Using as a criterion the expectation of the mean square deviation of realized Y from the target $\hat{Y}$, Poole has shown that, in the framework of the simple *IS-LM* model described by our system, whether M or r is a better intermediate target depends on the relative magnitude of the errors in the *IS* relation and in the money demand, or the *LM* relation, and on their correlation. By and large, an intermediate money target will tend to produce better results when the *IS* error is large relative to that of the money demand equation and when the two errors are positively correlated.

1. WILLIAM POOLE, 'Optimal Choice of Monetary Policy Instruments in a Simple Stochastic Macro Model', *Quarterly Journal of Economics*, vol. 84 (2), May 1970, pp. 197-216.

3. Shortcomings of the Traditional Paradigm

The above are the accepted views of the monetary mechanism, of the possible intermediate targets and of their likely effectiveness. Our criticism of these views may usefully begin with the observation that the descriptive and cognitive value of the traditional paradigm, and the effectiveness of money as an intermediate target, very much depends on a set of rather specific circumstances such as: i) that there exist some instrument identifiable as money in the sense that it performs primarily the function of a medium of exchange, and which is clearly distinguishable from other stores of value not having this property (one institution that clearly contributes to a sharp distinction is the absence of interest on money); ii) the Monetary Authority is in a position to control the money supply and chooses to do so; and iii) firms rely to a substantial extent for their financing on market instruments held directly by the public or by non-commercial-bank intermediaries.

These conditions appear to have been broadly satisfied for the United States, at least until fairly recently, and this may explain why the above paradigm has a distinct Anglo-Saxon bias. However even in the United States those conditions have been increasingly breached as the Central Bank's focus has shifted from money to broader aggregates, as other stores of value have acquired at least partial medium-of-exchange properties, and the spreading of interest payments on current accounts has increased the role of money as a store of value. With these developments the old paradigm is becoming less and less useful, both as a cognitive device and as a basis for policy.[1]

However, the inadequacy of the paradigm is even more evident if we look at other economies, as I realized some years ago in trying to apply it, in particular, to the Italian economy and later

1. PHILLIP D. CAGAN, 'Financial Developments and the Erosion of Monetary Controls', in WILLIAM FELLNER (ed.), *Contemporary Economic Problems*. Washington: American Enterprise Institute, 1979, pp. 117-51; WILLIAM L. SILBER, 'Monetary Policy Effectiveness: The Case of a Positively Sloped IS Curve', *Journal of Finance*, vol. 26 (5), December 1971, pp. 1077-82.

to many other economies, from France to Japan, from Spain to Sweden. In the case of Italy, for instance, the distinction between banks and savings institutions and between current and deposit accounts has always been imprecise; both types of accounts pay interest and, indeed, there have been times when, for complex technical reasons, interest on deposit accounts was reported to be lower on average than on current accounts; and, what matters most, much of the time the two types of accounts have been subject to the same reserve requirements. As a result, the $M1$ money supply is blurred, and while the Central Bank may be able to control the total of bank deposits through reserve requirements, it cannot control the way in which the public distributes that total between current and deposit accounts. This means that the money supply is demand-determined. Yet the price level has been well-behaved at least until recently. Finally, in Italy as in many other countries, bank deposits are by far the most important forms of credit instruments held by the private sector and, correspondingly, bank loans are by far the most common form of firms' debt financing.

4. Toward a Broader View of the Monetary Mechanism

In order to develop a broader view of the monetary mechanism, it is necessary to pay some attention to financial markets, and financial stocks and flows, other than the money market described by equation (1). These other markets are customarily suppressed in a basic macroeconomic model such as that of Part A because, given the traditional view of the monetary mechanism, they add nothing to an understanding of the determination of aggregate demand.

Certainly, the proposition that financial markets and institutions may play an important role in the transmission mechanism is by no means entirely new. It was emphasized some time ago by Gurley and Shaw[1] in their pioneering work which examined the role and implications of financial intermediaries on the saving-investment process; it is reflected in the portfolio-balance approach to monetary theory advanced by Tobin, Brainard and other members of the Yale school, as well as by Brunner and Meltzer;[2] and it has motivated and shaped the development of both the theoretical and empirical analysis associated with the construction of the MPS econometric model.[3] Much of this analysis, however, remains within the traditional

---

1. JOHN S. GURLEY and EDWARD S. SHAW, *Money in a Theory of Finance* (with a mathematical Appendix by ALAN C. ENTHOVEN). Washington: The Brookings Institution, 1960.

2. See: JAMES TOBIN, 'Commercial Banks as Creators of Money', in DEANE CARSON (ed.), *Banking and Monetary Studies*. Homewood, Ill.: Richard Irwin, 1963, pp. 408-19; JAMES TOBIN, 'A General Equilibrium Approach to Monetary Theory', *Journal of Money, Credit and Banking*, vol. 1 (1), February 1969, pp. 15-29; JAMES TOBIN and WILLIAM C. BRAINARD, 'Financial Intermediaries and the Effectiveness of Monetary Controls', *American Economic Review*, vol. 53 (2), May 1963, pp. 383-400; WILLIAM C. BRAINARD, 'Financial Intermediaries and a Theory of Monetary Control', *Yale Economic Essais*, vol. 4(1), Fall 1964, pp. 431-82; KARL BRUNNER and ALLAN H. MELTZER, 'The Meaning of Monetary Indicators', in GEORGE HORWICH (ed.), *Monetary Process and Policy. A Symposium*. Homewood, Ill.: Richard Irwin, 1967, pp. 187-217.

3. ALBERT K. ANDO, 'Some Aspects of Stabilization Policies, the Monetarist Controversy and the MPS Model', *International Economic Review*, vol. 15 (3), October 1974, pp. 541-71; ALBERT K. ANDO and FRANCO MODIGLIANI, 'Some Reflections on Describing Structures of Financial Sectors' (Appendix with KARL SHELL), in GARY FROMM and LAWRENCE R. KLEIN (eds.), *The Brookings Model: Perspective and Recent Developments*. Amsterdam: North-Holland, 1975, pp. 524-63.

framework in the sense that it is largely concerned with the working of an economy in which monetary policy takes basically the
form of control of the money supply. It is concerned either with
the way in which $M1$ control is transmitted through the financial markets on its way to affect spending decision or with the
way in which financial markets may undermine the achievement
of the authorities' targets through changes reflecting autonomous
developments, or even worse, a response to the authorities' policy
actions.

To illustrate this approach, Part B of the table highlights certain important financial flows. Here a distinction is made between a bank sector and a private non-bank sector, and within
the latter between "firms" and "households". What characterizes
"firms" in our formalization is that they, and only they, hold
physical capital. In addition, use will also be made, initially, of
the convenient simplifying approximation that firms hold no assets other than physical capital. Firms are financed in the first
place by equity capital, i.e., by the owners' funds. Insofar as this
wealth is insufficient to finance the firms' assets, the difference is
made up by borrowed funds. Units that have to have recourse to
borrowing in order to finance the capital of the firm will be labelled "deficit units". Those whose wealth is sufficient to finance
their firms will be called "surplus units".

This structure and assumption lead to the streamlined source-
and-use of funds set out in equation (7). There is but one use of
funds, investment (I), and two sources: the (net) increase in equity
E and the (net) borrowing, or increase in borrowed funds, B. (E
and B thus denote flows, like I). Equation (8) gives the demand
for credit. If some complications related to publicly-traded corporate enterprises are ignored, the net demand for credit can
be thought of as representing the difference between investment
and saving for the set of all (terminal) deficit units. It is, therefore, expressed as a declining function of r, and of income Y (as a
rise in Y should raise saving and hence the capacity for self-
financing). Note that equations (3), (7) and (8) imply that the
flow of equity financial investments is a decreasing function of
r and an increasing function of Y. In fact, if r increases, the self-
financed investment of surplus units decreases, while a rise in

income, by increasing saving, raises the self-financing of the deficit units.

Equation (9) is the source-and-use statement of the household sector. It is convenient to deal initially with a limiting type of financial structure in which there are no marketable debt instruments and, therefore, households can invest their saving only by increasing their holdings in money, m, and in deposit accounts balances, da, besides equity. Note that under these circumstances, (9) also implicitly yields the household demand for the increase in total liabilities – monetary and non-monetary – of the banking system, since S is given by (2) and, as has been noted above, E follows from (3) and (8). This demand, which consists of the excess saving over investment of the (terminal) surplus units, may be expected to increase with r, which encourages switching from real assets to bank deposits, and with income which increases saving. Actually, the rate relevant to this equation should be that on deposit accounts; however, for the moment it will be assumed that this rate can be expressed in terms of the loan rate, r, as competition between banks keeps the two rates close together, except for a spread covering the costs of intermediation.

The portion of the increment in total claims on banks taking the form of money is accounted for by the money demand equation which, however, must be rewritten in first-difference form. This is done in equation (1a) which replaces (1). It should be noted that interest on money is again assumed to be either zero or exogenously given. Finally, (10) is the streamlined source-and-use statement of the consolidated banking system (including the Central Bank). It states that the total increase in liabilities equals the increase in bank loans, L^b, the only assets available to the consolidated banking system. The remaining equation (11) sets forth the condition of equilibrium in the loan market; total borrowing, which is the same as firms' borrowing, must be equal to the lending by the only lenders, namely banks.

The enlarged system of Parts A and B contains eleven equations with as many unknowns, as five equations and four unknowns have been added to the original six equations with seven unknowns. However, as usual, one of the market clearing equations

(4), (6) or (11) is redundant. One more equation is thus needed to close the system.

In the standard monetarist-Keynesian formulation, the additional equation is of course (P. 1). In this case, the conventional paradigm holds since the monetary mechanism can be described by the equations of Part A alone.

It should be readily apparent, however, that condition (P. 1) – exogenously fixing the money supply – is by no means the only way of closing the system. Indeed, from a formal point of view, all that is required is an equation of the form $Z = \bar{Z}$, where Z could be any nominal variable of the system, and in particular any of the nominal financial variables. In our illustrative system, eligible variables would include money, m, deposit accounts balances, da, their sum, $m + da = M2$, bank lending, L^b, or firms' borrowing, B. Once such a variable (or linear combination of variables) has been fixed, all other financial variables will be endogenously determined. In particular, the money supply will be given by (1a) and hence will be demand-determined; and yet nominal income will be uniquely determined. It is also possible to show that if the assumption of price rigidity is dropped and replaced by the opposite case of perfect flexibility and the absence of any money or inflation illusion is assumed, then the quantity of money theory of the price level can be replaced by the more general proposition that the price level is proportional to the value of any appropriately chosen nominal stock (at least for zero inflation).

Thus the first basic proposition has been established. The purpose of the monetary mechanism, the determination and control of nominal income, can be achieved without exogenous control of the money supply and requires instead only exogenous control of some financial "aggregate", or of a linear combination of such aggregates. One obvious corollary of this proposition is that the traditional monetarist-Keynesian paradigm of the monetary mechanism cannot have general validity.

Nonetheless, for this implication to have empirical content it must be shown that the Monetary Authority is in a position to control aggregates other than the money supply. However, it should be obvious that this possibility exists, at least in principle.

Even in the case of the United States, for instance, the Federal Reserve has made extensive use of targets such as M_2 (monetary liabilities and other deposits at savings institutions) or even broader aggregates. However, many other possibilities exist, and in the following sections this proposition will be illustrated with examples based on the experience of other countries.

5. Controlling Nominal Income Through Bank Credit

To begin the use of total bank credit as the M.A.'s target must be considered. Can the M.A. control this target and how? Furthermore how does control of bank credit achieve control over nominal income?

The answer to the first question is clearly in the affirmative. One among several possible devices for controlling this aggregate is for the M.A. to require banks to hold reserves against total credit, and then to supply the reserves required to support a volume of bank credit equal to the target. Thus, the reserve required per dollar of credit is denoted by λ and bank reserves by MB^b (the monetary base held by banks), then bank credit must satisfy the following constraint:

$$L \leq \frac{MB^b}{\lambda}$$

Assuming that bank reserves yield less than the market rate, and allowing for profit maximization by banks, the above inequality constraint can be replaced, to a close approximation, by an equality. Thus, the M.A. can ensure any desired target value of bank credit, $\bar{L}^b$, by keeping bank reserves at $\bar{M}\bar{B}^b = \lambda\bar{L}^b$. Under these conditions the traditional policy equation (P. 1) can be replaced by the alternative:

$$(\text{P. 2}) \qquad\qquad L^b = \frac{\bar{M}\bar{B}^b}{\lambda} = \bar{L}^b$$

In the absence of government or private market instruments, it may be assumed that the M.A. creates reserves in the process of making loans to banks, so that (11) continues to hold.

It follows that equation (P. 2) closes the system and that it does not do so by exogenously limiting the money supply since, as is apparent from (10), it controls only the sum of bank liabilities. For given total bank credit, there is no limit to the money supply other than the demand of the public (as long as it does not exceed total deposits). Hence, it can be seen again that the standard paradigm is of no use. How, then, is aggregate demand kept under control?

To answer this question it should be recalled first that the essence of the traditional Keynes-Hicks paradigm lies in the interaction of simultaneous relations in the variables r and Y. The first is the *IS* relation expressing the conditions of equilibrium in the commodity market which is obtained by substituting (2) and (3) into (4):

$$(S.\ 1) \qquad\qquad S(Y) - I(r) = 0$$

The second is the *LM* relation derived from the money demand equation (1) (or 1a) and the policy equation (P. 1), and expressing equilibrium in the money market. However, from the financial equations in Part B it can be seen that an alternative way of closing the system is to replace the *LM* equation by an equation expressing the condition of equilibrium in the loan market. This alternative equation is given by (8) after using (11) and (P. 2) to replace B with $\bar{L}^b$. Thus:

$$(S.\ 2) \qquad\qquad \beta(r, Y) = \bar{L}^b$$

(S. 1) and (S. 2) again constitute a closed system in r and Y, with the policy variable $\bar{L}^b$ as a parameter.

To understand the working of this system it is useful to rewrite the above two equations in a way that highlights the role of surplus and deficit units. To this end it should be recalled that borrowing represents the difference between investment and savings of deficit units. Accordingly, (S. 2) can be restated as:

$$(S.\ 2') \qquad\qquad I^d\ (r) - S^d\ (Y) = \bar{L}^b$$

where the superscript d denotes deficit units.

Next (S. 1) can be replaced with the equation obtained by adding (S. 1) and (S. 2'), which yields:

$$(S.\ 1') \quad [S(Y) - S^d\ (Y)] - [I(r) - I^d\ (r)] \equiv S^s\ (Y) - I^s\ (r) = \bar{L}^b$$

Here S^s denotes the saving of the surplus units which is the difference between total saving and the saving of deficit units $(S - S^d)$; and similarly, I^s is the investment of surplus units. (S. 1') and (S. 2') have a straightforward interpretation. (S. 2') states the condition of equilibrium in the loan market in which deficit units operate, given the M.A.-determined supply of loans,

$\bar{L}^b$. (S. 2′) states the conditions of equilibrium in the lending market in which surplus units operate, given the exogenously determined volume of lending $\bar{L}^b$. However, since $\bar{L}^b$ is the same as M2, (S. 1′) can also be thought of as stating the conditions of equilibrium in the market for bank liabilities, given the exogenously determined supply, $\bar{M}2 = \bar{L}^b$.

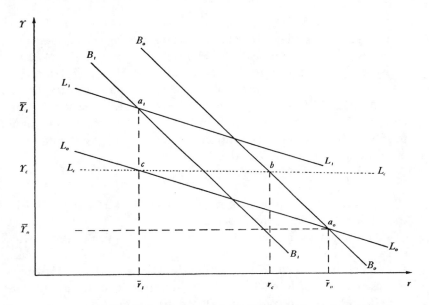

Figure 3. Income Determination and the Effects of Credit Rationing.

Figure 3 illustrates how the interaction of (S. 1′) and (S. 2′) determines income (and the interest rate). The steep solid curve labelled $B_0 B_0$ (for borrowing) is the graph of (S. 2′), the loan market equation, for $L^b = L^b(\text{o})$. For any given value of Y it shows what interest rate is required to clear the market of the supply $L^b(\text{o})$. Thus, for $Y = \bar{Y}_0$, the clearing rate is $\bar{r}_0$. Suppose that income were higher. From (S. 2′) it can be seen that a higher income implies more saving by deficit units, and therefore a smaller demand for credit at the initial rate r. Since the supply of credit is fixed along $B_0 B_0$, the higher income must lead to a lower r, as shown in the figure. Formally:

$$\left.\frac{dY}{dr}\right|_{B_0B_0} = \frac{I_r^d}{S_r^d} < 0$$

The graph of (S. 1′) corresponding to the same $L^b = L^b(0)$, is represented by the flatter solid curve labelled L_0L_0 (for lending). It shows the combination of Y and r which leads surplus units to lend the amount $L^b(0)$. To any given $\bar{r}$, such as r_0, there corresponds in the first place a certain amount of investment by surplus units, $I^s(\bar{r}_0)$. In addition, these units must be induced to lend $L^b(0)$. Hence, income for $r = \bar{r}_0$ must be such that their saving is as large as required to offset the sum of their investment $I^s(\bar{r}_0)$ and $L^b(0)$. In the figure, that income is $\bar{Y}_0$. If the interest rate were higher, their investment, and therefore their saving, would need to be lower, implying a lower income. Thus the graph of L_0L_0 is again downward sloping: formally

$$\left.\frac{dY}{dr}\right|_{L_0L_0} = \frac{I_r^s}{S_r^s} < 0$$

It can also be easily shown that, at least as long as the interest elasticity of investment and the income elasticity of saving of surplus and deficit units are not very different, then it must be the case that the LL locus is flatter than the BB locus, as in the figure. The equilibrium, or warranted, level of income and interest rate corresponding to the exogenously fixed bank credit, $L^b(0)$, is given by the intersection of B_0B_0 and L_0L_0 at point a_0 with coordinates $(\bar{r}_0, \bar{Y}_0)$.

This analysis serves to make clear the nature of the mechanism through which control of bank credit results in control over nominal income. It can be roughly described as follows: the flow of bank credit fixed by the M.A. directly determines the borrowing and investment of the deficit units and the interest rate in the loan market. This rate determines the deposit rate which controls the rate of investment of the surplus units. Finally, the sum of the investment of the two groups determines, in the usual manner, the level of income at which saving matches the investment.

The process can now be examined by which income responds to variations in bank credit, for example an expansion from $L^b(0)$

to $L^b(1)$. Consider first the loan market: if credit expands, then clearly the interest rate must fall, for any given Y. Hence, the B_0B_0 locus shifts to the left from B_0B_0 to B_1B_1. On the other hand, the LL locus must shift upward as shown by L_1L_1, because if credit creation increases, then surplus units must generate a higher rate of saving for any given r, and this requires a higher income. The intersection of the new loci, B_1B_1 and L_1L_1, generates a new equilibrium at a_1, with coordinates $(\bar{r}_1, \bar{Y}_1)$. As might be expected, the new equilibrium is characterized by higher investment and income, and by a lower interest rate.

It should be stressed again that control over nominal income is achieved without direct control over the money supply which is endogenously determined by the demand of the public expressed by equation (1). That demand is, of course, also determined, in the last analysis, by bank credit, which determines both the arguments of the demand for money, Y and r. Clearly, the opposite is also true: control of the money supply uniquely determines bank credit and income. It should be noted, however, that, at least with a simple financial structure of the type that has been assumed so far, the mechanism through which changes in money supply produce changes in income would be best described through the credit paradigm presented above rather than through the traditional Hicksian one. The M.A. cannot directly increase the money supply but can only increase the base, causing excess bank reserves and thus inducing an expansion of bank credit. This would produce an expansion of income and a fall in interest rates, along the lines described above, which would finally result in a rise in the outstanding quantity of money. It is on this mechanism that the M.A. would have to rely in tracking target M_1.

6. The Working of Bank Liabilities Targets

The conclusion that has been reached concerning the feasibility and workings of a bank credit target clearly applies directly to a target consisting of all bank liabilities, or $M2$, in our streamlined financial structure. Indeed, within that structure the two alternatives are simply indistinguishable. From a formal point of view L^b and $\bar{L}^b$ merely have to be replaced by $M2$ and $\bar{M}2$, whenever they appear in the policy equation (P. 2) and in the reduced forms (S. 1′) and (S. 2′). It follows from this that there is also a unique relation between nominal income and $M2$ which would provide the basis for the choice of an $M2$ target. However, it is suggested that for the purpose of understanding the mechanism through which an increase in $M2$ or bank liabilities is accompanied by an expansion of income, the relevant paradigm is again the bank credit paradigm of Section 5. This is because, in our system, bank liabilities can be created or destroyed only at the initiative of banks in the process of expanding or contracting bank loans. This proposition is of considerable interest in that it challenges a commonly held view, one that has been commanding growing support recently, namely that an increase of $M2$ is expansionary because it somehow increases "the liquidity" of the economy and perhaps because the non-$M1$ part of $M2$ is also endowed with moneyness properties and thus may be a better measure of money than the conventional $M1$. According to our paradigm, instead, a rise in $M2$ is expansionary because it is the unavoidable accompaniment – the other side of the coin – of a process of credit expansion. It is the credit expansion and resulting demand for investment that are expansionary both directly and through the consumption multiplier effect, and cause the positive association between $M2$ and nominal income.

It is worth noting in this connection that, in the traditional paradigm, an expansion of $M1$ leads to a fall in interest rates because the demand for money is a decreasing function of interest rates. However, in our model the demand for $M2$ is an *increasing* function of the interest rate, as can be seen from (S. 1′) – it takes a rise in interest rate to induce the surplus units to shift from physical capital (the competing asset) into bank liabilities.

The reason why a rise in M_2 will nonetheless tend to be accompanied by a fall in interest rates is that in order to expand liabilities banks must induce borrowers to borrow more, which will generally require a reduction in interest rates (except for the case of credit rationing; see below). Furthermore the reason why the public can be induced to expand its holding of deposit accounts balances despite the fall in interest rates, is that the expansion of credit raises income and saving.

7. The Role of the Deposit Rate, Interest Ceilings and Credit Rationing

So far no distinction has been made between the loan rate, r, and the bank deposit rate, r_d, on the assumption that, through competition among banks, the two rates differ only by a constant "intermediation margin." The effect of removing this limiting assumption can be examined. For example, it can be assumed that between these two rates there exists a functional relation:

$$(12) \qquad\qquad r_d = f(r)$$

This adds to the system one variable, r_d, and one equation, (12). This equation was implicit in our analysis so far, but was assumed to have unit slope ($f'(r) = 1$).

The effect of allowing for two distinct rates can be readily established by reference to equations (S. 1′) and (S. 2′). In the deficit unit equation, (S. 2′), since investment at the margin is financed by borrowing, the relevant rate is clearly the loan rate, r. On the other hand, for surplus units the opportunity cost of investing in physical assets is the deposit rate, r_d. Hence (S. 1′) should be rewritten as:

$$(S. 1'') \qquad\qquad S^s(Y) - I^s(r_d) = \bar{L}^b$$

This equation together with (S. 2′) and (12) form a closed system in Y, r, and r_d. However, using (12) to substitute for r_d in (S. 1″), the system can be reduced again to two equations in two unknowns, which can be graphed in a figure analogous to Figure 3. In fact, the graph of (S. 2′), BB is altogether unchanged. However, the graph of LL will be affected. In particular, the slope of the curve with respect to the r-axis is the product of the slope of Y with respect to r_d and of the responsiveness of r_d to r, i. e.,

$$\frac{dY}{dr}\bigg|_{L_0 L_0} = \frac{I_r^s}{S_Y^s} f'(r).$$

Since one would expect the intermediation margin to increase with the level of bank rates (i.e. $f'(r) < 1$), r_d moves less than r and the curve will be flatter than with a fixed margin.

One interesting implication of this result is that the imposition of a ceiling on the deposit rate by the M.A. tends to reduce the effectiveness of bank credit control in controlling income, in the sense that a given contraction in the bank credit target becomes less effective in reducing income. This proposition is illustrated in Figure 3. Suppose that, initially, the volume of bank credit is fixed at $L^b(1)$, that there is no ceiling, and that the position of the system is accordingly described by point a_1 at the intersection of B_1B_1 and L_1L_1. Now, let the bank credit target be reduced to $L^b(0)$. It is known that in the absence of ceilings a_1 would shift to a_0 with income falling from Y_1 to Y_0. Suppose, however, that at the same time as credit is reduced, the M.A. imposes a ceiling on the deposit rate which prevents it from rising above the initial level, $r_d(1) = f(r_1)$. From equation (S. $1''$) it can be seen that if r_d becomes a constant independent of r, i.e., $f'(r) = 0$, then Y is no longer a function of the loan rate but depends only on the parameters $r_d(1)$ and $L^b(0)$. However, this means that the graph of LL turns into the horizontal line represented by L_cL_c in the graph, going through the point c of intersection of L_0L_0 with the perpendicular through $\bar{r}_1$. Equilibrium is thus reached at point b where the horizontal L_cL_c intersects B_0B_0. The corresponding level of income Y_c is seen to be higher than Y_0, corresponding to point a_0 (and the loan rate is lower). That is, the ceiling reduces the contraction of income resulting from the restriction of bank credit.

One further noteworthy implication of the analysis is that the equilibrium level of income depends only on L_cL_c, that is, basically, on the behaviour of the surplus units; the behaviour of deficit units is relevant only to determination of the loan rate.

The reason why a ceiling reduces the effectiveness of credit policy can be readily understood. Holding the deposit rate artificially below r tends to encourage surplus units to shift away from bank deposits toward physical investment. It thus encourages disintermediation, and when the supply of bank credit is fixed by the M.A., disintermediation increases total investment, offsetting in part the deflationary effects of a reduction of bank credit. Conversely, the elimination of ceilings on deposit rates, with a fixed bank credit target, is contractionary.

The above analysis also provides the basis for understanding the effects of credit rationing. To see this, suppose again the system starts with $L^b = L^b(1)$ and no rationing or ceilings, so that equilibrium is at a_1, and let the M.A. lower the credit target to $L^b(0)$, while at the same time preventing banks from raising the lending rate above the initial level $\bar{r}_1$ and forcing them to ration the reduced supply. Under these conditions the deposit rate itself may be expected to remain fixed at the initial level, $r_d(1)$. Therefore the conclusion can be immediately reached that the LL curve turns again into the horizontal line, L_cL_c, and that equilibrium income is Y_c and is determined by the behaviour of surplus units. Since, in addition, the loan rate is exogenously fixed at r_1, the equilibrium may be regarded as described by point c, with coordinates $(\bar{r}_1, Y_c)$. What role, if any, can then be assigned to the B_0B_0 curve? To answer this question, it may be observed that B_0B_0 can be thought of as showing the demand price, or interest rate, that the deficit units would be prepared to pay, at various levels of income, to secure the amount of credit $L^b(0)$. In particular, r_c, corresponding to point b at the intersection of L_cL_c with B_0B_0, measures the demand price at the level of income, Y_c, which eventually prevails. It follows that the distance bc, or $r_c - \bar{r}_1$, provides an approximate "price measure" of unsatisfied demand to accompany the quantity measure, $L^b(1) - L^b(0)$. Finally, it is apparent from the graph and the previous paragraph that credit rationing, just like interest ceilings, reduces the effectiveness of credit policy – quite aside from its negative effects on the allocation of available credit.

It is worth noting that this conclusion that rate ceilings and credit rationing reduce the effectiveness of a given change in bank credit is diametrically opposite to the results that have been reported for the case in which the intermediate target variable is M_1.[1] In that case, in fact, ceilings and rationing tend to reduce the variation in market rates that accompanies a given reduction in income, which in turn reduces the required change in M_1.

---

1. Franco Modigliani, 'The Monetary Mechanism and Its Interaction with Real Phenomena', *Review of Economics and Statistics*, vol. 45 (1), Part 2, Supplement, February 1963, pp. 79-107; reprinted in Modigliani, vol. 1, pp. 69-97.

8. The Choice between Alternative Intermediate Targets: M_1, bank credit (or M_2), r

If the M.A. were confronted with a simple financial structure like the one described by our model, it could choose to enforce any one of a number of alternative intermediate targets and, in particular: i) the interest rate, ii) M_1, iii) bank credit, and iv) M_2 (which, however, in our case is the same as bank credit). It has already been noted that if the M.A. knew all the behaviour relations without error, then it would make no difference which of the three intermediate targets it chooses to pursue: indeed, provided they were chosen consistently, one could not infer which was being enforced. However in the presence of uncertainty, whether the result of either instability of behaviour or ignorance on the part of the M.A., any target would be subject to failure, measured by the discrepancy between targeted and realized Y. Furthermore, the failure would be different for each target. Hence, the question must be posed as to which target may be expected to result in the best performance.

This is a complex question which cannot be answered fully here, especially since recent developments in the theory of optimal control have pointed out that in general the best solution does not lie in enforcing any one target.[1] Nonetheless it will be useful to examine, if only briefly, the considerations that would be relevant to the choice of an intermediate target, if one were to be enforced, as this will help to provide some perspective about the relative merits of traditional targets, like r or M_1, versus credit, or M_2. In what follows, the customary assumption is made that "failure" can be measured by the error variances or squared deviations between targeted and realized income, $(Y-\bar{Y})^2$. Thus what follows is concerned with the question of which intermediate target can be expected to produce the lowest variance and how the answer is related to the financial structure of the economy and to other parameters.

1. BENJAMIN M. FRIEDMAN, 'Targets, Instruments and Indicators of Monetary Policy', *Journal of Monetary Economics*, vol. 1 (4), October 1975, pp. 443-74; BENJAMIN M. FRIEDMAN, 'The Inefficiency of Short-Run Monetary Aggregates for Monetary Policy', *Brookings Papers on Economic Activity*, 1977 (2), pp. 293-335.

It is well known[1] that when the intermediate target is the interest rate, the outcome error is simply the error of the *IS* equation. Specifically the relative error in income, given *r*, can be expressed as the difference between the relative error in investment, given *r*, and the relative error of saving, given income – both divided by the elasticity of saving with respect to income.

When the intermediate target is M_1, on the other hand, the relative error of income is a weighted average of the above error of the *IS* equation and of the relative error of the money demand equation (divided by the income elasticity of the demand for money). Thus, errors in the *IS* equation produce a smaller effect on income than under an interest target, an attenuation reflecting the so-called Hicksian mechanism examined in the first lecture. The attenuation is larger the greater the response of Y to *r* (through the elasticity of investment demand and the multiplier) and the smaller the elasticity of demand for M_1 with respect to interest rates. However, when this attenuated error is added to the error from the money demand equation, the outcome variance may be larger or smaller than that of a *r* target, depending on the relative magnitude of the errors in the *IS* and money demand equations, as well as on the above-mentioned parameters.

Consider now the case where the intermediate target is bank credit (assuming a stable spread between *r* and r_d). Clearly, control of bank credit ensures control of debt-financed investments. If debt-financed investment were a stable fraction of total investment, then bank credit would also ensure complete control of total investment. If so, the error of income, given credit, could arise only from instability in the saving function. However, in fact the level of investment, given credit, is subject to error because of the error in the rate of equity-financed investment which escapes direct control. The (relative) error of income can be expressed as the sum of the relative error in saving divided by the income elasticity of saving and the error in the ratio of equity

1. WILLIAM POOLE, 'Optimal Choice of Monetary Policy Instruments in a Simple Stochastic Macro Model', *Quarterly Journal of Economics*, vol. 84 (2), May 1970, pp. 197-216.

to total investment divided by the proportion of credit-financed investment. It should be noted that this last term depends explicitly on financial structure: other things equal, it will tend to be smaller the larger the proportion of investment that is debt-financed and thus directly controllable.

What can be inferred from these results concerning the effectiveness of a credit target as compared with the two traditional ones? In the case of the interest target, the answer is fairly straightforward since both credit and interest work entirely through investment. Accordingly, the credit target will dominate if, and only if, fixing credit provides a closer control over investment than fixing the interest rate. This, in turn, requires that the error in the equity share (divided by the share of credit-financed investment) is smaller than the relative error of the investment function. This condition is quite likely to be satisfied at least when the equity share is small. On the other hand, the conditions determining the relative effectiveness of credit versus money turn out to be more complex as they involve all the errors of the standard Keynesian functions, and their elasticities, as well as the error of the equity share which is related to financial structure. As a broad generalization, it can be said that the credit target would tend to be more effective if credit-financed investment is high, and if the error of the saving function is small relative to that of the investment and the money demand function.

It should be recognized that these results rest on a highly stylized and restrictive model, and furthermore, on the extreme assumption of absolute price rigidity. Clearly the analysis must be refined and generalized before it can be regarded as having prescriptive applications. Notwithstanding these limitations, our results seem to point to the type of interrelation that can be expected to exist between the effectiveness of alternative intermediate targets on the one hand and the financial structure on the other hand.

9. Some Implications of a More Complex Financial Structure

In this final section it is proposed to examine, if only in a brief manner, how far our analysis would be affected by allowing for a more complex financial structure.

a) *Firms' Financing from Non-bank Sources*

One relaxation that clearly deserves consideration is to allow for direct borrowing by firms from households (or non-bank intermediaries). In this case the M.A. has control only over a proportion of the total credit that firms can secure. If so, is it not to be expected that an endeavour by the M.A. to reduce bank credit would give rise to an expansion of non-bank credit which would enable firms to maintain their investment and thus frustrate the M.A.'s purpose to restrain total credit and income?

First one obvious circumstance may be noted in which direct lending would have little effect on the effectiveness of bank credit control, namely if the M.A. were in a position to control directly non-bank lending, for example by limiting the volume of direct loans that firms are allowed to issue. The power to limit direct market borrowing by firms exists in those countries, and there are many, in which the floating of marketable issues require the M.A.'s approval. In some countries, such as Sweden, that power has been used systematically as part of the monetary control. However, to be effective, the quota must be lower than the amount firms would like to issue – i.e., firms have to be rationed. Under these conditions it can be shown that the system can be described by Figure 3 and the underlying equations (S. 1′) and (S. 2′), except that $\bar{L}^b$ is replaced by $\bar{L}^b + \bar{L}^h$, where $\bar{L}^h$ is the quota on (net) new issues.

When there is no constraint on direct borrowing, the problem is more complex, but a qualitative answer is feasible even while keeping complexity to a minimum. To this end, we can conveniently retain the assumption that firms pay the same interest rate, r, on all debt, but will allow this debt to be bought not only by the bank intermediary sector, L^b, but also directly by households, L^h. Then L^h must be added to the right-hand side of the households' source-and-use statement (9). A new equation must be added to account for households' demand for L^h. Clearly, it will be of the general form:

$$(13) \qquad L^h = \pounds(r, r_d, Y)$$

with $\pounds_r, \pounds_r > 0$, and $\pounds_{r_d} < 0$, since r is the return from direct lending, and r_d the opportunity cost. Since r_d must be lower than r by the "intermediation spread", it must be assumed that direct claims on firms are less desirable than bank deposits for equal yield because of differences in liquidity, risk, divisibility, and transaction costs. These considerations suggest rewriting (13) in terms of r and the "intermediation spread" $s = r - r_d$. Thus:

$$(13') \qquad L^h = \pounds^*(r, s, Y)$$

with the properties:

$$\pounds_s^* = -\pounds_{r_d} > 0$$

because a rise in s, with r constant, means a decline in r_d which leads to a shift away from bank deposits into L^h, and:

$$\pounds_r^* = \pounds_r + \pounds_{r_d} < 0$$

because, with s held constant, a rise in r is a rise in both rates which may be expected to increase the demand for both nominal assets at the expense of physical investment.

Finally equation (11) needs to be modified as follows:

$$(11') \qquad B = L^b + L^h.$$

Thus, the description of this more complex financial structure requires an additional variable, L^h, and an additional equation, (13) or (13'). Thus there is confirmation that, even with this more complex financial structure, the system can be closed – i.e., nominal income can be controlled – by a policy of the form embodied in equation (P. 2), that is, by a limit on bank assets (or, quite equivalently, on bank liabilities).

The enlarged system can, again, be conveniently analysed in terms of the interaction of a borrowing and a lending market equation analogous to (S. 1') and (S. 2'). The right-hand side of the borrowing equation (S. 1') only needs to be added to the additional supply of direct loans, L^h, and L^h added to the right-hand side of (S. 2$'$) as representing an additional use of saving. If L^h is expressed in terms of (13$'$), we obtained two equations in Y, r and s. The graph of these two equations is basically the same as those shown in Figure 3, except that the slope of both curves now depends on the way in which L^h responds to r, s, and Y, and on the way in which s itself varies with r. Formally, we have:

(S. 3)   slope of BB: $\dfrac{dY}{dr}\bigg|_{BB} = \dfrac{I^d_r - \mathcal{L}^*_r - \mathcal{L}^*_s \frac{ds}{dr}}{S^d_Y + \mathcal{L}^*_Y}$

(S. 4)   slope of LL: $\dfrac{dY}{dr}\bigg|_{LL} = \dfrac{I^s_r + \mathcal{L}^*_r + \mathcal{L}^*_s \frac{ds}{dr}}{S^s_Y - \mathcal{L}^*_Y}$

The change in slope, or "rotation", in the two market equations resulting from the additional terms in the numerator and denominator, turns out to be critical in determining how and to what extent the presence of direct lending tends to affect the control over nominal income that the M.A. can exercise through bank credit.

Suppose, first, that the banking system is competitive so that the spread is roughly constant, i.e., $ds/dr = 0$, and reflects the cost of intermediation. In this case the presence of direct lending affects the slope of BB in two offsetting ways. On the one hand the numerator of (S. 3) becomes greater in absolute value as a rise in interest rate reduces the demand for bank loans, not only by reducing the investment of deficit units but also by increasing the supply of direct loans. However, at the same time the denominator, too, becomes larger as a rise in income reduces the deficit units' demand for bank loans not only by raising their saving, but also again by increasing the supply of direct loans. Thus, in principle, the slope of BB could change either way. If it is accepted that, to a first approximation, direct lending is a fraction of total lending depending on the spread, then it can be shown that, on balance, BB will tend to become steeper. The slope of LL is also affected in two offsetting directions. The absolute value of the numerator becomes smaller, as the effect of a rise in the interest rate in reducing investment is partly offset by its effect on raising direct lending; but also the denominator becomes smaller as part of the rise in saving produced by a higher income is absorbed by increased lending. Again, the balance is uncertain though, on the above assumption about the nature of the lending function, the two effects cancel each other out, leaving the slope unchanged.

Suppose that the M.A. brings about a contraction of bank credit. Then, as in Figure 3, both curves shift down, and to the extent that BB is steeper and LL is unchanged (or flatter) it can be verified that the resulting fall in Y (and rise in r) will be smaller than in the absence of direct lending. If so, the effectiveness of credit policy would be reduced by direct lending, as might have been expected. However, our results suggest that this effect would be *small* and even its sign is not entirely clear.

What accounts for this rather surprising outcome? The answer is not difficult to find. When the M.A. reduces $\bar{L}_0^b$ by ΔL to $\bar{L}_1^b$, the availability of bank loans will tend to raise r. It might be expected that the rise in r would induce firms to turn to the public for credit and the public to shift from bank deposit to direct loans. To the extent that this happens, the reduction of bank loans would be offset by disintermediation, and the total supply of credit, $L^b + L^h$, would remain unchanged. As a result, Y and r would not be significantly affected by the contraction of bank credit. However, in reality there is no reason to expect a significant rise in disintermediation if, as is assumed here, competition, or other institutional forces, leads banks to increase the deposit rate, r_d, *pari passu* with r. In this case, the spread between r and r_d being constant, there will be no incentive to increase disintermediation. Lenders will find that the higher rate firms are willing to pay is matched by the higher r_d paid by intermediaries and, similarly, firms will find that what they have to offer for non-bank funds rises as fast as the cost of bank loans. There will be, at most, a modest increase in L^h as the overall rise in rates encourages the deficit units to switch from physical to nominal assets. A certain fraction of this additional lending would take the form of L^h, and accounts for a likely steepening of the BB curve.

However the situation is quite different when we move to the opposite extreme where, because of either collusion or a ceiling on deposit rates imposed by the M.A., either r_a is constant or $ds/dr = 1$. Then, of course, the rise in r will increase either direct lending or disintermediation, tending to offset the restrictive move and the intended rise in r and fall in Y. In terms of our graph, the BB curve tends to become less steep because of the term $-\pounds_s^*$ in the numerator of (S. 3). Similarly the addition of $\pounds_s^*$ in the numerator of (S. 4) makes the LL curve steeper and may even change the sign of the slope and make it positive. The degree of rotation of the curves BB and SS depends on the magnitude of $\pounds_s^*$, which essentially measures how close a substitute direct lending is for deposits. In the extreme case of perfect substitutability, $\pounds_s^*$ would tend to infinity, and both BB and LL tend to become vertical, as LL rotates clockwise and BB counterclockwise. In this situation bank credit would become an almost powerless tool for the control of income and interest rates.

In summary, it would appear that under a highly competitive banking structure the presence of direct lending would not significantly affect our earlier analysis about the effectiveness of bank credit as an intermediate target, except for the additional uncertainty created by errors in equation (13). However, once again it is found that if regulation and perhaps collusive practices prevented r_a from responding to changes in market rates, the effectiveness of a credit target could be considerably impaired by disintermediation as well as by added uncertainty.

b) *Bank Sources other than Deposits*

This case is worth a short examination because when banks can finance themselves with non-deposit sources (e.g., commercial paper in the United States), control of M_2 and control of credit are no longer synonymous. Equation (P. 2) can take either the form:

(P. 2a) $\qquad\qquad L^b = \bar{L}^b \qquad\qquad$ or

(P. 2b) $\qquad\qquad M_2 = \bar{M}_2$

Not surprisingly, it can be shown that, if the M.A.'s control takes the form (P. 2a), then the availability to banks of non-deposit sources does not substantially affect the analysis and conclusions of Sections 5 and 6.

If, on the other hand, the control is of the form (P. 2b), then the implications are similar to those of Section 6: (i) because the M.A. now controls but a fraction of bank credit, it has less effective control on the total, both in the sense that raising or reducing $M2$ will tend to be partly offset by variations in the banks' other sources, and because of the added uncertainty of the contribution from these sources. (ii) The loss of effectiveness will be increased if regulation or collusion prevents adjustment in the deposit rate r_d but not in the rate paid for other sources. If, for example, market rates rise in response to a reduction in $M2$, banks will have an incentive to raise their rate on other liabilities, increasing their supply and offsetting the fall in $M2$. One obvious implication of these results is that if the M.A. aims at controlling nominal income through credit, then a strong case can be made for imposing limitations on total bank assets (whether through reserve requirements or otherwise), rather than on some particular class of liability such as current account balances or $M2$.

FOURTH LECTURE
The Accumulation of Individual and National Wealth and the Role of Social Security

1. Historical Perspective on the Role of Accumulation. – 2. Keynesian Views of the Determinants of Saving. – 3. The New Theories of the Consumption Function. – 4. Implications for Propositions 2, 3 and 4. – 5. Propositions 1 and 5 and the Role of Growth. – 6. The Role of Bequests. – 7. Proposition 6. – 8. The Effect of Pension Funds on Saving, Private and National: i) The LCH Perspective, ii) Some empirical evidence, iii) Replacement versus induced retirement effects, iv) Some considerations on the Italian case.

1. Historical Perspective on the Role of Accumulation

In this last lecture a number of issues related to the process of accumulation (or decumulation) of wealth by households, and its relation to the accumulation of national wealth will be surveyed. It is a subject to which I have devoted a large proportion of my research over the last twenty-five years, and it is one area that I have particularly enjoyed because it demonstrates in an unusual way the usefulness of a disciplined systematic approach based on the foundation of economic analysis. The usefulness of theory has been demonstrated by the fact that its application has led to a number of conclusions that were not intuitive, and sometimes even counter-intuitive, but were later proven consistent with the empirical evidence.

In addition, the topic is central to economics in that the accumulation of wealth is on the whole necessary and sufficient for the accumulation of capital, and capital in turn is a crucial factor of production which controls the productivity of labour and its growth over time. In other words, the growth of capital is an indispensable part of the process of economic development. It is partly for this reason that alternative views of the accumulation of wealth have also come to play a major role in the controversies between classical and neoclassical economics, and various schools critical of this tradition, including in particular the Marxist school and more recently the Kaldorian attack. Between these competing schools there are not only differences of substance but also interesting differences in terminology; the traditional economists like to refer to saving and wealth, but the Marxist economists use the more suggestive terminology of "the process of the capitalistic accumulation".

The fact that capital is a necessary condition for economic development, and that it is in very limited supply, has been widely recognized in the post-war period. More recently the oil crisis has heightened the appreciation of the scarcity of capital by making people aware that a large amount of capital may be required to replace oil as a source of energy. However this attitude toward capital can be traced back to the origins of economics and it is for this reason that saving has typically been regarded as a virtuous social act.

Nonetheless, it must be borne in mind that there has been a brief but influential interval during which, under the impact of the Great Depression and Keynes' *General Theory*, saving came to be regarded with suspicion, as potentially economically disruptive and harmful to social welfare. The period in question was between the mid-1930s to the late 1940s or early 1950s. Thrift was a potential enemy because it might result in an "inadequate" demand – that is, in an aggregate demand lower than the capacity of the economy. Indeed, the act of saving was seen as reducing one component of demand, consumption, without systematically and automatically giving rise to an expansion of the other component, investment. This failure was attributable to a combination of reasons which have been partly discussed in the first lecture: wage rigidity, liquidity preference, fixed capital coefficients, and investment being controlled by animal spirits rather than by the cost of capital. In particular, oversaving was seen as having played a major role in the Great Depression, and there was widespread fear that it might occur again in the post-war period. These fears were encouraged by the widely held conviction that, on the one hand, in the future, there would not be a great need for additional accumulation of capital while, on the other hand, as income grew with technological progress, the saving ratio would rise, leading to faster and faster accumulation. This combination could be expected to result, sooner or later, in saving outstripping the "need" for capital. It was these fears that gave rise to the "stagnationist" school that was prominent in the late 1940s and early 1950s.

It is interesting that the impetus for the systematic study of saving behaviour was largely the result of this concern with the role of saving and the danger of oversaving. Oversaving was seen both as contributing to short-run cyclical fluctuations related to variations of investment and as providing the potential for long-run stagnation. This concern encouraged both the assembling of factual evidence and the development of paradigms useful to interpret and organize that evidence. Furthermore, in view of the concern at that time, it is not surprising that the emphasis was placed on the determinants of consumption as a component of aggregate demand. Thus, the subject came to be known as the study of the "consumption function" rather than of the saving function.

2. Keynesian Views of the Determinants of Saving

It is for this same reason that the early attempts to model individual and aggregate saving behaviour were dominated by the views expressed on this subject by Keynes in the *General Theory*, and in particular by his well-known basic "psychological" (rather than "economic") law to the effect that the increase in income can be relied on to lead to a positive but smaller change in consumption. Even when the analysis followed the more traditional line of demand theory, it relied on a purely static framework in which saving was seen as one of the many "goods" on which consumers could spend their income. Thus, income was seen as the main systematic determinant of saving which, in line with Keynes' law, was regarded as a superior commodity (i.e., one on which expenditure rises with income) or possibly as a luxury, characterized by "expenditure" rising faster than income. Furthermore, in contrast to other goods, the "expenditure" on saving could be negative – and, accordingly, dissaving was seen as the norm for people below some "break even" level of income, a view encouraged by the findings of budget studies.

It was, of course, recognized that other forces could influence the share of income devoted to saving (or dissaving), but the further hypotheses put forward were not systematically derived from economic analysis, but instead rested typically on *ad hoc*, plausible considerations of a psychological or sociological nature.

Even after the work of Kuznets[1] and others had provided clear evidence for the long-run stability of the saving ratio despite the growth of per capita income, the initial attempts by Duesenberry[2] and myself[3] at reconciling this long-run stability with the

1. SIMON S. KUZNETS, *National Income. A Summary of Findings*. New York: National Bureau of Economic Research, 1946.
2. JAMES S. DUESENBERRY, *Income, Saving and the Theory of Consumer Behavior*. Cambridge, Mass.: Harvard University Press, 1949.
3. FRANCO MODIGLIANI, 'Fluctuations in the Saving-Income Ratio: A Problem in Economic Forecasting'. Paper prepared in connection with a Research Project of the Institute of World Affairs and presented at the Conference on Research in Income and Wealth; in *Studies in Income and Wealth*, vol. 11. New York: National Bureau of Economic Research, 1949, pp. 371-443; Sections I-VII (pp. 371-402) and XIII (pp. 427-31) reprinted in MODIGLIANI, vol. 2, pp. 3-40.

observed positive cyclical association of saving and income proceeded along similar empiricist lines. The reconciliation was achieved by hypothesizing that the preference for saving versus consumption was determined not only by current income but also by the highest past level of income (or consumption).

However, common sense, intuition, and casual empiricism did not prove adequate to provide a solid foundation for an understanding of saving behaviour either at a microeconomic or, even more so, at a macroeconomic level. Indeed, as mentioned earlier, saving behaviour frequently appears to defy intuition and to run counter to plausible, or even self-evident hypotheses. However, according to the so-called "new theories of the consumption function" which were advanced in the mid-1950s, namely my own Life Cycle Hypothesis (LCH)[1] and the Permanent Income Hypothesis (PIH) of Milton Friedman,[2] that behaviour can be accounted for by a systematic application of the hypothesis of rational (or consistent) economic behaviour.

It is proposed to demonstrate these claims here by stating a number of propositions which were generally regarded as obviously valid before the new theories, and which, it is believed, would still be regarded as highly credible by the non-expert. After stating these propositions, the intention is to show that only two of the six are consistent with the Life Cycle Hypothesis, and that these are the only two that are also consistent with the evidence – while the remaining four, though equally plausible, are inconsistent with the LCH as well as with the empirical evidence.

Proposition 1. Rich countries save a larger fraction of income than poor ones.

Proposition 2. At a given level of income, farm families save more than urban families.

Proposition 3. Within the urban families, those with a lower status, such as the black families in the United States, save less at any level of income.

1. FRANCO MODIGLIANI, *The Life-Cycle Hypothesis of Saving*, in MODIGLIANI, vol. 2, edited by Andrew Abel. Cambridge, Mass.: MIT Press, 1980.

2. MILTON FRIEDMAN, *A Theory of the Consumption Function*. Princeton: Princeton University Press, 1957.

Proposition 4. Families who expect a higher income in the future tend to consume a larger proportion of their current income.

Proposition 5. It follows that countries whose income is rising and is expected to continue to rise tend to save a smaller fraction of their income.

Proposition 6. Wages earned by poor workers are largely consumed, whereas property income, which is the income of rich capitalists, is largely saved. Or equivalently, the rate of accumulation of wealth will rise substantially if income is redistributed from labour to property income.

3. The New Theories of the Consumption Function

In order to appreciate what the new theories of the consumption function, and in particular the LCH, have to say about the validity of these propositions, the basis of these models needs to be briefly reviewed.

The basic assumption is that consumption and saving decisions can be accounted for within the framework of the classical theory of consumers' choice. Consumers are assumed to have well-defined preferences between alternative paths of consumption over their lifetime and to choose the preferred path subject to the constraint represented by their life earnings in addition to any asset received by bequests or gifts. According to this view, saving (or dissaving) in any given interval is the difference between the receipts for that period and the relevant segment of the chosen life-consumption path which reflects *life* resources. Thus, saving has no direct utility but is only the means through which resources are carried back and forth to enforce the chosen consumption path. The only other important assumption is that the proportional allocation of total life consumption to any and every portion of the life cycle is independent of the total to be allocated.

Let it also initially be assumed that the representative family does not plan to leave or receive bequests. The model incorporating this additional assumption may be labelled the "Elementary LCH". It then follows that consumption at any age, t, is proportional to life resources, with a proportionality factor independent of resources.

It might be further expected that the chosen consumption path would be reasonably smooth and therefore close to annualized life resources (with proper allowance for the life cycle of family size). Under these conditions the saving rate at any point of time, representing the difference between current income and the chosen consumption path, would reflect primarily the extent to which current income differed from the life average – that is, the size of "transitory" income. Thus, a high saving ratio should be associated not with a high income in absolute terms but rather with an income that is high in relative terms – that is, relative

127

to a person's life income. Similarly, it should not be the poor who dissave but rather the temporarily poor. It should be noted that deviation of current from average life income could be the result of either unforeseen random occurrences such as sickness, unemployment, overtime, or systematic, foreseeable and even partially controllable events such as schooling early in life, or retirement.

The PIH is quite similar in spirit except that it makes the approximation that life is of indefinitely long duration. Accordingly, the notion of life resources is replaced by that of permanent income, defined as the maximum flow of consumption that could be sustained indefinitely. For many purposes, the assumption of an infinite planning horizon is an excellent approximation to a life-cycle horizon. Accordingly, the LCH and the PIH turn out to have many implications in common – at least at the micro level – such as those that follow from the association of saving with transitory income. It is for this reason that they give the same answer to Propositions 2, 3 and 4.

4. Implications for Propositions 2, 3 and 4

With respect to Proposition 4, one of the two propositions that are warranted in terms of empirical support, the conclusion rests on the consideration that for a family which expects a higher or rising income in the future, current income is below average; hence, the family is transiently poor and therefore will tend to save less than one with expectations of stable income.

Proposition 2 is the other valid one, while all the remaining propositions are rejected by the evidence. The evidence for Proposition 2, and against 3, goes back to a well-known budget study financed by the United States government during the Great Depression as a form of unemployment relief. The findings in support of Proposition 2 were readily accepted because that proposition fitted with the prejudice that country life encourages traditional virtues such as parsimony, while city dwellers cannot resist the temptations and the pressures of "keeping up with the Joneses" inherent in urban living. However, the finding that black families, just like farm families, saved more than white urban families at given levels of income was quite perplexing because, in terms of the prejudices of the time, blacks, in addition to being poor, were generally supposed to be spendthrifts by nature, incapable of thinking of the future.

Instead, according to the new theories, the findings for both farmers and blacks are accounted for by a common phenomenon, namely that transiently rich people save more than transiently poor ones. To see this point, suppose a group of consumers is taken whose income is subject to significant transitory disturbances that cause it to deviate from permanent income. If they are classified into current income classes, then it can readily be shown that the proportion of current income that is transitory in nature will tend to be larger as we move to higher income classes. However, this means that the proportion of income saved in any income class will tend to be higher, the more that income class exceeds the mean. It then follows immediately that if two groups of people are compared which differ appreciably in terms of their mean permanent income (for example, blacks with whites or rural with urban families) then it can be assumed that, at any given level of current income, the poorer group will tend to exhibit more saving (or less dissaving). It might also be noted that the ratio of transient to permanent income depends not only on the distance from the mean but also grows with the variability of the transitory component of income. Since the income of rural families is typically much more variable than that of urban families, the saving differential at given levels of income above the mean between rural and urban families will be more pronounced than between blacks and whites; however, below the mean rural families could dissave more than the others.

One further implication of the new theories that directly follows from the above considerations is the following: because productivity growth implies that successive generations enjoy a higher average life income than earlier ones, it should be the case that, for a developing economy, the proportion of income saved at any given level of (real) income should gradually decline in time. This is precisely the finding – at that time quite puzzling – of a classic paper of Dorothy S. Brady and Rose D. Friedman.[1]

It should be mentioned at this point an alternative hypothesis that has been put forward to explain the above findings, namely the so-called Relative Income Hypothesis (RIH) of Duesenberry.[2] This hypothesis retains the conventional view that the rich consume less and the poor more than their income but holds, on sociological grounds, that being rich or poor is not a matter of absolute level of income but rather one of standing in relation to the social norm of an appropriate reference group, approximated by the group's mean income or perhaps mean consumption. This hypothesis is appealing but it has two major shortcomings as compared with the LCH:

i) according to the RIH, people who are permanently poor would permanently dissave. This is obviously absurd, since in this society people are unable to dissave for any length of time unless they have saved and accumulated some assets before; that is,

---

1. DOROTHY S. BRADY and ROSE D. FRIEDMAN, 'Savings and the Income Distribution', in *Studies in Income and Wealth*, vol. 10, New York: National Bureau of Economic Research, 1947, pp. 250-97.

2. JAMES S. DUESENBERRY, *Income, Saving, and the Theory of Consumer Behavior*.

while it may be more or less easy to borrow, it is nearly impossible to have a negative net worth, except perhaps temporarily, pending some later saving. Under the LCH, on the other hand, dissaving is always a transitory phenomenon related to income transiently below life average;

ii) the LCH, besides providing an alternative explanation for the set of phenomena explained by the RIH, can also highlight many other aspects of saving behaviour, from the life cycle of wealth to a great number of macroeconomic phenomena.

Nonetheless, as will be seen later, the RIH may still be applicable in some circumstances when the assumption of no bequests is dropped.

5. Propositions 1 and 5 and the Role of Growth

The macroeconomic Propositions 1 and 5 can now be considered. To begin with, it is clear that the highly credible Proposition 1 is inconsistent with the LCH, at least in its elementary form, because according to that model the proportion of permanent income saved (or dissaved) at any age is independent of income and, over the entire life-span, is equal to one. If this is so, the proportion of aggregate national income saved could not depend systematically on whether the country was rich or poor, as measured by, for example, per capita income. At the time this counter-intuitive inference was derived,[1] there was little evidence to test it, because national income statistics were available for only a small number of countries and suffered from serious comparability problems. However, since then a large body of national income account statistics have been assembled, through the work of the United Nations, and research by Summers, Kravis and Heston,[2] and these data have tended to provide clear support for the conclusion. This statement is illustrated by Figure 4 which exhibits, for a sample of 40 countries, the relation between an estimate of the saving ratio – private net-of-tax income less consumption, divided by income – and of per capita net-of-tax income, expressed in terms of purchasing power. To minimize the impact of cyclical and purely erratic movements that can greatly affect the saving rate, the observation for each country is an average of the years 1960–1970, or of as many years within that interval for which information was available. The list of countries included in the graph is given at the bottom; each is identified by a number that is also used to identify the points in the graph.

1. See FRANCO MODIGLIANI and RICHARD BRUMBERG, 'Utility Analysis and the Consumption Function: An Interpretation of Cross-Section Data', in KENNETH K. KURIHARA (ed.), *Post Keynesian Economics*. New Brunswick, N.J.: Rutgers University Press, 1954, pp. 388-436; reprinted in MODIGLIANI, vol. 2, pp. 79-127; and 'Utility Analysis and Aggregate Consumption Functions: An Attempt at Integration' in MODIGLIANI, vol. 2, pp. 128-97.

2. ROBERT SUMMERS, IRVING B. KRAVIS and ALAN HESTON, 'International Comparison of Real Product and its Composition: 1950-77', *Review of Income and Wealth*, Series 26 (1), March 1980, pp. 19-66.

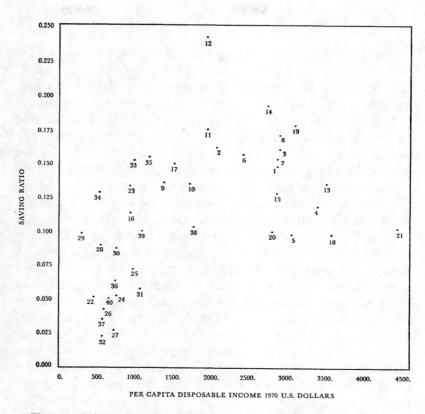

Figure 4. Relation between the Saving Ratio and Real Per Capita Income in the 1960s for 40 Countries.

Country	Index	Country	Index	Country	Index
Australia	1	Netherlands	14	Honduras	28
Austria	2	Norway	15	India	29
Belgium	3	Portugal	16	Nicaragua	30
Canada	4	Spain	17	Panama	31
Denmark	5	Sweden	18	Paraguay	32
Finland	6	Switzerland	19	Peru	33
France	7	United Kingdom	20	Philippines	34
West Germany	8	United States	21	South Africa	35
Greece	9	Bolivia	22	Turkey	36
Ireland	10	Brazil	23	Tunisia	37
Italy	11	Colombia	24	Venezuela	38
Japan	12	Costa Rica	25	Jamaica	39
Luxembourg	13	Ecuador	26	Malaysia	40
		Guatemala	27		

In interpreting the graph, an allowance must be made for the serious limitations of the data which arise from problems of comparability as well as of measurement, and which affect particularly the per capita income estimate. However, the errors are unlikely to account more than marginally for the four striking facts highlighted by the graph: i) the enormous disparities in per capita income, which, of course, have already received a great deal of attention; ii) the similar extreme variability of the saving rate – even when averaged over ten years. It ranges from a huge 24 per cent (Japan) down to approximately 2 per cent (Paraguay); iii) the fact that all countries, rich or poor, report positive saving, and that many countries appear to save a surprisingly large fraction of income – half the countries in the sample save 12 per cent or more of their disposable income; iv) the fact that there is no systematic positive association between the saving rate and real per capita income. While some of the low income countries have low saving, others have fairly high saving rates; more significant is the fact that the one country, distinctly ahead of all others in terms of per capita income (especially during the 1960s), that is to say the United States (21), had a saving rate below the median. Furthermore, much of the same applies for four of the six countries with per capita income above $3,000 – Sweden (18), Canada (4), Denmark (5), besides the United States. Italy (11) is seen to have one of the highest saving ratios (it ranks fifth in our sample) even though its per capita income is below $2,000, and the same applies to the highest saver, Japan.

However, if zero over-life saving can account for the observed lack of association between the saving ratio and per capita income, does it not also imply zero aggregate saving, contrary to the evidence of Figure 4 – or for that matter, zero aggregate wealth? Naturally the answer is negative; indeed, under the LCH the forces that control individual and national saving are to a large extent unrelated. In particular, according to the LCH, zero individual life saving can result in both positive and negative aggregate saving, and, in either case, is consistent with a large stock of wealth.

This conclusion can be most easily understood by referring to Figure 5, which is intended to highlight the essential implications of the elementary LCH by conveniently relying on a highly stylized description of the relevant aspects of the life cycle. Age is measured on the horizontal axis, and various dollar stocks and flows on the vertical axis. The upper solid line, *ee'*, represents income earned, which is assumed to be constant at the rate, *e*, through the working span, terminating at *W*, and then to fall to zero through the retirement period, which ends with death at age *T*. With the return on assets assumed to be zero, total life resources are given by the rectangle, *ee'WO*, and these resources can support the constant rate of consumption, *c*, through

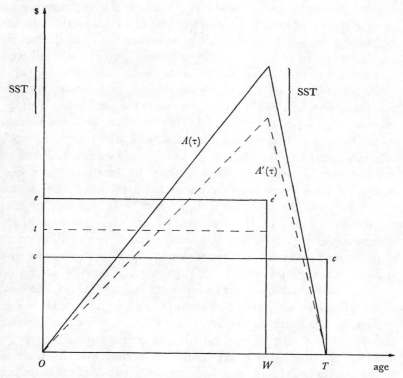

Figure 5. Income, Saving and Wealth and the Effect of Social Security
in the Elementary LCH

—————— $A(\tau)$ = wealth at age τ in absence of social security

– – – – $A'(\tau)$ = wealth at age τ with social security benefits equal SST life. Accordingly, the household is saving at the rate *e-c* up to *W*, and its wealth grows linearly from zero to a peak at *W*, along the path indicated by the solid line $A(\tau)$. This wealth is then decumulated linearly back to zero in the retirement period, as the household dissaves at the rate *c*.

What would control *aggregate* saving in a community of households whose individual behavior over the life cycle was approximated by the graph of Figure 5? The answer is basically: the rate at which the economy is growing. Indeed, if productivity and population are constant, and this has been the case for a sufficiently long time, zero life saving implies zero aggregate saving. For, while those in the working span will be accumulating, their savings will tend to be offset by the dissaving of those in the retirement span. At the same time, as is obvious from the figure, even in this zero-aggregate-saving economy, individuals will tend to hold substantial amounts of wealth relative to their income throughout their lives. This will be true as long as, for the representative household, income tends to fall well below average with old age, while the preferred rate of consumption stays closer to average. For the economy as a whole, the aggregate stock of wealth and the annual income flow, representing the sum of income and wealth over all ages, can be inferred from Figure 5. They are given respectively by the area under the wealth curve $A(\tau)$ and the income rectangle *ee'WO*. It is apparent that for the elementary LCH, where the main systematic reason for accumulation is retirement, the wealth-income ratio will be quite sensitive to the length of the retirement period. Indeed, for the stylized earning and consumption profile of Figure 5, it can be shown that the ratio of total wealth to income is equal to half the number of years in the retirement span – or approximately 5.

Suppose next that population is growing. Then each successive cohort is more numerous than the preceding ones. Hence, the number of those in their accumulation period will rise relative to the number of the retired dissavers, with the result that saving becomes positive. Thus, the LCH implies that aggregate saving should depend on the demographic structure of the population, declining with the proportion of aged (and hence retired) households, and more generally with the dependency ratio which includes not only the retired but also those who have not yet entered the labour force. Many studies have found empirical support for this implication (see Leff,[1] Modigliani,[2] Modigliani and Sterling,[3] Mikessel and Zinser,[4] and Feldstein[5]).

However, even with a stationary population, the LCH is consistent with positive saving if per capita income is growing because of productivity. The reason in this case is that each successive age cohort is richer in terms of life resources than the preceding ones. Accordingly, the dissaving of the currently retired, that is based on a lower life income, will be more than offset by the saving of the richer cohorts currently in the labour force. Thus a rising income should tend to result in a higher saving ratio *for the economy as a whole*. This tendency may be partly offset by the fact that the expectation of a rising income may raise consumption relative to life income early in life (Proposition 4), but limitations on the ability to borrow against future saving should seriously limit this offsetting mechanism.

The conclusion that the saving ratio should rise with the rate of growth of income contradicts Proposition 6 and, for once, also the PIH, which, because of the assumption of infinite life, cannot handle differential cohort saving and dissaving. However, it has been confirmed in a number of empirical studies which suggest that, in fact, this variable is of prime importance in accounting

1. NATHANIEL H. LEFF, 'Dependency Rates and Savings Rates', *American Economic Review*, vol. 59 (5), December 1969, pp. 886-96.
2. FRANCO MODIGLIANI, 'The Life Cycle Hypothesis of Saving and Intercountry Differences in the Saving Ratio', in WALTER A. ELTIS, MAURICE FG. SCOTT and JAMES N. WOLFE (eds.), *Induction, Growth and Trade: Essays in Honour of Sir Roy Harrod*. Oxford: Clarendon Press, 1970, pp. 197-226; reprinted in MODIGLIANI, vol. 2, pp. 382-412.
3. FRANCO MODIGLIANI and ARLIE STERLING, 'Determinants of Private Saving with Special Reference to the Role of Social Security – Cross-country Tests', in FRANCO MODIGLIANI and RICHARD HEMMING (eds.), *The Determinants of National Saving and Wealth*. Proceedings of a Conference held by the International Economic Association at Bergamo, Italy, 9-14 June 1980. London: Macmillan, 1983, pp. 24-55.
4. RAYMOND F. MIKESELL and JAMES E. ZINSER, 'The Nature of the Savings Function in Developing Countries: A Survey of the Theoretical and Empirical Literature', *Journal of Economic Literature*, vol. 11 (1), March 1973, pp. 1-26.
5. MARTIN FELDSTEIN, 'Social Security and Private Savings: International Evidence in an Extended Life-Cycle Model', in MARTIN FELDSTEIN and ROBERT INMAN (eds.), *The Economics of Public Services*. London: Macmillan, 1977, pp. 174-205.

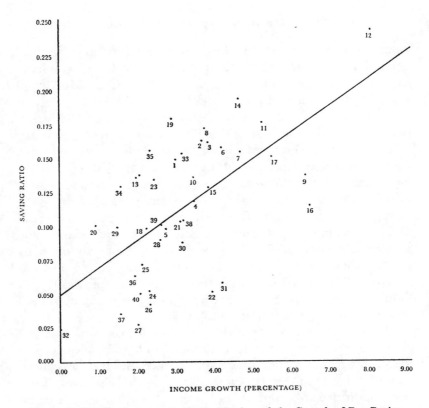

Figure 6. Relation between the Saving Ratio and the Growth of Per Capita
Income in the 1960s in a 40-country sample.

for differences in saving ratios. Support for this statement is
provided by Figure 6 which shows for the 40 countries in our
sample, the saving ratio averaged over the decade plotted against
the growth of per capita income in the course of the decade.
The association of the two variables is surprising, especially bearing in mind that even within the LCH there are a number of
variables besides per capita income growth that can be expected
to influence saving. My own estimations[1] suggest that an increase

1. FRANCO MODIGLIANI, 'The Life Cycle Hypothesis of Saving and Intercountry
Differences in the Saving Ratio'; FRANCO MODIGLIANI and ARLIE STERLING, 'De-
terminants of Private Saving with Special Reference to the Role of Social Security –
Cross-country Tests'.

in productivity growth by one percentage point tends, *ceteris paribus*, to be accompanied by a rise in the saving ratio by between two and three percentage points, an effect which is consistent with the slope of the line fitted to the scatter of Figure 6, which is 2.0. A response of this magnitude can be shown to be in line with the implications of the elementary LCH model.[1]

The basic implications of the LCH to the effect that the saving ratio is independent of income but depends on its growth rate, can be related to a well-known proposition in growth theory, that is to say that, if the wealth income ratio is constant, then, with stable growth, the saving ratio is proportional to it, and the proportionality factor equals the rate of growth. This follows from the consideration that saving is the product of wealth multiplied by its rate of growth and, with a constant wealth-income ratio, income, wealth, and thus saving, all rise at the same rate. In particular, when the growth rate is zero, saving is zero. The above relation is quite informative because it implies that one way to understand the effect of a variable on the saving ratio is to analyse its likely effect on the wealth-income ratio.[2]

1. FRANCO MODIGLIANI, 'The Life Cycle Hypothesis of Saving and Intercountry Differences in the Saving Ratio'.
2. *Ibid.*

6. The Role of Bequests

The above analysis is based on the elementary LCH, which assumes no bequests left or received. This assumption is clearly counter-factual – it is well known that bequests take place and that leaving an estate is a motive for saving – even if not the principal one. Furthermore, casual observation and some systematic evidence indicate that this motive tends to become more important at high levels of permanent income. This tendency is consistent with some evidence that the saving ratio increases not only with current but also with permanent income, and with growing evidence that the wealth of older people relative to their life resources tends to increase more than in proportion to life resources (see, e.g., Feldstein and Pellechio,[1] Kotlikoff,[2] Diamond and Hausman[3]). Therefore the question may be asked whether the new theories of saving can accommodate a bequest motive, and with what consequences.

As far as it is known, for the PIH the answer is basically negative for, with infinite life, there can be no meaningful bequests. However there is no difficulty in generalizing the LCH by recognizing that at least certain classes of households might plan to leave bequests which other households will receive. This means that some households may turn out to be positive life savers – if they left bequests in excess of what they received – and others negative. Allowance must also be made for the possibility that the share of life resources bequested may rise with the size of life resources. These generalizations will not affect the major macroeconomic implications of the LCH – and in particular the independence of saving from per capita income – as long as the bequest motive can be assumed to satisfy two "reasonable" postulates. The first is that the share bequeathed

1. MARTIN FELDSTEIN and ANTHONY J. PELLECHIO, 'Social Security and Household Wealth Accumulation: New Microeconometric Evidence', *Review of Economics and Statistics*, vol. 61 (3), August 1979, pp. 261-368.

2. LAURENCE J. KOTLIKOFF, 'Testing the Theory of Social Security and Life Cycle Accumulation', *American Economic Review*, vol. 69 (3), June 1979, pp. 396-410.

3. PETER DIAMOND and JERRY HAUSMAN, 'Individual Savings Behavior', Paper prepared for the U. S. National Commission on Social Security, May 1980.

depends not on absolute but on relative life resources. The second is that the share of resources bequested remains below an appropriate ceiling. These postulates are sufficient to ensure that there is some critical ratio of bequests received to labour income such that bequests left equal those received and life saving becomes zero. It follows that if productivity and population were stationary, then the amount of aggregate wealth associated with bequests left and received would tend to some critical, "equilibrium" level, just as in the case of that part of wealth associated specifically with the life cycle. Once wealth had reached the critical level, total saving would again be zero in a stationary society, independently of the level of income. On the other hand, income growth for any reason would cause the equilibrium level of bequeathed, as well as life-cycle, wealth to grow at the same rate as income, generating saving at a rate depending on the growth rate but not on the level of income. Of course, because the bequest motive will raise the wealth-income ratio, it will also raise the saving ratio for any given growth rate. Thus, a society that discouraged inter-generational transfers might be expected to have a smaller saving ratio, for given growth.

Of course, once the bequest motive is taken into account, it must also be recognized that the rate of saving and the stock of wealth consist of two parts: one related to the life cycle and the other to bequests. An interesting question is how to measure these two components and how to assess their relative importance. Clearly, the LCH would lose much of its relevance if it could be established that assets and saving related to bequests represent a large portion of the total. In reality, the measurement problem is a complex one, and is currently under debate. The basic issue is whether, in computing at any point of time the total amount of current wealth that has been inherited, the inheritances are valued (i) as of the time they were received, or instead (ii) are capitalized to the date of measurement. Because of the power of compound interest and considering the substantial gap between the receipt of inheritance and the giving of bequests, it makes an enormous difference which of these two measures is used. In my view, approach (i) is the appropriate one in that it is consistent with defining life saving as the difference between wealth bequeathed and inherited (or equivalently, with including in life-time income and life-time saving, property income earned on inherited assets). There is evidence from both survey data and estate data to suggest that, with this measure, the bulk of wealth is life-cycle related: inherited wealth would appear to account for possibly around 15 percent of total private wealth with a possible range of plus or minus five percentage points. On the other hand, reliance on measure (ii) could give very different results with inherited wealth accounting for three-quarters or more of total wealth.[1]

1. LAURENCE J. KOTLIKOFF and LAWRENCE H. SUMMERS, 'The Role of Intergenerational Transfers in Aggregate Capital Accumulation', *Journal of Political Economy*, vol. 89 (4), August 1981, pp. 706-31.

7. Proposition 6

There remains to consider the last proposition. It is not only intuitively appealing, but in addition it has become respectable through its adoption by Kaldor[1] and later by Pasinetti[2] as an important component of their theoretical constructs. It leads to an aggregate saving function in which saving depends (linearly) on labour and property income, and the coefficient of labour is small and possibly zero, while that of property income is large and possibly close to unity. Its most important implication is that the saving ratio depends on the share of property in total income, i.e., on the so-called functional distribution of income.

The first thing to observe is that the LCH implies an aggregate saving function that looks somewhat like the Kaldorian one. That is, according to the LCH, saving can be shown to depend (linearly) on labour income and wealth. However, with a reasonably stable rate of return on wealth, property income and wealth will be roughly proportional to each other.

In what sense can it be asserted that the Kaldorian Proposition 6 is inconsistent with the LCH (and the evidence)? The answer is that while both models imply a possible difference between the coefficients of labour and property income, they provide a radically different interpretation of the *reason* for the difference, and as a result, they also lead to very different predictions about the size and even the sign of these differences. These predictions can be validated empirically.

In Kaldor's model, the propensities to save out of the two kinds of income are different because the two incomes accrue to people belonging to two different social classes. The workers save a small proportion of their wages primarily because they are too poor to do so and also perhaps because they are short-sighted and have no stake in society. The property owners consume little because they are so rich they do not know what else to do with

1. NICHOLAS KALDOR, *Essays on Value and Distribution*. Collected Economic Essays, vol. 1. London: Duckworth, 1960.
2. LUIGI L. PASINETTI, 'Rate of Profit and Income Distribution in Relation to the Rate of Economic Growth', *Review of Economic Studies*, vol. 29 (81), October 1962, pp. 267-79.

their income, and also perhaps because they are looking forward to improving their lot and expanding their empire by accumulating wealth.

In the LCH, on the other hand, workers and property owners are indistinguishable. Broadly speaking, all people earn non-property income until they reach retirement age, but, at the same time, all people accumulate property at some time of their life as a reserve for contingency and to support retirement, and to a limited extent, for the purpose of making bequests. This wealth may be invested in financial assets, directly or through pension funds, or in physical assets providing direct services, such as houses and consumer durables and sometimes may represent equity in their own business. The only people living entirely on property are likely to be retired and, of course, have worked for most of their lives.

In view of this role of wealth, and not just of the income derived from it in supporting future consumption, it is wealth rather than property income that appears as the main determinant of consumption (and hence saving). Furthermore, its contribution to consumption should be substantial – its coefficient in a "consumption function" should be as large as, and could very well be larger than, the rate of return on property. On the other hand, for the Kaldorian model the coefficient of property income should be small, and therefore if property income is replaced by wealth, its coefficient should be a small fraction of the rate of return. Tests of the two alternative predictions based on the inclusion of wealth in a consumption function have been generally consistent with the LCH prediction as opposed to the Kaldorian one.[1] Alternatively, suppose that we fit a consumption function using property income, instead of wealth; if the LCH prediction that the wealth coefficient is likely to exceed the rate of return is valid, then the coefficient of property income appropriately measured so that the effect of short-run fluctu-

---

1. FRANCO MODIGLIANI, 'The life cycle hypothesis of saving twenty years later', in MICHAEL PARKIN and A. ROBERT NOBAY (eds.), *Contemporary Issues in Economics*. Manchester: Manchester University Press, 1975, pp. 2-36 (especially Sections 5 and 8); reprinted in MODIGLIANI, vol. 2, pp. 41-75.

ations is eliminated, might well exceed unity. Thus the coefficient of property income should not be much smaller than that of labour income as hypothesized by Kaldor and could even be substantially larger. This result has been reported, in particular for Italy[1] where the coefficient of property income has been found to be well in excess of unity (around 1.5).

1. Franco Modigliani and Ezio Tarantelli, 'The Consumption Function in a Developing Economy and the Italian Experience', *American Economic Review*, vol. 65 (5), December 1975, pp. 825-842; reprinted in Modigliani, vol. 2, pp. 305-322.

8. *The Effect of Pension Funds on Saving, Private and National*

i) *The LCH Perspective*

It is proposed to conclude with one more application of the LCH, this time to an area that has recently become very popular and controversial, that is to say the impact of social security and private pension funds on private and national saving, including implications for public policy.

The essence of pension systems, whether public or private, is that they take away some of the participants' income during their working years and then provide them with a stream of benefits during their retirement (or after some specified age). They thus take over some of the function otherwise filled by life-cycle saving and wealth.

This proposition is illustrated in Figure 5. The amount withheld is represented by the distance *e-t*. Insofar as this amount is eventually paid back to the participants (with accrued interest) during retirement – which can be assumed to be roughly the case, at least for private pensions – the existence of the pension fund does not change a person's life resources. It may be assumed, therefore, that it should not change the optimal consumption path, that remains at *c* in the graph. However, this means that the individuals' personal accumulation are reduced from the initial rate *e-c* to the lower rate *t-c*; accordingly, personal wealth will trace a path lower than $A(\tau)$, represented by $A'(\tau)$.

The difference between the macroeconomic effects on private and national wealth of private as opposed to state pension funds lies firstly in the way in which the contribution to, and benefits from, the fund are assessed in the national income accounts and, secondly, in the fact that a private system is typically fully funded – i.e., accumulates assets matching the pension liability of the fund – whereas a state system may be funded partially or not at all.

In the case of a private system, contributions are treated as part of private income and the fund's use of the contributions to accumulate assets is treated as private saving. On the other hand, benefits are not treated as income but as a return on capital (except for the amount representing current interest). Thus, in our figure, disposable income remains at e, total private saving at e-c, and total wealth (the sum of the personal and the pension fund accumulation) remains at $A(\tau)$, even though personal accumulation is $A'(\tau)$. It would appear, therefore, that, to a first approximation, private pension arrangements should have no effect on private saving and wealth, as their accumulation merely displaces saving that would otherwise be done by individuals. However, this conclusion presupposes a world of perfect markets and rationality. As has been stressed by Dolde and Tobin,[1] the major inadequacy of this assumption arises from the fact that accumulation in pension funds is completely illiquid and cannot be utilized for any purpose except retirement. In particular, it cannot be used either to maintain consumption in the face of major disruptions in income or to cover exceptional needs, or to provide equity for investment in a house and other durables, or even as a collateral for such loans. For this reason a dollar of pension saving and wealth is likely, on average, to displace less than a dollar of private wealth. In addition, compulsory participation in a pension system may induce more accumulation for retired consumption than the individual would have chosen; indeed, while it is always possible for individuals to supplement the pension saving, if they prefer a larger or longer retired consumption, it would be very difficult to offset pension saving that they regarded as excessive by borrowing against their reserve to support current consumption.

A number of cross-section studies have been conducted in the United States to assess the extent to which private pensions do in fact displace private saving and wealth, and the estimates have ranged between 60 cents and nearly a dollar per dollar. This suggests that pension schemes may, on balance, increase private saving – a conclusion that could be strengthened by the so-called "induced retirement" effect discussed below. On the negative

---

1. WALTER C. DOLDE JR. and JAMES TOBIN, 'Mandatory Retirement Saving and Capital Formation', in FRANCO MODIGLIANI and RICHARD HEMMING (eds.), *The Determinants of National Saving and Wealth*, pp. 56-88.

side, however, the possibility of private pensions being under-funded, which would act in the direction of reduced aggregate saving, should be considered. It would be desirable to check the results based on cross-sections of households with data based on a cross-section of countries, but at present the difficulties in as-sembling the relevant data seem forbidding.

The effect of state pensions is rather different because the amount withheld, e-t, is treated in the national income accounts as a tax, and thus excluded from disposable income, whereas the pension benefits are included. Insofar as the social security system is balanced in the sense that individual (or at least cohort) contributions match benefits, consumption will again be un-changed at c. It is then apparent from Figure 5 that the LCH implies that private saving during the working span will be re-duced by the extent of the social security tax, or e-t. Accordingly, private wealth should follow the lower path $A'(\tau)$; the lower accumulation is sufficient because at retirement the household can rely on the equivalent of a "social security wealth" (to be paid out in instalments) in the amount marked SST in the figure. However, this wealth, in contrast to private pension reserves, does not appear as part of private assets. In other words, a bal-anced social security system should reduce *private* wealth relative to disposable income, much as private pensions should reduce individually-held wealth. Now, as has been pointed out, a decline in the wealth-income ratio means a proportional decline in the *private* saving rate, for a given rate of growth of income and demo-graphic characteristics.

A useful way to measure how large an impact a social security system should tend to have on private wealth and saving is in terms of the so-called replacement rate, the ratio of average benefits to average income. Suppose that planned consumption in retirement were of the order of average income (as with a constant planned consumption). The replacement rate can be thought of as an approximation to the ratio of benefits to retired consumption. Thus, because the accumulation of life-cycle wealth is designed to finance consumption in retirement, a replacement rate of x per cent should reduce the path of wealth over life, and hence also saving, by x per cent. Allowing for the fact that, for a number of reasons, consumption in retirement would probably fall short of average income, this suggests that one percentage point rise in the replacement rate might lead to a decline in saving by an amount larger than one per cent (estimated at 1.4 per cent in Modigliani and Sterling).[1] It should be noted that this reduction in private saving could in part take the form of a fall in the amount of private pension schemes.

However, there are a number of considerations suggesting that the replacement effect might be appreciably lower than indicated above. The discussion above of how private insurance might actually increase saving, and hence reduce individual wealth less than the increase in pension funds wealth, implies that the effect of social security on private wealth could be less than one for one. Another factor that could tend to produce the same effect is that, in the absence of social security, a portion of consumption in retirement may tend to be financed not from life-cycle wealth accumulation but by transfer from children – the equivalent of a private pay-as-you-earn system. If so, the introduction of social security might not affect the accumulation of private wealth as the old come to be provided for by social security and the children provide for themselves through social security taxes. The overall conclusion may be reached that social security should tend to reduce considerably private wealth – or saving – but, possibly, by appreciably less than by a dollar per dollar.

What do these results imply with respect to the impact of social security on *national* as distinguished from *private* saving and wealth? The answer depends entirely on how the system is financed. If it is funded, then the reduction in private wealth and saving will be offset by the rise in public wealth and saving, much as in the case of private pensions. However, if it is of the pay-as-you-earn type (with the growth in contribution due to population and productivity growth used to pay benefits larger than contributions) then the reduction of private wealth would be reflected in the national total.

1. Franco Modigliani and Arlie Sterling, 'Determinants of Private Saving with Special Reference to the Role of Social Security – Cross-country Tests'.

ii) *Some empirical evidence*

How far are these predictions supported by empirical evidence? Casual observation does not appear favourable. While over the last fifty years social security has spread in coverage and size of benefits within countries and has been adopted by more and more countries, there is no obvious evidence of a serious decline in the saving or in the private wealth ratio; if anything the opposite is true. However, casual evidence could be misleading because over the same period other forces were pushing in the direction of more saving, such as faster economic growth, through population and productivity increases, and longer retirement caused by both earlier retirement and greater longevity. More rigorous analyses are needed and to some extent have been carried out, but the results have been elusive and have given rise to much controversy.

Feldstein,[1] using aggregate data for the United States for the period 1929 to 1971, concluded that social security had a large negative effect which by the end of the period was reducing the saving rate by one half. However, these results have since been refuted by several other authors who could find no appreciable effect from social security.[2] Studies of a few other individual countries have produced similar negative results.[3] On the other hand, analysis by a variety of authors of data on individual households – especially older ones – with different rates of social security cover, have consistently shown that social security wealth displaces private wealth, with an estimated effect ranging from some 60 cents to 90 cents per dollar.[4]

1. MARTIN FELDSTEIN, 'Social Security, Induced Retirement, and Aggregate Capital Accumulation', *Journal of Political Economy*, vol. 82 (5), September/October 1974, pp. 905-26.

2. ROBERT J. BARRO, *The Impact of Social Security on Private Saving. Evidence from the U.S. Time Series.* Washington: American Enterprise Institute, 1978; DEAN R. LEIMER and SELIG D. LESNOY, 'Social Security and Private Saving: A Re-examination of the Time Series Evidence Using Alternative Social Security Wealth Variables', Paper presented at the 1980 American Economic Association Meeting, Denver, Col., 6th September 1980 (see also 'Social Security and Private Saving: New Time – Series Evidence', *Journal of Political Economy*, June 1982, vol. 90 (4), pp. 606-629).

3. GEORGE M. VON FURSTENBERG (ed.), *Social Security versus Private Saving.* Cambridge, Mass.: Ballinger Press, 1979.

4. PETER DIAMOND and JERRY HAUSMAN, 'Individual Savings Behavior'; MARTIN

Another series of tests has been based on a cross-section of countries, a method that, in principle, has the considerable advantage of providing direct evidence on the effect of social security on *aggregate* saving. Its main weakness is lack of comparability of national income accounts data in general and especially the difficulty of measuring crucial inter-country differences in social security benefits, both in terms of coverage and replacement rate. The first study, by Feldstein,[1] was based on a sample of 15 developed countries for which the required information was available and used averages for the decade of the 1950s. He found again a clear impact of the social security replacement rate on the saving rate. The estimated coefficient implied a displacement effect not far from two thirds and suggested that, in the absence of social security, the saving rate would have been on average one third larger. However, in this case too, later cross-country studies by other authors have failed to find evidence of a saving-reducing effect of social security (Barro and MacDonald,[2] Kopits and Gotur[3]).

These results are rather puzzling and, on balance, do not support clearly the implications of the LCH. Nonetheless a reconciliation of these results among each other and with the LCH might be found within the LCH itself along lines first suggested by Feldstein.[4] He has pointed out: (i) that according to the LCH the length of retirement plays a crucial role in determining the wealth-income and hence the saving ratio, and (ii) that the length

FELDSTEIN and ANTHONY J. PELLECHIO, 'Social Security and Household Wealth Accumulation'; ROGER H. GORDON, DONALD E. WISE and ALAN S. BLINDER, 'An Empirical Study of the Effects of Pensions on the Saving and Labor Supply Decisions of Older Men', Study prepared for the U.S. Labor Department, May 1980; LAURENCE J. KOTLIKOFF, 'Testing the Theory of Social Security and Life Cycle Accumulation'.

1. MARTIN FELDSTEIN, 'Social Security and Private Savings: International Evidence in an Extended Life-Cycle Model'.

2. ROBERT J. BARRO and GLENN M. T. MACDONALD, 'Social Security and Consumer Spending in an International Cross Section', *Journal of Public Economics*, vol. 11 (3), June 1979, pp. 275-90.

3. GEORGE F. KOPITS and PADMA C. GOTUR, 'The Influence of Social Security on Household Savings: A Cross-Country Investigation', *International Monetary Fund Staff Papers*, no. 27, March 1980, pp. 161-90.

4. MARTIN FELDSTEIN, 'Social Security, Induced Retirement, and Aggregate Capital Accumulation'.

of retirement cannot be taken as physiologically or institutionally given. It is instead an economic decision that must be chosen simultaneously with consumption and hence with the path of wealth, in response to a number of variables. Among these, the availability of a pension, private or public, is likely to be an important one. In particular, social security could be expected to be an important force making for earlier retirement. There are many considerations suggesting such an effect, ranging from the fact that a pension system forces the individual to make provisions toward retirement, to the fact that social security taxes and benefits tend to reduce the cost of retirement in terms of foregone consumption. In addition, social security schemes often have redistributive elements within cohorts and thus make retirement accessible for relatively low earners who might not have been able to afford as much of it before.

To the extent that this is the case, social security could be expected to have two offsetting effects on wealth and saving. For given length of retirement, it would tend to reduce the need for private accumulation – an outcome that Feldstein has labelled the "replacement effect". However, it would also have an "induced retirement effect" – that is, it would make for a longer retirement period tending to increase saving. The former effect might be expected to dominate, leading on balance to a negative impact of social security on saving. However, it can be shown that the opposite result is not inconsistent with the LCH and rational behaviour.

The hypothesis that social security tends to encourage retirement agrees with casual observations. Certainly the improvement and expansion of social security in recent decades have tended to go together with a noticeable increase in frequency and length of retirement. In terms of systematic statistical analysis, there have been some cross-section studies of United States households. Kotlikoff[1] finds some positive and some negative results, though the negative ones are questionable because of the way the impact of social security was measured. Another study by

---

1. LAURENCE J. KOTLIKOFF, 'Testing the Theory of Social Security and Life Cycle Accumulation'.

Boskin and Hurd[1] finds strong support for the hypothesis. Supporting evidence is also found in some cross-country studies such as that of Pechman, Aaron and Taussig[2] and Feldstein's[3] analysis of the 15-country sample mentioned earlier. His coefficient estimate implies an elasticity of retirement, measured by the labour force participation rate of men over 65, with respect to the social security replacement rate of approximately 0.4.

These results suggest that in order to test whether and to what extent social security replaces private wealth, it is necessary to control explicitly for the effect of retirement; if this is not done, what is measured is not the replacement effect but instead the net result of that effect and the offsetting one caused by social security, inducing earlier retirement and thereby increasing accumulation. The Feldstein contribution mentioned above, in which he had found a strong replacement effect, did include a retirement variable, thus controlling explicitly for the incidence of retirement. He found that that variable was quite important in explaining saving and that its quantitative contribution was also large – a rise of 10 percentage points in his retirement variable (which, in Feldstein's sample, averages approximately 60 per cent) was estimated to increase saving by 2.5 to 3 percentage points – a response that turns out to be broadly consistent with the prediction of a stylized LCH (see Modigliani and Sterling[4]). The fact that two later studies could not find confirmation for the effect of social security could be a result of their failure to include a retirement variable.

In a paper with Arlie Sterling,[5] we have attempted to check the earlier studies using data for the more recent decade of 1960–1970 and a sample of 21 OECD countries, all those for which

1. MICHAEL BOSKIN and MICHAEL D. HURD, 'The Effect of Social Security on Early Retirement', *Journal of Public Economics*, vol. 10 (3), December 1978, pp. 361-378.

2. JOSEPH A. PECHMAN, HENRY J. AARON and MICHAEL K. TAUSSIG, *Social Security. Perspectives for Reform*. Washington: Brookings Institution, 1968.

3. MARTIN FELDSTEIN, 'Social Security and Private Savings: International Evidence in an Extended Life-Cycle Model'.

4. FRANCO MODIGLIANI and ARLIE STERLING, 'Determinants of Private Saving with Special Reference to the Role of Social Security – Cross-country Tests'.

5. *Ibid.*

Row	Determinant (1)	Estimated coefficient (2)	Sample Mean (3)	Estimated Effect			Deviation from Sample Mean		
				Sample Mean (4)	Maximum Value (5)	Minimum Value (6)	U.S. (7)	Japan (8)	Italy (9)
1	Constant	8.0 (0.9)	1	8.0			0	0	0
2	Dependency Ratio	-0.13(4.3)	90.7	-11.8	-15.5	-9.1	-2.6	-0.2	0.4
3	Proportion of men over 65	-0.50(1.3)	15.2	-7.5	-9.5	-5.0	-0.1	2.5	0.1
4	Retirement	0.26(2.5)	70.0	18.2	23.6	10.4	0.2	-6.5	2.4
5	Productivity Growth	2.70(5.2)	4.04	10.9	21.1	2.6	-2.4	10.7	3.2
6	Subtotal			17.8	24.3	13.5	-4.9	6.5	6.1
7	Effect of Social Security Replacement Rate[1]	0.40(2.5) 0.81(2.4)	49 24	-19.5	-26.8	-3.2	2.0	16.6	-4.4
8	Computed Saving Rate			14.3*	23.6	10.2	-3.8	9.1	3.7
9	Actual Saving Rate		14.5	14.5	24.1	10.0	-4.2	9.6	3.0

Table 2. Estimated Determinants of the Saving Ratio[2]

* $14.3 = (6) \times [1-|(7)|/100]$; i.e. $17.8 \times [1-19.5/100]$.

1. Two figures are shown in columns (2) and (3) because two alternative measures of the replacement rate were used, depending on the availability for each country, and hence there are two estimated coefficients, and means, one for each measure.

2. Based on FRANCO MODIGLIANI and ARLIE STERLING, 'Determinants of Private Saving with Special Reference to the Role of Social Security – Cross-country Tests'.

the required data for that period were available. In so doing we have included a measure of retirement similar, but in our view somewhat preferable, to Feldstein's, namely the percentage decline in the labour force participation rate of men over 65 relative to the participation rate of men aged 25–54. In addition, we have sought to correct a mis-specification common to all previous studies – namely the assumption that social security has a simple additive effect. In reality, as has been seen above, the LCH implies a multiplicative effect: one percentage point increase in the replacement rate should reduce the wealth-income ratio by approximately one per cent, or perhaps more, and similarly for the saving ratio. Thus, if a country had no growth and hence no saving to begin with, social security should reduce the *wealth-income* ratio but not the *saving* ratio which would remain zero.

With these specifications and using for the replacement rate what appeared to be the most reliable measure available for each country, we obtain results roughly matching those of Feldstein, as can be seen from the information reported in Table 2. The first column shows the variables used to explain the private saving ratio, and they will all be recognized as characteristic LCH variables. The second column shows the corresponding estimated coefficients from Modigliani and Sterling, equation (1.4″). (The figures in parenthesis following the coefficients are *t*-ratios, a measure of the reliability of the estimates). The third reports the sample mean value for each variable, while column (4) shows the contribution of each variable to the explanation of the average saving ratio, which is shown in the bottom line, estimated by multiplying the coefficients of column (2) by the sample mean value of column (3). Row 4 relates to the retirement variable and clearly confirms its importance; the coefficient implies that a rise of 10 percentage points in our retirement variable (that averages 70 per cent) would increase saving by as much as 2.6 percentage points, a result that accords well with Feldstein's (2.4 per cent).

The sum of the first five rows of column 4, reported in row 6, represents what saving would have been in the absence of social security. Next, row 7 reports the estimated percentage by which savings are reduced because of social security. The average reduction for the sample is nearly 20 per cent, or 3.5 percentage points. Stated differently, according to our estimate, in the absence of social security, the saving ratio would have been higher by $0.21/0.79 = \frac{1}{4}$, which is only slightly lower than Feldstein's estimate[1] of $\frac{1}{3}$. These are large effects, though in Modigliani and Sterling[2] we estimated that a dollar per dollar displacement would imply more nearly a 50 per cent reduction in the saving rate.

The figures of column (4), however, are not very enlightening except when related to those in columns (5) and (6) which show for each variable the maximum and minimum effect over the sample. The spread between the figures of the two columns provides a hint of how important each variable is in accounting for cross-country variations of the saving rate. It is apparent that each of the variables makes a contribution, and a surprisingly large one, to the variation of the saving rate, which itself exhibits quite a large spread of 14 percentage points. For the two demographic variables, the variability is similar, amounting to 5 to 6 percentage points. Much greater variation comes from differences in retirement practices, amounting to 13 percentage points, while difference in growth rates account for the largest spread, nearly 20 percentage points. The spread resulting from the social security effect in row 6 also appears to be large (25 per cent). However, this figure is not directly comparable with the other rows since it is 25 per cent of the saving rate before social security, which averages 18 per cent. The spread, therefore, is more likely to amount to 5 percentage points – still a substantial number.

In the remaining columns of the table, we show estimates for the differential saving behaviour of three countries which may be considered to be of special interest, namely the United States, the most powerful economy and yet at the very bottom of the group in terms of saving rate; Japan, the country with by far the highest rate, and, of course, Italy.

The low saving ratio of the United States appears to be attributable to a productivity growth that is one percentage point

1. MARTIN FELDSTEIN, 'Social Security and Private Savings: International Evidence in an Extended Life-Cycle Model'.
2. FRANCO MODIGLIANI and ARLIE STERLING, 'Determinants of Private Saving with Special Reference to the Role of Social Security – Cross-country Tests'.

below average, and to a relatively high dependency ratio (reflecting in part the post-war baby boom) – only partially offset by a below average social security replacement rate. In the case of Japan, by contrast, the main factor behind the high saving is the extraordinarily high growth rate and the favourable age structure in addition to the extremely low social security benefits, although the low rate of retirement produces a significant counterbalancing effect. Italy has a high rate of growth in common with Japan but in contrast to Japan has a relatively early retirement. As a result, the saving rate in the absence of social security is estimated to be nearly the same in the two countries. The large difference of 6.5 percentage points might thus be attributed to the large difference in the social security replacement rate. However, this interpretation could be rather misleading in view of the systematic positive association between the retirement and social security which is examined directly below.

iii) *Replacement versus induced retirement effects*

To summarize, our study confirms the conclusion of Feldstein (and others) about the wealth replacement effect, for given length of retirement, even though our estimate implies a less than a dollar effect as calculated from the elementary LCH. It also confirms his findings of a significant positive effect of retirement on wealth and saving (in addition to Feldstein, see Kotlikoff[1]). In order to complete the analysis of the *total* effect of social security, another look must be taken at the remaining link, the effect of social security on retirement.

As noted earlier, Feldstein's international cross-section study[2] provided clear evidence for such an effect and yielded some estimates of its magnitude. Using our 21-country sample, an attempt has been made to secure an independent estimate of this effect. Feldstein found that the main variable determining retirement, besides social security, was a non-linear function of per capita

---

1. LAURENCE J. KOTLIKOFF, 'Testing the Theory of Social Security and Life Cycle Accumulation'.

2. MARTIN FELDSTEIN, 'Social Security and Private Savings: International Evidence in an Extended Life-Cycle Model'.

income (a dummy variable measuring whether the system required a person to be retired to receive benefits was generally not significant). A similar specification has been used except for the addition of a variable measuring the incidence of dependants. As expected, this variable contributed to reducing retirement. However, again the attempt to measure the differential effect of provisions or different social security systems in encouraging retirement was unsuccessful.

On the whole, our results conform closely to those of Feldstein; retirement increases with income though at a decreasing rate and, most important for our purpose, is affected to a very significant extent by the social security replacement rate – the coefficients imply that an increase of 0.1 in the replacement rate increases retirement by 6 to 7 percentage points. This corresponds to an elasticity of the mean of around 0.3, somewhat higher than Feldstein's estimate which is below 0.2.

The implications of these results for the total direct and indirect effects of an increase in the social security replacement rate by 10 percentage points are conveniently summarized in Table 3. Column (2) shows the effect implied by the Modigliani and Sterling estimates, at the mean of their sample. The replacement effect given in row (1) amounts to a 1.3 percentage point change in the saving ratio per 0.1 percentage point increase in the replacement rate, which is not large but still quite significant. However, somewhat surprisingly, the indirect effect through induced longer retirement (row 2) leading to higher saving (row 3), turns out even larger, 1.4 percentage points, as shown in row (4). Our estimates are thus seen to imply that the *net* effect of increasing social security on saving is actually positive, though minute. A 0.1 increase in the replacement rate would increase the saving ratio by 0.1 percentage points. In column (1) of the table, the estimates of Feldstein, which led him to the opposite conclusion, are reported. His estimate of the replacement effect (row 1), and of the effect of retirement on saving (row 3), are very similar to ours. The difference lies in the estimated effect of social security on retirement, which is only around 2.5 as against our 6 to 7 percentage points. Thus, his induced retirement effect comes to 0.6, implying that the effect of a rise in the social security replacement rate is negative, though again small, and amount to − 0.5. Feldstein cites the same result but makes it sound more impressive by stating that an increase in the replacement rate of 25 percentage points reduces saving by 1.2 percentage points. The fact is that a 25 percentage point increase in the replacement rate is quite a large one.

In conclusion, it can be said that there is no real contradiction between Feldstein's and our results − both show that on balance the negative replacement effect of social security, which is large, is mostly offset by the retirement effect, leaving a net impact

	Feldstein Sample Average (1)	Modigliani-Sterling Sample Average (2)	Italy (3)
1. Replacement	− 1.1	− 1.2[1]	− 1.4[2]
2. Effect of Social Security on Retirement	2.5	6.5	6.0
3. Effect of Retirement on Saving	0.24	0.26	0.26
4. Effect of Social Security on Saving Through Retirement (row 2 × row 3)[3]	0.6	1.4	1.2
5. Total	− 0.5	0.2	− 0.2

Table 3. Estimated Impact of Social Security on Saving − Replacement, retirement and total effect per 10 percentage point increase in replacement rate

1. This figure is obtained by multiplying the estimated average saving ratio before social security (Table 2, column 4, row 6) by 0.7. The latter coefficient is derived from the two coefficients reported in row 7 of column (2) assuming that a 10 percentage point rise in the average replacement rate is equivalent, on the average, to a 14 percentage point rise in the Olsen measure (based on the ratio of the Olsen to the ILO measure); Leif HAANES-OLSEN, 'Earnings Replacement Rate of Old Age Benefits, 1965-75, Selected Countries', *Social Security Bulletin*, vol. 41 (1), January 1978, pp. 3-14; ILO (International Labor Organization, *Yearbook of Labor Statistics*, various issues).

2. The saving rate [derivable from column (9), row (6)] times 0.6, assuming a 14 percentage point change in the Olsen measure − see footnote 1.

3. For columns (2) and (3), the product of rows (2) and (3) is further multiplied by (1 − Replacement effect), given in Table 2, row 7.

which is negligible, whether it is slightly positive or slightly negative. Furthermore, this conclusion can also serve to reconcile Feldstein's and our findings of a clear replacement effect with the findings of others, including Barro and MacDonald,[1] and Kopits and Gotur[2] of no effect (or even a modest positive effect). For their estimate measures not the replacement effect but instead the total effect of social security which, according to our own findings, is small at best and even of uncertain sign. To substantiate further this conjecture, the basic saving ratio equation has been re-estimated without the retirement variable. It is then found, as in the case of other authors, that the coefficient of the social security variable, now measuring the combined replacement and induced retirement effects, does fall to around zero.

iv) *Some considerations on the Italian case*

What implications can be drawn from this analysis of the effects of social security for the specific case of Italy? There are a number of considerations suggesting the need for considerable caution in applying the results of our cross-country analysis to Italy. Italy is a country that already in the 1960s offered exceptionally favourable social security benefits, especially relative to its degree of development. Now, according to our analysis, the replacement effect of social security on saving is not linear, but instead tends to be greater (in absolute value) the higher the replacement rate and saving ratio, which in the case of Italy is again unusually high. Thus, even if the coefficient estimates of our cross-country equation are applied mechanically to Italy, some different conclusions can be expected when these coefficients are applied to the sample mean values. This proposition is illustrated in the last column of Table 3. It is seen that the replacement effect in the first row is relatively large, reflecting the high saving ratio (especially without social security), while the induced retirement effect is smaller, for the same reason.

1. ROBERT J. BARRO and GLENN M. T. MACDONALD, 'Social Security and Consumer Spending in an International Cross Section'.
2. GEORGE F. KOPITS and PADMA C. GOTUR, 'The Influence of Social Security on Household Savings: A Cross-Country Investigation'.

The result is that the net effect of raising social security is now negative though still quite small and amounts to − 0.3.[1]

These estimates, taken at face value, suggest that the exceptionally favourable benefit arrangement existing even in the 1960s may have had some unfavourable effect on saving, but certainly not of major magnitude or justifying serious concern. Similarly, they do not point to changes in social security benefits as a particularly promising way of influencing private accumulation. However, in our view, there are reasons for casting doubt on the reliability of this conclusion and for suspecting that the Italian social security system may after all be encroaching on the accumulation of capital, especially when allowance is made for the further substantial liberalization of benefits that has occurred since the 1960s. With these changes the Italian system is well on its way to becoming one of the most generous of the world in terms of replacement rates and other features (such as indexation). Successive improvements in benefits increasingly produce a more unfavourable effect on saving, because of the non-linear nature of the replacement effect noted above.

Another reason for caution in relying on our cross-section results is that the social security system of Italy (as well as many other countries) has been in rapid evolution, and there are a number of reasons why the social security effects during the break-in period could be different from the steady state effects, including the fact that people may not have full confidence about the system delivering the promised pension on schedule. (This mistrust, incidentally, appears to be widespread in many countries, including the United States, as well as Italy). Unfortunately, our cross-section study was unable to throw any light on these transitional effects, but this does not mean that they can be simply dismissed.

One consideration justifying a lack of concern for the possible detrimental effects of the expanding social security on Italian saving is that the saving ratio in the 1970s has been even higher than the very high levels of the 1960s. However, recent work

---

1. FRANCO MODIGLIANI and ARLIE STERLING, 'Determinants of Private Saving with Special Reference to the Role of Social Security – Cross-country Tests'.

has highlighted the fact that the figures on which this conclusion is based are misleading because they do not make proper adjustment for inflation – they include in income the nominal return on debt instrument, without making correction for the loss of real principal caused by inflation. Some recent attempts at re-estimating the saving ratio using appropriate measures suggest that in fact the ratio has tended to fall somewhat in the late 1970s. There may, of course, be many other reasons for this behaviour, but at the very least it suggests that the issue should be kept under observation.

One further potentially serious consequence of rising benefits is related to the fact that the growth of outlays has tended to outstrip the receipts of the system. Thus, not only has the system failed to accumulate assets to cover future liabilities, but instead it has been accumulating debts, adding to the huge overall deficit of the government. Clearly this deficit is reducing the flow of private saving available for capital formation.[1]

Finally, it should be borne in mind that even though the evidence suggests that social security does not have a major effect on the saving ratio, our analysis still implies that it will have substantial effect in reducing each of the two components of the ratio – saving and income. This is because the saving reducing replacement effect is countered by lengthening retirement which implies a reduction of income.

To summarize, our review of the implication of the LCH for the impact of social security on the saving ratio and of the empirical evidence, in the light of that model, would suggest that there is no real ground for fearing a major negative effect or even one worth any concern. Nonetheless, for reasons stated above, I feel that, especially in the case of Italy, the question bears close continued observation to ensure that an over-generous system, unfunded or deeply in debt, will not result in the withering away of one of the main resources which, together with the ingenuity and hard working character of the people, made the "Italian miracle" possible, namely an abundant supply of private saving.

---

1. FRANCO MODIGLIANI and ARLIE STERLING, 'Determinants of Private Saving with Special Refernce to the Role of Social Security – Cross-country Tests'.

DISCUSSION

GIAMPIERO FRANCO[1] shared Professor Modigliani's overall economic and institutional premises but expressed reservations about some of his specific assertions. Professor Modigliani had maintained that, since it was the level rather than the composition of aggregate demand that determined the level of employment and of the balance of trade, the choice between monetary and fiscal policies had no relevance to the control of inflation and to the external deficit. While acknowledging that this proposition might be true for economic systems of the North American variety, Professor Franco denied that it applied to the Italian economy. A sharp rise in wages in 1962–1963, unmatched by a corresponding increase in productivity, had set in motion an inflationary spiral, which was first fuelled by increases in consumption (resulting in a large deficit of the balance of payments) and then fanned by the increase in the money supply of 1962–1963. The only result of the strict controls imposed by the Bank of Italy had been to bring about a fall in investment. As Professor Franco understood it, this process indicated that some key economic variables (such as consumers' expenditure and the quantity of money) exerted a much greater cumulative influence in Italy than elsewhere. Although Italy had not been the only country to feel the impact of rising energy prices and of falling world demand, her different productive structure, the nature of public spending and specific institutional and behavioural features of her political and social structure had meant that Italy had been affected by these changes with exceptional severity.

Professor Franco maintained that, apart from the obvious differences in economic capacity, the differences in social and political philosophy were such that economic conditions and policies in Italy could not be compared with those of other countries. Inflation and unemployment had weakened even the mighty economy of the United States, but their effects on the weak Italian economy had been shattering and had pushed it to the brink of collapse.

Professor Modigliani had rejected the neo-monetarist arguments and their resulting anti-inflationary policies as a response

1. Professor of Economic and Financial Policy, Università degli Studi, Venice.

to the twin assault of unemployment and inflation on the economic and social stability of Western economies. Instead he had considered a neo-Keynesian approach, with its in-built inflationary consequences, to be the appropriate strategy for Italy. Professor Franco believed that Professor Modigliani's neo-Keynesian prescription, which was designed on the one hand to manage private consumption by means of a combination of monetary and credit controls and a deflationary fiscal policy, and on the other hand to stimulate investment through changes in interest rates and increased public expenditure (resulting in a large deficit in the government budget), was misconceived.

Turning to the theoretical model used by Professor Modigliani to underpin his policy prescriptions, Professor Franco felt that its underlying assumptions were applicable to the North American economy and to some European industrial nations, where the relationship between inflation and unemployment conformed to the original Phillips Curve, but did not pertain to the Italian situation. In his opinion Italy was unique in many respects: in her extreme inter-regional differences, in the dualism of her productive structure, in the inefficiency of her administrative apparatus, in the irresponsible policies followed by some employers and in the overwhelming power of the trade unions.

However, it was not only on the account of the political constraints implicit in Italy's social background that Professor Franco felt that Italy could not rely on the formalized models propounded by Professor Modigliani. He also doubted whether operational models which depended on precise correlations and elasticities of selected variables could ever be applied in the real world. The inappropriate nature of models based on assumptions about the predictable behaviour of certain key variables was particularly obvious in the case of Italy, a country whose markets, and above all whose financial markets, functioned badly.

GIOVANNI BELLONE[1] referred to Professor Modigliani's article on 'Consumption Decisions under Uncertainty'[2] and asked whether

1. Professor of Economics, Università degli Studi, Padua.
2. JACQUES H. DRÈZE and FRANCO MODIGLIANI, *Journal of Economic Theory*, vol. 5 (3), December 1972, pp. 308-36; reprinted in MODIGLIANI, vol. 2, pp. 198-226.

the experience of repeated bursts of unexpected inflation could have an influence on saving behaviour and on the separability of consumption and portfolio decisions.

GIUSEPPE PELLICANÒ[1] sought some clarification on the proposition, put forward by Professor Modigliani in his second lecture, that the shareholders of industrial companies were protected from inflation because investment in fixed assets undertaken by industrial companies maintained its real value in spite of inflation.

In recent years, added Mr Pellicanò, share prices had failed to keep in line with inflation, as could be ascertained by examining the trend of indices such as the Dow Jones. Mr Pellicanò was inclined to explain this phenomenon with the fact that the real value of fixed assets could only remain unaffected by inflation if firms provided for depreciation at replacement value rather than, as they normally did, at book value, so that cash flows were often insufficient to provide for the renewal of plant and equipment. In such a situation, firms, in order to remain competitive, had to borrow from banks, which usually lent at interest rates higher than the rate of return on capital. As a result, self-financing became more difficult and the real value of cash flows, and of share prices, was negatively affected. Mr Pellicanò was interested to know how Professor Modigliani would explain the recent trend of share prices in Italy and recalled that in Italy mere rumours of a rise in the inflation rate or in M_1 were enough to trigger a bear market.

GALEAZZO IMPICCIATORE[2] argued that many of the policy prescriptions advanced by Professor Modigliani were based on an unsatisfactory theoretical model, which assumed that either market forces or government intervention would eventually steer the economic system in the direction of an efficient equilibrium (or equilibria). Professor Impicciatore referred to the approach

---

1. Chairman and Managing Director of Tecnomasio Italiano Brown Boveri S.p.A., Milan.
2. Professor of Economic Policy, Università degli Studi 'La Sapienza', Rome.

developed by Clower, Leijonhufvud, Patinkin and others, aimed at reformulating the traditional model in terms of optimizing individual behaviour. According to this approach, decisions taken by individuals were based not only on relative and absolute prices but also on expectations regarding the feasibility of selling and buying plans so that, if transactions were allowed to take place at non-market-clearing prices, the system might fail to converge to a full-employment equilibrium. Professor Impicciatore referred explicitly to an article by Hal Varian,[1] which had proved that a simple dynamic model produced two equilibria, one unstable and characterized by full employment, the other (locally) stable and inefficient. In such circumstances, the prospects for economic policy were rather bleak: if the economy happened to be in a full-employment equilibrium, then any intervention would be de-stabilizing, whilst, in the case of an inefficient equilibrium, there existed no economic policy capable of leading the economy to full employment.

Professor Impicciatore admitted that the degree of correspondence between these theoretical models and the reality of modern economies was low, but no lower than was the case with the traditional models and concluded that this new approach had uncovered problems that could no longer be ignored by the theorists of economic policy.

GABRIELE GAETANI D'ARAGONA[2] offered an explanation of a phenomenon that had puzzled Professor Modigliani, namely the fact that in Italy, in spite of substantial increases in social security payments and especially in index-linked retirement and disability pensions, the propensity to save had remained quite high.

Professor Gaetani d'Aragona recalled that disability and retirement pensions had increased considerably in recent years, but pointed out that the most significant improvements had occurred at the very bottom of the pension scale. He went on to say that the major proportion of the recipients of State pensions for the

1. HAL R. VARIAN, 'Non-Walrasian Equilibria', *Econometrica*, vol. 45(3), April 1977, pp. 573-90.
2. Professor of Economic and Financial Policy, Università degli Studi, Naples.

disabled and the self-employed with low incomes were from the poorest regions of Southern Italy and that, although the increase in nominal value had outstripped inflation, basic pension benefits were still at a very low level, especially if compared with the salaries of civil servants and the wages of industrial workers. This disparity in relative incomes, coupled with the aspiration for the affluent life-style propagated by the mass-media, made State pensions look very inadequate and hence led the middle-aged and those near retirement to save at a high rate in order to supplement their pensions after retirement.

GIANLUIGI MENGARELLI[1] agreed with Professor Modigliani that it would be wrong to forsake stabilization policies, since the business cycle was not obsolete but, on the contrary, was the inevitable result of the economic activity. In a capitalist economy, said Professor Mengarelli, a period of recession was necessary to re-adjust the system and to overcome the de-stabilization caused by speculative expectations which had arisen during the expansionary phase. The role of stabilization policies, in Professor Mengarelli's view, was to slow down the expansion and to prevent the ensuing recession from becoming a prolonged depression. Nevertheless he was not optimistic about the effectiveness of the policy of low interest rates advocated by Professor Modigliani in initiating an economic recovery and therefore wished Professor Modigliani to expand on his remarks on this point.

ORLANDO D'ALAURO[2] referred to the remarks made by Mr Pellicanò and argued that the "Pellicanò effect", i.e., the poor performance of the stock market under inflationary conditions, was the consequence of stagflation which, in turn, was the inevitable consequence of inflation. Professor D'Alauro went on to emphasize that, given the rigidity of wages, any increase in the rate of inflation and even a situation of stable inflation always generated a fall in employment.

The "Pellicanò effect" could be explained easily by recalling

1. Professor of Economic Policy, Università degli Studi, Venice.
2. Professor of Economic and Financial Policy, Università degli Studi, Genoa.

that if the monetary authorities permitted inflation to take place, then business would be adversely affected since, as a rule, costs rose faster than returns. And, concluded Professor D'Alauro, if shareholders expected companies to make losses, how could anyone be surprised if they tried to sell their shares?

GIORGIO ROTA[1] concentrated his remarks on inflation and its effects, arguing that neither monetarist nor neo-Keynesian theories provided an explanation for the Italian inflationary experience. Monetarist theory, whilst formally correct, was hardly applicable to Italy, where the velocity of circulation, however measured, had always shown wide fluctuations. Neo-Keynesian theory had many features that applied to the Italian case but, as Professor Modigliani had acknowledged, it had been developed in countries that complied with the canons of economic theory much more closely than Italy. As an example of how unsuited to Italy these theories could be, Professor Rota quoted Professor Modigliani's reference to "fallacious belief that the harmful effects of inflation contribute significantly to reducing it". Professor Rota was convinced that, under certain circumstances, this belief might not be fallacious at all. He recalled that inflation was all too often conceived in an unduly narrow fashion, as nothing more than the average increase in prices, although in reality deviations from the average were much more significant, for they focused attention on who stood to lose and to gain out of inflation. When Professor Modigliani had touched upon the redistribution of income brought about by inflation, he had stated that it could be either random or systematic. Professor Rota felt that, apart from random (i.e., poorly predictable) and systematic (i.e., consistently predictable) redistribution, there existed a third type, which was deliberately sought by certain interest groups and whose final outcome could not be foreseen.

If it was accepted that inflation was subject to the interactions of social groups, then – continued Professor Rota – it had to be acknowledged that inflation might be actively supported by those who thought they would benefit from it and, conversely,

---

1. Professor of Economic Policy, Università degli Studi, Turin.

might be opposed by those who felt they would be hurt by it.

From this Professor Rota concluded that if inflation became harmful to the groups which had previously supported it, then this could indeed have a stabilizing effect. In the long run even the harmful effects on the groups who lost from inflation might also have a stabilizing effect, in so far as these groups were motivated to build up their anti-inflation defences. If inflation was advocated and used as a mean of redistributing income, its ultimate fate was the same as that of any other instrument that wore out of use and was eventually given up.

Finally Professor Rota asked Professor Modigliani whether it would be possible to design anti-inflationary policies that had the capacity to curb deviations from the average and thereby turn inflation into a stabilizer.

FRANCO BRUNI[1] felt that Professor Modigliani in his Lectures had provided a clear negative answer to the question posed in his 1976 American Economic Association Presidential Address, namely "Should We Forsake Stabilization Policies?".[2] Professor Bruni took this to mean that the monetary authorities should play an important role in stabilizing the economy and should not aim at targets expressed in terms of monetary aggregates. Instead they should set targets regarding those variables that people understood and cared about, such as income, employment and prices. This meant, continued Professor Bruni, that the authorities should seize the opportunity of stimulating income growth regardless of fixed monetary rules established without reference to the business cycle. In Professor Modigliani's view the monetarists' opposition to this way of thinking did not rest on an altogether different theoretical model but rather on a different expectation regarding the value of some crucial parameters of a common model; hence empirical evidence could help to prove the monetarists wrong.

Professor Bruni felt that a feature of this common model was

1. Assistant Professor of Economics, Università Commerciale Luigi Bocconi, Milan.
2. 'The Monetarist Controversy or, Should We Forsake Stabilization Policies?', 17th September 1976, *American Economic Review*, vol. 57 (2), March 1977, pp. 1-19; reprinted in MODIGLIANI, vol. I, pp. 3-21.

worth highlighting: it ignored the degree of efficiency of the allocation of resources. On the one hand Friedman assumed that, provided the model was in equilibrium, resources would be allocated optimally; on the other hand, Keynesians maintained that resources could be underutilized even in equilibrium but, to the extent they were utilized, this was done optimally. Professor Bruni wondered whether the type of active monetary policy advocated by Professor Modigliani in opposition to Friedman's would be appropriate in the case in which a mere re-allocation of resources would produce a significantly higher level of real income. He felt that the question was relevant, especially in Italy's institutional context, and asked for Professor Modigliani's opinion on the brief and necessarily incomplete answer that he was about to sketch.

It was well known that if the economy could be partitioned in two sectors, one efficient and the other inefficient and the latter had a more inelastic demand for loans than the former, then a *restrictive* monetary policy, even if appropriate on demand-management grounds, should be postponed for as long as possible, for it would worsen the allocation of resources. This should not be taken to imply that an *expansionary* monetary policy would be doubly beneficial, in so far as it would lead not only to a higher level of activity in the short run but also to a long-run improvement in the allocation of resources. On the contrary, Professor Bruni believed that, in the presence of allocative distortions, there was an even stronger case against expansionary monetary policies. In fact, in order to ascertain whether a monetary expansion was the appropriate response to a decrease in economic activity, it was cardinal to determine whether the depression itself was the long-term outcome of a worsening of the allocation of resources. If so, an expansionary monetary policy would lead to those phenomena that characterized an economy pushed beyond its long-term rate of growth, i.e. inflation and an external imbalance.

This argument against stabilization policies was different from Friedman's, in so far as the latter was grounded on the detrimental effects of mis-timed intervention, whilst the argument outlined by Professor Bruni was based on the observation that, because of the misallocation of resources, it would be difficult for the monetary authorities to detect the true value of the natural rate of unemployment. In a distorted economy the natural rate of unemployment could vary quite suddenly and these variations prevented the authorities from disentagling the structural (i.e., natural) component of the actual rate of unemployment from its cyclical (i.e., transient) component.

Professor Bruni suggested that in some countries the main source of inefficiency was the behaviour of the public sector; the magnitude of public expenditure was determined more by uncontrollable political and bureaucratic processes than by reference to cyclical conditions and by a proper assessment of net social benefits. As a result, the allocation of resources *between* the public and the private sector was distorted. In addition to this, there was the misallocation of resources *within* the public sector itself: all these problems, continued Professor Bruni, were neglected by macroeconomic models which concentrated on aggregate demand and ignored aggregate supply.

Once the inefficiency of the public sector was taken into account, another assumption of the models aimed at analysing the appropriateness of stabilization policies had to be jettisoned. These models, in fact, assumed not only perfect allocative efficiency, but also that the authorities were in control of the instruments pertaining to them and would act in concert. In other words, the monetary authorities were supposed to act *alongside* those in charge of public expenditure and taxation in an attempt to stabilize the private sector. However, if the quantity and quality of public expenditure were in fact beyond control and public services were produced inefficiently, the monetary authorities would find themselves up *against* both the public and the private sector.

In conclusion, Professor Bruni believed that, in addition to the technical difficulties mentioned earlier, there was a political reason for refraining from using monetary policies as a stabilization tool. An uncontrolled expansion of unproductive public expenditure, coupled with a stable money supply, would tend to crowd out the private sector, thus depressing its level of activity. If the monetary authorities reacted by stabilizing interest rates in an attempt to shield the more efficient sector from the consequences of the expansion of public expenditure, the latter would expand even further. As a result, there might well be a short-term gain in the general level of economic activity, but the underlining structural situation would become more difficult to detect and the required structural transformations more difficult to implement.

FRANCO COTULA[1] recalled that in his third lecture Professor Modigliani had discussed the controllability of monetary aggregates and the most appropriate choice of intermediate objectives for monetary policy. He had made a distinction between countries with highly developed financial markets in which there was a clear boundary between M_1 and other bank deposits, and countries in which this clear separation did not exist. In the former group, the central bank was able to regulate the monetary base and control deposits in current accounts (i.e., M_1) and, furthermore, the relationship between these deposits, the level of income and the rate of interest paid on the only category of credit existing in the "standard" model would remain stable. In the latter countries, where there was only one compulsory reserve coefficient for all forms of deposits, the central bank could control the total, but not the composition of bank deposits. As a result, the relationship between the central bank instrument (the monetary base), income and rate of interest was no longer stable.

Dr Cotula considered that if the various forms of bank deposits were perfect substitutes, the demand for total deposits would not necessarily be more unstable, though it was likely that the degree of inertia of the system would be greater than when the demand for money was only for transaction purposes (though still elastic with respect to the rate of interest). If this were the case, the difference would be one of degree – to be assessed empirically – and there would be no invalidation (on these grounds) of the standard model. In particular, if the yield on total deposits were constant, the standard model would enable the rate of interest to be determined. Conversely, if the deposit rate varied in accord-

1. Director Research Department Bank of Italy, Rome.

ance with the credit rate, the demand for money would depend on the differential between the two rates of interest, and the supply of money would have to be made explicit in a more complex manner. In this case, if the operating target of the Central Bank were the quantity of *bank reserves*, as was substantially the case in Italy (so that the rate representative of money market conditions adjusted itself in consequence), the variability of the deposit rate would tend to *amplify* (possibly to an undesirable extent) the effect on interest rates of a given change in *bank reserves*.

Dr Cotula went on to explain the considerable importance which he attached to Professor Modigliani's next step: the extension of the standard model so as to include the gross flows of finance between households and firms, rather than the net flow. The enlarged model had been used by Professor Modigliani to demonstrate the greater stability of the relationship between credit and income compared with that of the relationship between other intermediate and final objectives.

Dr Cotula thought that, because of the particular hypotheses and simplifications involved, the enlarged version of the model, at least in the version presented in the lectures, was not the most appropriate one for demonstrating the greater stability of the relationship between credit and final objectives. For example, in this version of the model financial assets did not appear in the balance sheet of the firms' sector, which included only investment and two types of credit.

It was of crucial importance that firms should also be allowed to borrow in order to buy financial assets, which varied over time, a fact which resulted in an unstable relationship in the short term between credit and real flows. This was of great importance if the amount of firms' money (and financial assets) happened not to be the equilibrium one at the beginning of the period, or if the differential between credit and deposit rates changed over the period, or, finally, if there were shifts in the demand for financial assets themselves.

In Dr Cotula's view, in order to assess the relative effectiveness of monetary and credit aggregates in pursuing final objectives, one had to compare the *relative stability* of the demand for deposits to that of the demand for bank credit. As a first step, it was necessary to take into account substitutability of deposits with respect to total financial assets, and of bank credit with respect to total financial liabilities.

Finally, he felt that rather than speaking of the choice of one single intermediate objective it would be better to speak of the most suitable (and mutually compatible) values to be assigned to various intermediate objectives. For the firms' sector, which was a net borrower, an objective related to credit might be most appropriate; for the household sector, which determined the composition of wealth, the amount of money available might be most appropriate. Dr Cotula believed that in order to define an intermediate objective in a meaningful way, vis-à-vis a final objective, it was necessary to take account of the relation between the quantity of financial assets and a given amount of credit and of the fact that both aggregates were associated with that final objective. It was well known, concluded Dr Cotula, that in the case of an open economy there were good reasons for not choosing an intermediate target related to money. On the other hand, in a closed economy – like that portrayed in Modigliani's model – money could be taken as a proxy for bank credit, because money and bank credit (including Treasury financing) were equal.

PAOLO BAFFI[1] alluded to Professor Modigliani's remarks concerning the relationship between the Central Bank and the Government. Certainly the situation was highly complex, but not, he thought, one in which the Central Bank could be described as a servant of the Government. However, he conceded that in Italian legislation the Bank was not attributed as strong a position as in some other countries. In Italy there was no law entrusting the Central Bank with the task of defending the purchasing power of money, as an independent objective of monetary policy, whereas laws of this nature did exist, and were part of the Constitution, in other countries. For instance, in Germany, the United States and Sweden the Central Bank's position was strengthened by the fact that it was responsible not to the Executive but to the Legislative.

Dr Baffi went on to stress that in Italy there was no law compelling the Central Bank to purchase Government securities.

1. Governor, Bank of Italy, Rome.

Indeed, the object of the ceiling placed on the Treasury's indebtedness via its current account with the Central Bank (as a ratio of current budget expenditure) was to restrict recourse to the Central Bank. If the Bank of Italy were to take up whatever stock of securities the Treasury offered, it would betray the purpose of this law.

Nevertheless on some occasions the Bank of Italy had been under pressure to purchase Government securities that were difficult to place on the market.

However, under present legislation, the one moment when Government and Central Bank might come into conflict was at the Treasury bill auctions, because existing regulations were open to two interpretations. The general rule was that the Treasury could not compel the Central Bank to purchase its securities, but when Treasury bill auctions were first introduced the Interministerial Committee on Credit and Saving had issued a resolution ensuring that the monthly issues would be covered by the Central Bank. There was some similarity here with the situation in the United Kingdom, where a syndicate ensured coverage.

This resolution further stipulated that the Treasury's offer price for these bills had to reflect fully market conditions. To Dr Baffi's mind, in this case "fully reflect" should be taken to mean that the offer price had to represent a higher yield than equilibrium market rates, so that if the Central Bank purchased Treasury bills at issue, it could subsequently place them on the secondary market without incurring any loss.

Indeed, the Bank had successfully fought to impose the latter interpretation and Governor Baffi was sure that it would not have escaped notice that over the previous six months, i.e., since March 1977, the yield on Treasury bills had fallen from around 18 to 12 per cent, while the Treasury's offer prices had not changed so that the Bank of Italy, acting as a free agent, had been able gradually to increase its bid prices. The Central Bank had thus been able to place on the secondary market what it considered an amount of Treasury bills sufficient to ensure a regular supply of the money stock. In fact, one could almost say that placement on the secondary market had overtaken auction placements.

Professor Modigliani had also stated that the Treasury Minister fixed the discount rate. This remark too should be qualified: the Treasury Minister fixed the discount rate following a proposal by the Governor of the Bank of Italy. Such a proposal had always been made. Dr Baffi recalled that exactly a year previously, when the Treasury Minister and he were leaving for Manila during a serious foreign exchange crisis, the then Director-General of the Treasury caught him at the airport to ask him to initial the decree issued by the Treasury Minister. It was in fact the Bank of Italy that had proposed to raise the discount rate from 12 to 15 per cent.

Thus, Italian legislation was not very clear on this point; it did not solve the problem one way or the other. It was a question of personal relationships. And also a question of the support given to the Central Bank by public opinion and academics, so that it could form its own long-term outlook beyond that held by Government. Governor Baffi therefore called on them for their support.

Having cleared up these institutional issues, the Governor touched on some of the points covered in this series of lectures. Although he had unfortunately not been able to attend the lectures, he had carefully read through Professor Modigliani's Presidential Address to the American Economic Association and checked with Dr Cotula that these points were actually covered in the lectures. He stressed that he wanted to address himself to points of analysis, rather than policy. This should not surprise the audience since, as academics rightly tried to draw conclusions from their analyses in terms of rules for economic policy, he, as a policy maker, was trying with equal validity, he thought, to discover the analytical roots of his actions.

His first point concerned the nature of the shocks which occur in an economy. Usually these were divided into shocks originating in the "real" sector and those generated in the monetary sector.

From his point of view, the difficulty raised by a shock such as the Italian economy was then experiencing, entailing, among other things, a drop in inventory demand, lay in the fact that in an open economy the "real" event is the mirror image of the monetary event and vice versa, making it difficult to distinguish between the two events. By this Dr Baffi meant that, since Italy was heavily dependent on imports, a reduction in inventory demand resulted in a drop in demand for imported goods and hence a balance of payments surplus on the current account, produced both by a reduction in inventory demand and by low levels of productive activity. A current balance of payments surplus generated money, which could remain in the system. It was thus difficult to establish which came first: the desire to hoard money, which shaped inventory demand, or the desire to sell off inventories, which led to money creation.

Since the remedies might well differ according to whether the origin of the shocks was monetary or real, he asked for Professor Modigliani's help in defining the shock which Italy was then experiencing and the consequences for economic policy.

His second point concerned Milton Friedman's prescription for the constant expansion of the money stock.

One might have imagined that monetarists were to be found within the Central Bank, but this was not so. In the Governor's opinion, the Central Bank had, if anything, gone too far in the past in stabilizing interest rates rather than the money stock. He considered this prescription totally unsuited to the problems of an open economy, because it presupposed that foreign accounts were in equilibrium. Obviously, if they were not, a central banker could always keep monetary expansion on a given course for a certain period by restoring to the system – via domestic money creation, such as Treasury financing or Central Bank operations – what the balance of payments had destroyed.

However, with this method a time would come when reserves and international credit dried up. It would then no longer be possible to keep to that course and there would be a crisis on the exchange market. In a highly indexed economy such as Italy's a foreign exchange crisis affected prices; there was a jump in all prices, the real value of the existing money stock decreased and it therefore became necessary to cause a jump also in the money stock. So the path ahead did not slope smoothly upward, but was broken up in a series of large steps.

Dr Baffi felt that in an open economy a constant expansion of the money stock did not provide a feasible alternative, not even if the hypothesis of fixed or periodically adjustable exchange rates was replaced by that of a completely floating rate. In a highly indexed economy, the effects on domestic prices would cause costs to soar so that the money stock had also to be increased to meet the increase in prices.

His third and last point concerned the interest-rate elasticity of demand for money. Here again he had no wish to disagree with Professor Modigliani, but simply wanted to describe the reality of the situation in Italy.

It seemed to him that the solution to the problem of the interest-rate elasticity of money demand depended on whether it was assumed that money was not interest-bearing or that there was a variable differential between the interest rate on money and that on other financial assets.

Italian bankers had acted in such a way that the yield on current accounts had been close to, and on occasion had exceeded, that on saving deposits. These yields had come closer to the rate prevailing on the financial market, to the point where the differential between the yield on money and non-money had either narrowed or disappeared. Obviously, in these circumstances the interest-rate elasticity of money demand could become nil or even positive, because if all interest rates on financial assets were to increase there might be a shift towards investment in financial assets, including money.

Turning back for a moment to the institutional problem, he wished to add something of importance which he had omitted to mention earlier. Professor Modigliani had said that it was the Treasury Minister who fixed the discount rate and Dr Baffi had explained how the Minister did it. However, it had to be pointed out that even when the Treasury Minister had established the discount rate, there was still no regulation which obliged the Central Bank to discount.

MARIO BALDASSARRI[1] examined the effects of monetary policies employed as a response to demand and supply shocks, an issue that Professor Modigliani had dealt with in his first two lectures.

1. Professor of Economics, Università degli Studi, Bologna.

Professor Baldassarri pointed out that, on the one hand a restrictive monetary policy tended to raise interest rates, thereby lowering the demand for both consumer and capital goods: because of the resulting decrease in the level of economic activity the demand for credit would tend to fall. Professor Baldassarri defined this sequence of events as a demand shock brought about by a restrictive monetary policy. On the other hand, a restrictive monetary policy, apart from leading to the postponement or even the cancellation of investment projects, could also affect the stock of productive assets. As a result, production costs could increase, because of higher financial charges. Firms could respond to such an increase by going out of business altogether, by falling back on "internal funds" or by increasing their demand for credit per unit of assets. This meant, explained Professor Baldassarri, that one needed to ascertain the net effect of the short-term reduction in the demand for credit as compared to the medium-term increase in the demand for finance. In technical terms, this meant evaluating the second derivative of the net effect. In other words, one had to ascertain whether a sustained restrictive monetary policy tended to depress economic activity at a slower rate than the rate of increase in the demand for finance by the firms that managed to remain in business. Thus another dimension had to be worked into the design of monetary policies, i.e., their duration and timing. Indeed, warned Professor Baldassarri, there might come a point beyond which a restrictive monetary policy, introduced to curb inflation, would in fact create inflationary pressures. In view of this assessment, Professor Baldassarri felt that he could agree with Professor Modigliani that there was little sense in setting intermediate monetary targets and that setting such targets for a "long" period of time was positively detrimental.

Objectives had to be revised over time in order to adjust them to the changing state of the economy.

MARIO MONTI[1] commented that Professor Modigliani had dealt with the problem of indexation in two separate contexts, al-

1. Professor of Monetary Theory and Policy, Università Commerciale Luigi Bocconi, Milan.

luding to the indexation of wages (labour market) and the indexation of long-term financial assets (financial markets). Professor Monti wished to raise three questions, regarding the *spread* of indexation, the *technique* of indexation and perhaps the very *notion* of indexation.

Regarding the spread of indexation, Professor Modigliani had referred more than once to the problems raised by the *existence* of wage indexation as "diabolical" or "infernal" and at the same time had spoken of the *absence* of indexation of the yield on long-term financial assets as no less serious.

Professor Monti thought that he understood the reasons for this different stand but was anxious that it should not engender confusion in the minds of some observers in Italy at a time when both terms of the problem were under active consideration by the public.

He therefore asked Professor Modigliani whether his negative assessment of the situation confronting both the labour market and the financial assets market as far as indexation was concerned depended on a lack of symmetry between the two markets or on the specific nature of these markets. He wondered whether Professor Modigliani would regard a situation in which there was no indexing at all as optimal as a situation with full indexation in all markets and indeed whether either case could be seen as "optimal".

Professor Monti felt that economic analysis and economic policy should pay more attention to the allocative aspects in addition to the aggregate effects of indexation, or lack of it. In the case of Italy at least, the indexing of wages and the lack of indexation of long-term interest rates – often kept low by "suitable" monetary policies as well as by subsidized credit – had exerted a somewhat artificial pressure on the cost of capital compared to the cost of labour. This may have been one of the causes of the comparatively low growth of employment with the medium- and long-term growth of the gross domestic product. This discrepancy had arisen following the adoption of excessively capital-intensive techniques of production together with an undue "debt intensity" in the financial structure of firms.

His second question concerned the technique of indexation.

Almost incidentally, Professor Modigliani had given a fairly discouraging prospect to Italian observers when he had said that the worst of all possible worlds was one in which financial assets were subject to a hybrid form of indexation which tied them to short-term interest rates rather than to price indices.

These were the only modes of indexing long-term financial assets that had been tried in Italy, by firms, credit institutions and, recently, by the State through the issue of Treasury credit certificates.

Professor Monti wished to know why Professor Modigliani regarded this formula as unsatisfactory.

The last question related to the concept of indexation itself. When considering its effects, the extent and the rate of adjustment of some prices (wages or interest rates) to the general level of prices should be borne in mind. Professor Monti had the impression that the effects of indexation were often assessed on the (implicit) assumption that the frequency of transactions and their built-in inflation expectations in the economy were *given*.

And yet, if there were no indexation, transactions would probably be more frequent and so he wondered whether the benefits, in terms of lower inflation, of measures aimed at reducing the degree of indexation may not somehow be offset, beyond the very short term, by more frequent trading. To cite an example, if people were not aware that the worsening of the terms of trade could involve the need to reduce real incomes, it would surely make little difference, beyond the very short term, whether there was indexation or not. Admittedly, if the sliding scale ceased to compensate for the effects of changes in the terms of trade, then awareness of this need would probably be sharper.

As an additional point on a somewhat different subject, Professor Monti asked Professor Modigliani for his view on the other outstanding difference of opinion between monetarists and neo-Keynesians. He recalled that in his presidential address to the American Economic Association Professor Modigliani, true to his neo-Keynesian conviction, had argued that in the recent past there had been many convergences of views between the two schools, and that the only outstanding fundamental divergence was on the role of stabilization policies.

On the other hand, an economist with monetarist sympathies, Thomas Mayer, had reached the conclusion that basically "every single proposition of monetarism is one which a Keynesian could accept while rejecting others, and still maintain his adherence to basic Keynesian theory. In particular, the policy propositions are readily detachable from the theoretical propositions of monetarism, and can be accepted without qualms by a Keynesian".[1]

Thus for Professor Modigliani there was a *divergence* between monetarists and neo-Keynesians regarding the role of stabilization policy, whereas for some monetarists there was a *convergence* between them and the neo-Keynesians on this same issue. Professor Monti asked for Professor Modigliani's comments on Mayer's statement and wanted to know if it would be true to say that the rival schools (monetarists and neo-Keynesians) could agree that there was a growing agreement between them but disagreed as to the points on which they agreed.

LUIGI PASINETTI[2] said that he had drafted a couple of contributions to the discussion but realized that there would not be time to deliver them in full. He began on a personal note and recalled that the previous time he had been able to listen to a series of lectures by Professor Modigliani was in 1957-58, when he was a graduate student at Harvard University, and Professor Modigliani was spending a sabbatical year there. Twenty years since, he was pleased to find Franco Modigliani the same as ever – bouncing, smiling, always provocative, charmingly extravagant in vaunting the merits of his own models and a bit unfair when demolishing those of others; ever shrewd and ready with intelligent replies to any objection, whether it came from renowned theoretical economists like Samuelson or from people dealing with concrete reality like the Governor of the Bank of Italy. He tought we should all thank the organizers of the Mattioli Lectures. At such a chaotic moment in the country's history

1. 'The Structure of Monetarism', *Kredit und Kapital*, vol. 8, 1975, pp. 191 ss. and pp. 293 ss.; reprinted in THOMAS MAYER, *The Structure of Monetarism*. New York-London: W.W. Norton and Company, 1978, pp. 1-46 (the quotation on pp. 45-6).

2. Professor of Economic Analysis, Università Cattolica del Sacro Cuore, Milan.

as the present one, the commencement of these Lectures was an important cultural event, filling a conspicuous gap. Professor Pasinetti had known Mattioli personally in the last years of his life, and from a very special angle, through his friendship with Piero Sraffa, and considered the institution of these lectures in his honour to be a very happy and appropriate initiative.

Professor Pasinetti went on to say that Franco Modigliani would not be surprised by the critical nature of the contributions he had prepared. For, an integral part of Professor Modigliani's own teaching method had been to instil a consistently critical attitude in his pupils.

Professor Pasinetti wanted to say a few words on the life-cycle model of savings and on the exposition of Keynesian thought which had been presented in the First Lecture. The life-cycle model of savings was a very interesting model, attempting to provide a theory of consumer behaviour in conditions of certainty. He was a little surprised that Modigliani should have used by way of introduction a reference to Smith's theory of capital accumulation. He felt that it was entrepreneurs who accumulate wealth and consumers who spend it. Thus, in order to be able to make inferences on the accumulation of wealth, one could not confine oneself to consumer behaviour but had to concentrate one's attention *on the production side* of economic activity.

Naturally the life-cycle model of savings led to some extremely interesting results. However, it would seem counterproductive to present it as the best of all models, which solved all the theoretical problems that arose in the study of savings. There existed other, much simpler, models, like the one, familiar to all, based on income-bracket differentiated propensities to save, which, among other things, could not be faulted for neglecting the production side of an economic system. One of the weakest points in the life-cycle model of savings seemed indeed to be the fact that it completely ignored what was happening on the production side.

Professor Pasinetti also found that the way in which Professor Modigliani had presented his model lent itself to criticism. Modigliani always mixed up the very important notion that consumers may decide to defer consumption from one period to another with certain specific assumptions regarding the distribution of consumption over time – in the case in point, a rectangular distribution – that was supposed to be independent of income levels.

In this respect Professor Pasinetti felt that the idea of a distribution of consumption through time independent of income levels counters to common experience, if only because of the influence of income levels on personal attitudes to inheritance. Surely people in the low income brackets did not even think about such things whereas those in higher income brackets thought a great deal about how they would leave their wealth to their heirs.

Thus, on the one hand, the basic idea was an important one, so important that Modigliani had been able to draw extremely interesting conclusions regarding the determinants of aggregate savings quite independently of individual savings. The subsidiary assumptions, on the other hand, were very particular and could lead to bitter disappointment, as had been seen in the case of social security.

The other point worth touching on briefly concerned the traits in the development of Keynesian economic thought that Franco Modigliani had described in his first lecture – the lecture perhaps most in keeping with the spirit of the Mattioli Lectures. Modigliani had presented this development as starting in the years preceding World War II but – very significantly – he had traced its evolution not from the *General Theory* of Keynes, published in 1936, but from the presentation of the Keynesian theory given by Hicks in 1937. Of course Modigliani was perfectly consistent, in that the whole evolution of his own economic thinking had taken the Hicksian reformulation of Keynes as its starting-point.

However, when Modigliani had said that there were no basic analytical differences between Keynesians and monetarists, he clearly had in mind Hicks' reformulation. He could not have had in mind the Keynes of the *General Theory*.

Professor Pasinetti felt that there were two very different ways of looking at the contribution of Keynes: one was to regard it as an upsetting phase that would in due course be absorbed into the mainstream of traditional formulations (Hicks was a typical example of this). The other was to regard the *General Theory* as a break with traditional theory. The latter seemed to him to be closer to Keynes' own view and to have proved to be the more fruitful.

Modigliani, by adopting the former approach, had deprived himself of the possibility of making an effective critique of Friedman. Modigliani criticized Friedman from the standpoint of exactly the same analytical apparatus, and Friedman had an easy run when he said that we are all Keynesians now. If one were to take one's cue from Keynes' *General Theory* however the conclusions would be quite different.

Professor Pasinetti said that it would be presumptuous of his to start here proposing alternative elaborations. Fortunately in the next series of Mattioli Lectures a true authority on Keynesian thought would be speaking: Professor Kahn, who is thought by some to have been the coauthor of the *General Theory*. This discussion might well be resumed on that occasion.

Finally Professor Pasinetti felt that a further point needed to be made at this juncture: when Keynesians of different persuasions came down from the level of theory to that of practical applications there was a considerable convergence of opinions. The crucial difference here was between those who thought that nothing should be done and those convinced that, in the face of unemployment, something had to be done. On this, Modigliani clearly belonged to the latter category and, from this point of view, between him and Friedman there really was a wide gap. For, at depth, Modigliani had remained a man of action. On this respect, perhaps, there was no closer man to Keynes in the lecture-room than Franco Modigliani.

FABRIZIO ONIDA'S[1] first question referred to the theoretical definition and the empirical measurement of the "natural" rate of unemployment, a concept that had played a prominent role in Professor Modigliani's second lecture on the trade-off between inflation and unemployment.

---

1. Professor of Economic Policy, Università degli Studi, Modena and Università Commerciale Luigi Bocconi, Milan.

He wondered whether Professor Modigliani agreed with the proposition that in the 1970s the "full employment rate of unemployment" had increased appreciably in the Western economies. Professor Onida was not referring to the argument derived from search and information theory used by Professor Modigliani himself, which held that a cyclical slack, by creating few jobs, lengthened the time-period required to find a new job. Such an argument contributed to the explanation of the cyclical behaviour of unemployment, but not to explaining the average rate of unemployment over the cycle. What Professor Onida had in mind was an argument pertaining to two structural factors, concerning the aftermath of the oil crisis and recent demographic trends.

Because of the worsening of the terms of trade forced by OPEC upon oil-consuming countries, the latter had been compelled to engage in a rapid re-allocation of resources between various production processes (from non-tradeable to tradeable goods, from energy-intensive to energy-saving production techniques, etc.). The urgency of these adjustments had been increased by the reluctance of financial markets to accommodate the resulting "equilibrium" deficit in the current accounts of industrial countries by means of capital transfers and reserve pooling.

These sudden inter-sectoral shifts, argued Professor Onida, had worsened the mis-match between supply and demand for labour and had resulted in a higher natural rate of unemployment. As indirect evidence for this, Professor Onida cited West German data according to which actual vacancies (600,000) outstripped by far registered vacancies (250,000).

The other structural factor that might account for a higher natural rate of unemployment was the rising average rate of participation in the labour market, due to demographic trends and re-inforced by a considerable increase in the supply of female labour. Professor Onida argued that more women were seeking jobs in an attempt to offset the fall, or the slower rate of increase, in real after-tax household incomes that had occurred during the recent period of stagflation.

Professor Onida's second question related to the "front-loading" policy derived by Professor Modigliani from his application of the turnpike theorem to the Phillips Curve model. In this respect Professor Onida had two objections to make and wished to know Professor Modigliani's reply to them. His first criticism was that the increased instability of the investment function in Western economies since 1973 could hardly be accounted for in terms of the marginal efficiency of capital projects. The demand for capital goods and inventories had been greatly affected by inflationary expectations: it seemed that firms had reacted to the persistent and erratic waves of inflation by adjusting the time-profile of their buying and selling programmes so as to hedge against price risks. This type of behaviour had more to do with Keynes' "animal spirits" than with marginalist criteria.

Professor Onida's second objection, which he believed to be fully applicable to Italy and to a growing extent to the United States too, was that an expansion in domestic demand could lead to an external deficit and hence to devaluation and inflation. In an economy with a shortage of foreign reserves and with downward price-rigidity, it had to be acknowledged that, under a flexible exchange-rate regime, the integral of expected inflation in a given period was directly proportional to the leads and lags in the time-profile of the expansionary measures employed within that same period. In conclusion Professor Onida asked Professor Modigliani whether he, as an experienced adviser to Italian policy-makers, felt safe in assuming that his policy of "rapid recovery now, slowing down thereafter" would guarantee the attainment of the optimal unemployment-inflation mix in the medium term.

COMMENTS BY FRANCO MODIGLIANI

Professor MODIGLIANI began his response to the discussion by answering the question posed by Mr PELLICANÒ, namely why share prices failed to keep up with inflation, not only in Italy, but also in the United States and apparently in many other countries.

Mr Pellicanò had ascribed this to the failure of cash flows to keep up with inflation, which rendered firms unable to finance the replacement of their equipment and plant. Mr Pellicanò had offered two reasons why this would remain true even if profits before tax and interest were a stable fraction of sales and hence kept up with inflation. Firstly, taxes were levied on accounting income computed by deducting depreciation at historical rather than replacement cost, so that tax payments rose faster than inflation. Secondly and more importantly, the heavy indebtedness of Italian firms meant that even if gross profits kept pace with inflation, net profits would be significantly reduced, simply because of the rise of nominal interest rates in line with inflation. Thus, commented Professor Modigliani, a change from a situation with no inflation and a 5 per cent rate of interest to a situation with a 20 per cent inflation rate and no change in the *real* rate of interest would entail a five-fold increase in interest charges (from 5 to 25 per cent). This would indeed reduce what Mr Pellicanò had called "cash flows", as measured by conventional accounting methods. The flaw in Mr Pellicanò's argument, however, came from the fact that, under inflationary conditions, these conventional methods of measuring cash flows were plainly inappropriate. The proper method would be to allow for an unchanged real amount of debt, or leverage, in the capital structure of the firm. This meant, explained Professor Modigliani, that with a 20 per cent inflation rate, debt should also rise by 20 per cent. If this 20 per cent annual increase in debt were added to the conventional measure of cash flow it would provide the resources necessary to take care of replacement at current costs, as could easily be verified. Furthermore, Professor Modigliani added, the tax system allowed firms to deduct interest charges at *nominal* values, even though, in the example given above, the 20 per cent inflation premium added to the real interest rate of 5 per cent was in fact a repayment of principal. In this sense at least, argued Professor Modigliani, inflation tended to lower the tax burden on firms. Whether or not this outweighed the unfavourable effect inflicted by inflation via depreciation at historical cost depended on the relative importance of the fixed asset-debt ratio as compared to sales. Given that European – and especially Italian – financial structures were so heavily burdened with debt, the tax advantage accruing from the treatment of interest charges ought to outweigh the tax disadvantage due to the calculation of depreciation at historical cost.

Professor Modigliani could not therefore agree with Mr Pellicanò's explanation of the poor performance of the stock market, although he conceded that the latter might be the result of an instance of "money illusion", in that even though firms were better off in terms of taxation and no worse off in terms of cash flows (if these were correctly measured), nonetheless, in the eyes of investors who fail to make the adjustment so as to allow for the effects of higher nominal interest rates on cash flows, the profitability of firms might appear to have worsened, thereby justifying a lower valuation on the stock market. Similarly, bankers who failed to realize that there was nothing wrong with lending more, as long as the growth of loans was in line with inflation and the volume of business, might respond to inflation by refusing to lend the additional resources necessary to finance the replacement of equipment and plant.

Professor Modigliani felt that Mr Pellicanò's complaint that banks were charging interest rates well in excess of profit margins reflected once again a certain measure of money and inflation "illusion". Although nominal interest rates were very high, there was no evidence that, once inflation had been taken into account, *real* rates had in fact increased. Indeed, Professor Modigliani maintained that real after-tax interest rates had never been so low as in recent years. According to him the explanation of the poor performance of the stock market had to be sought in "inflation illusion" which, as he had argued in the lectures, took two forms: (i) the failure of the public, including perhaps some managers and bankers, to compute correctly the cost of debt and, hence, of profits; and (ii) the tendency to confuse real with nominal rates and thus to capitalize at nominal rates.

Professor Modigliani found that Professors FRANCO and MEN-GARELLI's contributions had some elements in common, in that they both doubted whether interest rate management was as effective in stimulating a depressed economy as it was in restraining an expanding one. It was by no means the first time this view had been expressed, observed Professor Modigliani. In fact its origins could be traced back to Keynes' "liquidity trap". Professor Modigliani doubted that such a syndrome was a major factor at work in the current circumstances, even though it might have been of some importance in the Great Depression. He conceded that an expansionary monetary policy might not have an immediate effect, because its initial impact would tend to be on short-term interest rates and would spread only gradually to long-term interest rates, which were the more significant in terms of controlling aggregate demand. However, monetary policy needed not be restricted to interest rate management; it could work directly through credit expansion and thereby ease market interest rates, since the latter reflected to some extent the tightness of credit in the system. Professor Modigliani suggested that an expansion of credit could bring results quite rapidly. On the whole he could see no reason why, under current circumstances, an expansionary monetary policy would not be effective in expanding demand, even though there were possible exceptions. For instance, it was reasonable to expect that lower interest rates would stimulate investment in capital-intensive, labour-saving devices. However, such an effect might fail to occur in a country such as Italy, in which there was no labour mobility and employers were unable to reduce the workforce, even when more efficient methods of production had lowered labour inputs. Other problems could arise in an open economy with a fixed exchange-rate regime, added Professor Modigliani. Assuming that interest rates in the rest of the world were given, any attempt to implement an expansionary monetary policy would inevitably cause outflows of capital, thus creating balance-of-payments problems and little domestic expansion. Under a floating exchange-rate regime, on the other hand, an expansionary monetary policy would create an additional channel for the expansion of demand, since currency devaluation would stimulate exports, even if at the cost of some inflation.

Professor Modigliani concluded that in cases in which monetary policy was likely to be less effective it had to be coordinated with appropriate fiscal measures.

Of the two questions posed by Professor BELLONE, on the effects of unanticipated inflation on savings and on the separability of consumption and portfolio decisions, Professor Modigliani found the latter easier to answer: separability was wholly dependent on the nature of preferences as reflected in the cardinal utility function. In general one would not expect circumstances affecting opportunities, such as inflation, to have an influence on preferences, as described by the utility function. The former question was much more difficult to answer. As he had pointed out in the second lecture, the main effect of unanticipated "pure" inflation (i.e., inflation that did not affect relative prices) was to redistribute income between creditors and debtors, because such inflation was not fully reflected in nominal interest rates. Moreover, this effect was reinforced by the presence of taxes and of government intervention (in the form of interest rate ceilings, etc.). If there was no government debt, it was impossible to establish whether or not such redistribution would have a systematic effect on saving. Where there was government debt, however, there would certainly be some redistribution from the private to the public sector (i.e., to future generations). In Professor Modigliani's view this redistribution was likely to reduce consumption and hence to increase saving, unless it was accompanied by an increase in government consumption. On the other hand, if measured correctly, private savings would show a fall, since the reduction in consumption would be less than the loss of wealth suffered by the private sector. However, according to the conventional measure of savings, i.e., with nominal rather than real interest included in income, savings might be expected to rise. Finally, concluded Professor Modigliani, the uncertainty about returns associated with the uncertainty of inflation could, but did not have to, increase savings.

Professor Modigliani had no difficulty in accepting Professor IMPICCIATORE's proposition that, by applying enough ingenuity, models could be constructed that would not tend to a stable equilibrium and in which disequilibria might not be a temporary phenomenon. The real problem, however, was whether these "ingenious" models provided a useful description of the "real world". Professor Modigliani had some doubts about this, especially in view of the assumption which these models made of complete rigidity of prices and wages and of their failure to take into account the role of money and of financial markets. Professor Modigliani could not see any convincing evidence for the existence of markets in a permanent state of disequilibrium; furthermore, the persistent disequilibria that could be observed were of the Keynesian variety, i.e., were caused by deficient aggregate demand. Such disequilibria, of course, could be eliminated through appropriate fiscal and monetary policies, even though, if given enough time, they would eventually disappear without any intervention. Other types of permanent, or long-run, unemployment called for quite different explanations, such as "insufficient capital".

Professor Modigliani concluded that if he was correct in suggesting that the real world did not conform to the predictions of Professor Impicciatore's models, then he ought to change the assumptions on which these models were based so as to be able to account for what was observable in the real world.

Professor Modigliani was grateful for the consolation that Professor GAETANI D'ARAGONA had offered him for the fact that the existence of a social security system in Italy did not appear to have produced some of the effects posited by the life-cycle hypothesis. In the lectures Professor Modigliani had suggested that social security transfers would reduce savings, not necessarily because of the high propensity to consume of the recipients of social security but rather because it reduced the need to save of those people who had not yet reached pensionable age. Professor Modigliani found Professor Gaetani d'Aragona's explanation for the high saving rate in Italy somewhat surprising, namely that the marginal propensity to save of social security recipients was very high, in spite of the very generous provisions of social security benefits. Professor Gaetani d'Aragona had argued that most social

security transfers, including disability pensions, went to the poorest strata of the population in the poorest parts of Italy and that
these people would save at a very high rate in order to achieve the
affluent life-style propagated by the media. To Professor Modigliani this sounded like the "relative income hypothesis" in reverse: the saving rate was assumed to *rise* with "relative" income.
Professor Modigliani had had some reservations about the original relative income hypothesis, but confessed to have even more
serious doubts regarding Professor Gaetani d'Aragona's "reverse"
formulation.

Professor Modigliani had two comments to make on the hypothesis put forward by Professor D'ALAURO to explain the unfavourable effects of inflation on the stock market. He had argued
that inflation would inevitably engender stagflation; thus, as
stagflation meant a lower level of economic activity in general and
of profits in particular, this would provide a justification for the
observed decline (in real terms) of the stock market in the face of
increasing inflation. Moreover he had claimed that in an inflationary environment costs would tend to rise faster than
returns.

In reply to this argument Professor Modigliani pointed out
that the evidence did not suggest that in inflationary conditions
costs rose faster than prices, at least as far as the United States
were concerned. On the whole, during the recent spate of inflation in the United States profit margins had not been eroded,
after allowance was made for the effects of changes in the level of
economic activity. However, Professor Modigliani conceded that
inflation, in so far as it was fought by producing a slack in the
economy, was likely to affect negatively corporate profits. Nonetheless Professor Modigliani believed that this fall played only a
minor role in accounting for the poor performance of shares.

Furthermore he considered the main reason for the decline in
the stock market in the United States to be the substantial decline
in price-earning ratios that had taken place there. Professor Modigliani recalled that between the late 1960s and the late 1970s
P/E ratios had been approximately halved in the United States in
line with the rise in inflation and in nominal rates. In Professor

Modigliani's view this phenomenon was due to the misunderstandings surrounding real and nominal rates as well as to the underestimation of profits of highly levered companies.

Referring to Professor ROTA's comments, Professor Modigliani recalled that in the lectures he had indicated his disagreement with those who claimed that all measures to reduce the painful effects of inflation would sap the will to fight inflation itself and should therefore be opposed. Professor Rota had challenged this position by arguing that the most important effects of inflation were redistributive and that, as a result, the persistence of inflation might be supported by those who stood to gain from it and resisted by those who stood to lose from it. In his view the more pain was inflicted upon the losers, the more likely it was that they would take action to fight inflation. In this respect Professor Modigliani pointed out that, at least in the case of the United States, it could be said that, taking into account stagflation and the effects of inflation on financial assets, bonds and equities, almost everybody had been hurt by inflation. It would be difficult to find one single interest group who would be inclined to favour the persistence and exacerbation of inflation. The only group that might be conscious of gaining something from inflation were home-owners benefitting from pre-inflation low interest rates, and even this group could hardly be said to have been vocal in its support for inflation. Professor Modigliani concluded from this that the persistence of inflation had to be attributed to the substantial cost of reducing it, measured in terms of unemployment and lost output. Professor Modigliani acknowledged that the same need not apply to other countries, Italy included. His own impression was that in Italy there were important interest groups that, while not favouring inflation as such, had been willing to support policies that could only result in inflation. On the one hand, the trade unions had continued to demand higher wages – even though they knew that inflation would increase as a result – on the ground that workers were protected from inflation by the wage-indexation mechanism. On the other hand, industry and other business interests, once confronted with higher wages, had supported an expansionary monetary policy that, by leading to higher domestic prices and eventually to the devaluation of the currency, had enabled them to pass the higher costs onto prices. This lack of real will to fight inflation on the part of Italy's most powerful social groups, coupled with the fact that the people most hurt by inflation had so little power, explained why inflation had been so stubbornly high and so slow to come down. Professor Modigliani agreed with Professor Rota that, if a powerful coalition of people who stood to lose from inflation could be formed, then a rigorous dis-inflation plan might have a better chance of being actively pursued, but he could not see any such coalition on the horizon.

Professor Modigliani expressed substantial agreement with Dr COTULA's observations. However, he wanted to make it clear that the aim of his analysis had not been to invalidate the traditional approach that focused on the money supply, but rather to point out that there were many other possible aggregates which in principle could be used to control money and real income. Nor had he tried to indicate which of these aggregates had the most stable relation to income in a stochastic environment; he had merely suggested that stability was an empirical matter that depended, among other things, on the financial structure of the economy involved. Finally Professor Modigliani acknowledged that in his illustrative model he had omitted a variable whose importance Dr Cotula had rightly underlined, namely the demand by firms (or other deficit units) for nominal assets, especially money. Professor Modigliani explained that this variable could be expected to play an important role in empirical investigations since the higher the demand for nominal assets by firms, the smaller the amount of investment that could be financed out of a given supply of credit.

Professor Modigliani was reluctant to express an opinion on the complex political issues involved in Professor BRUNI's questions. However, Professor Bruni appeared to have put together a number of quite separate questions, such as: (i) whether there ought to be *any* discretionary policy; (ii) if not, whether discretion ought to be replaced with a fixed rule either in the form of a constant growth of some aggregates or in some other form; and (iii) assuming that discretionary policies were adopted, whether discretion ought to be exercised by the Central Bank in a completely independent fashion or whether there should be a measure of government control. Professor Modigliani's own view was that the Central Bank ought to be given full independence to use the tools it considered to be appropriate and should bear full responsibility for the success or failure achieved by means of those tools. On the other hand the targets to be achieved ought to be determined by the government, with the participation and support of the Central Bank. In attempting to attain these targets, the Central Bank had to take into account the fiscal policy chosen by the government. In order to expedite the achievement of the agreed targets, the Central Bank might find it convenient to announce intermediate growth targets for certain money aggregates; these "intermediate" targets, however, had to be flexible and should be changed in line with changing circumstances. Professor Modigliani noted incidentally that the framework he had just sketched was in broad terms the one which had recently been adopted in the United States in the form of the so-called Hawkins-Humphrey Act. Although the Act had not been fully implemented, it was nevertheless a step in the right direction. In this regard Professor Modigliani felt that, in the light of the approach outlined in the lectures, it should be clear that there was no necessary relation between the budget deficit resulting from the fiscal policy of the government and the creation of money, which ought to be determined exclusively by the Central Bank as part of its overall strategy to achieve the ultimate targets. This meant, in particular, that there was no need to impose upon the Central Bank any obligation to "support" the issue of government debt at any given rate of interest.

Professor Modigliani hesitated to give his own views on the Italian legal provisions and practice because of their typically Italian complexity and the presence in the audience of someone much better qualified than himself in these matters, namely the Governor of the Bank of Italy, Dr Baffi. However, Professor Modigliani ventured to suggest that in one sense the Bank of Italy appeared to be under the Treasury's influence in so far as the

Governor served at the discretion of the Treasury Minister and the Bank required the Treasury's approval in fixing the discount rate. With respect to financial policy, on the other hand, the Treasury was under the control of the Central Bank in so far as the issue of government debt required the Bank's approval. Professor Modigliani defined this complex system of controls as "checks and balances", but remained unclear as to which institution had the final word on the overall shape of monetary and credit policies.

Professor Modigliani began his reply to Governor BAFFI by expressing his satisfaction with the fact that, by referring in the debate to the relationship between the government and the Central Bank, he had succeeded in inducing the Governor to participate in the discussion. The audience had been enlightened by the Governor's presentation of his views on the nature of the links between the Central Bank and the government and had also been able to hear about some of the Governor's current policy concerns.

Professor Modigliani pointed out that the Governor had once again shown up the full complexity of the statutory relationship between the government and the Bank of Italy. Professor Modigliani re-iterated his view that the essential aspect of the Bank's independence was its freedom in the choice and utilization of tools, which meant specifically its ability to select a monetary and credit policy directed not at supporting the market for government debt, but at generating the amount of money, credit and the level of interest rates appropriate for the achievement of the aggregate targets chosen by central government with the advice of the Central Bank. If one followed Governor Baffi's account one would have to draw the conclusion that the Bank was indeed independent in this essential sense. Professor Modigliani remained unclear as to why the discount rate had to be set by the Treasury, even if this did take place on the recommendation of the Bank of Italy. In any case the Governor had made the point that discount policy had not been a particularly important tool for Central Banks in modern times and that the Bank of Italy was not in any case under an obligation to provide discounting facilities.

Professor Modigliani then took up the last of the Governor's analytical questions, that related to the interest-elasticity of the demand for money. He agreed completely with the Governor's insistence that the answer depended on whether the interest rate paid on money was zero (or, more generally, exogenously fixed) or, on the contrary, it was determined on money market.

Professor Modigliani was aware that in Italy the rate of interest paid on current accounts moved in line with that paid on savings accounts and, on occasions, had been even higher. Indeed the fact that in Italy current and savings accounts deposits had been often almost indistinguishable, both in terms of reserve requirements and in terms of remuneration, had been a motivating force in the development of the analysis set out in the third lecture. Under such conditions although the Central Bank could still control total bank liabilities or assets such as total bank credit it was no longer able to control directly the quantity of demand, deposits and hence of money. In these circumstances it was more useful to think of the interest rate as determined on the credit market rather than on the money market.

Professor Modigliani understood the Governor's anxieties about the feasibility of a policy based on a constant growth of the money supply under a fixed exchange-rate regime. At least for a "small" country with high mobility of capital, the domestic money supply ought to be consistent with interest rates and price levels in the rest of the world.

Professor Modigliani pointed out that it was precisely the difficulty with controlling the money supply under fixed exchanges that led Milton Friedman, who might be expected to favour the more orthodox fixed exchange-rate regime, to oppose it and favour floating exchanges. Friedman's Supreme God, to which everything else – including fixed exchange rates – had to be sacrificed, was the rule that money growth should be constant. In the light of the fact that floating exchanges were supposed to be necessary and sufficient to permit an independent policy with respect to the quantity of money and in particular a policy of constant growth, Professor Modigliani was puzzled by the Governor's apparent rejection of that conclusion, at least in the case of a highly indexed economy. Of course under a constant money growth rule, the stock of money would not "be adjusted to changes in prices". Professor Modigliani was unclear as to whether under these conditions Governor Baffi thought that a policy based on a constant rate of growth of money was not feasible because the money stock had to be adjusted to changes in prices or because it would not produce desirable results.

Professor Modigliani admitted that he had not fully understood the nature of the dilemma posed by Governor Baffi in his last question. Apparently the basic observable fact was that inventories were being liquidated and this, together with a low level of productive activity, was generating a surplus on the current account balance which in turn was giving rise to an expansion of the money supply. The question seemed to be whether this phenomenon resulted from a real cause – a fall in inventory demand which had given rise to an increase in the money supply via the effect on the balance of payment – or instead whether the expansion of money was to be interpreted as reflecting an increased desire to hoard money which in turn had led to the reduction in inventories.

In attempting to provide an answer to these questions, Professor Modigliani made the observation that, in his view, neither an increase in the demand for hoarding nor a surplus in the balance of payments resulting, for instance, from a liquidation of inventories, could be regarded, in themselves, as causes of increase in the money supply. The money supply increased if and only if the Central Bank allowed it to happen, and accordingly engaged in an expansion of reserves. It was of course true that in a system of managed float the Central Bank could be forced to acquire the inflow of foreign currencies generated by the surplus. However, there was no reason why this purchase should be accomplished through an expansion of Central Bank liabilities, that is to say of high-powered money. On the contrary, unless the Bank felt that it was appropriate to expand the money supply, the inflow should be "sterilized" by selling some other assets on the Bank's balance sheet in order to make room for the increase in the assets consisting of foreign reserves. Finally, Professor Modigliani could not see why a reduction in the demand for inventories should be interpreted as an increase in the demand for hoarding.

In the absence of specific information on the current situation which might suggest that the above considerations were not relevant, Professor Modigliani was inclined to conclude that the phenomenon which was being observed was a real one, expressing a reduced desire to invest in inventories and probably in other physical assets. He also felt that this phenomenon was related to an increase in the money supply engineered by the Central Bank. On the basis of the available information, Professor Modigliani did not feel himself to be in a position to say whether or not this expansion of the money supply was an appropriate response under the circumstances.

Professor Modigliani noted that, despite some reservations about certain points of detail, he was in basic agreement with Professor BALDASSARRI, who had provided an elaborate illustration of why a monetary growth target set for a long period of time could generate problems.

Professor Modigliani had found the comments made by Professor MONTI characteristically sharp and relevant, and was grateful to him for having drawn attention to some points in the lectures which could appear puzzling to the reader and thus providing the opportunity to clarify them.

The first question that Professor Monti had asked Professor Modigliani was how he had found it possible to give whole-hearted support to the indexation of financial assets while at the same time opposing the indexation of wages as fraught with danger. Professor Modigliani was concerned to correct a wrong impression which might have been left by the lectures. As a matter of fact he did not regard the indexation of wages as an unqualified disaster. What he did believe to be an unqualified disaster was the kind of indexation which had been in force in Italy for some time, under which everybody received the same absolute amount of money whenever the cost of living rose by one per cent. This system was, as he had pointed out countless times, deeply destructive. It implied that the lower income brackets received a compensation for inflation which appreciably exceeded the rate of inflation; it was even possible for the overall indexation to exceed one hundred per cent (though the extent to which this happened depended on the growth of real wages and had been decreasing in time). As for conventional indexation, it had been shown by many authors to have both desirable and undesirable properties. Generally speaking, indexation was stabilizing with respect to demand shocks, but was destabilizing with respect to supply shocks. Since in recent years the important shocks had been coming mostly from the supply side, indexation had, on the whole, contributed to maintain the momentum of inflation coming from these shocks. These considerations, in turn, suggested that wage indexation could have a positive rather than a negative impact if it could be designed in such a way as to exclude from the basket used for the indexation goods subject to large supply shocks, such as those associated with oil and with changes in the external value of the currency.

Professor Modigliani then turned to the subject of the indexation of financial assets, which he did not, by any means, regard as indiscriminately desirable. Indeed, he felt there were relatively few cases in which indexation would be a significant improvement, and these were invariably cases involving very long-term contracts.

Two instances in which Professor Modigliani thought that indexation could be extremely helpful were two annuity-type contracts, namely the fully amortized level mortgage and the pension contract. As he had pointed out in the Lectures, in these cases, the lack of indexation meant that inflation resulted in a most serious distortion in the real outcome produced by these contracts. In the mortgage contract debtors had to pay at a very uneven real rate which started at a very high level and made it hard for them to acquire a house. Pensions suffered from the opposite "tilt"; the annuity started at a very high level to end at a very low real level. In both cases, indexation would solve the problem. Professor Modigliani recalled that he had also pointed out that there were other ways in which the problem could be largely alleviated, if not completely solved. Computing the annuity by using an "appropriate" real rate, together with debiting – or crediting – the relevant account with a nominal market rate would eliminate to a large extent the "tilt" problem brought about by inflation.

Professor Modigliani went on to point out that in the case of long-term bonds, with a life of 10 to 30 years, reliance on conventional nominal contracts created disturbingly large risks for both lenders and borrowers. Here, again, indexation was a possible solution. However, in this case, too, there were alternatives which might not be quite as satisfactory but would still greatly reduce uncertainty. They consisted in using a variable, or floating, interest rate tied to an appropriate short-term rate.

Professor Modigliani insisted that Professor Monti's impression that he was against these types of contracts reflected a misunderstanding. Professor Modigliani's objections were to a type of contract that had been used in Italy under which the variable interest rate paid by the instrument was tied not to short-term rates but to long-term rates. If one accepted the basic proposition that long-term interest rates were basically an average of expected future short-term rates, then it was clear that this instrument was a hybrid which made no economic sense and created quite unnecessary risks for both lenders and borrowers. Professor Modigliani did not believe that this instrument had any future, but re-iterated his support for a policy of tying the rate to a short-term instrument. For some time he had been suggesting that one should distinguish between two aspects of the problem of the term of an instrument. One was the length of time it took for the instrument to reach maturity, and the other was the term of the interest rate to which the interest paid by the instrument was tied. Because short-term interest rates, by and large, tended to adjust to inflation, by combining a long maturity with a short-term reference rate, one could secure the economies of a long instrument – that is, a reduction of transaction costs – while eliminating at least some of the inflation-induced risk to both borrowers and lenders.

Professor Modigliani then moved to the last question posed by Professor Monti, that is whether the agreement between monetarists and Keynesians included the question of what the agreement was about. Professor Modigliani submitted that the difference with Tom Mayer arose primarily from a difference in the definition of the essence of monetarism. To him the essential monetarist was Friedman, and the distinctive component of his view was that governments could not be trusted with discretionary powers. Therefore the money supply had to grow mechanically at a rate given once and forever, and the failure of the money supply to grow at a constant rate was the source of all macroeconomic problems. On the other hand, the essence of the Keynesian position, in his view, was that they did not regard the system as sufficiently stable, if left alone, and held that discretionary policy, or at any rate more complex stabilization rules, could be used by the government to improve the situation. Most other differences were to be regarded as "quantitative" rather than qualitative.

Professor Modigliani had been gratified to hear Professor PASINETTI's reactions to the lectures. Professor Pasinetti had been one of his best students, which meant that he had been a student from whom Professor Modigliani himself had learnt a good deal. His only regret was that Professor Pasinetti had felt that, because time was short, he had to cut back his remarks. It was always enjoyable to exchange ideas with Professor Pasinetti despite, or perhaps because of, the fact that his criticisms tended to be on the sharp side.

Professor Modigliani had been criticized by Professor Pasinetti for preferring his own life-cycle model to much simpler models, like the one based on absolute income, as the main explanation in variations in the saving-income ratio. Professor Modigliani pleaded guilty to Professor Pasinetti's accusation. However, the fact remained that the simpler models had long been given up for the simple reason that they could not account for most of the more interesting aspects of saving behaviour. Professor Modigliani submitted that no one knowledgeable of the facts would maintain that the saving ratio depended on absolute income. The so-called relative income hypothesis might fare considerably better. However, it should be noted that the existence of an association between the saving ratio and relative current income was among the implications of both the life-cycle and the permanent income hypotheses. On the other hand, the relative income hypothesis as such did not lead very far. In particular, it could not account for any of the six propositions in his lecture except possibly the first.

It had also appeared to Professor Modigliani that Professor Pasinetti felt that the life-cycle model was open to criticism on the ground that it ignored what was happening on the production side. However, Professor Pasinetti had not explained why this should be a defect rather than a merit, and, in any case, Professor Modigliani did not find the accusation justified. In the life-cycle model the overall flow of saving depended both on aggregate production and on its rate of growth.

Professor Modigliani then confronted Professor Pasinetti's criticism that, in illustrating the essential implications of the life-cycle model, he had made use of very convenient simplifying assumptions such as a constant rate of income until retirement and a smooth consumption through life. However, it should have been clear, Professor Modigliani thought, that these assumptions had been used only for illustrative purposes. The crucial aspect of the life-cycle model was that the observed life path of consumption reflected the preferred allocation of life resources and that the preferred consumption path was smoother than that of income, and, in particular, remained significantly above it, as income declined in the retirement period. These assumptions were sufficient to provide a unified explanation for a good deal of saving behaviour both at the individual and at the aggregate level. Furthermore, contrary to what Professor Pasinetti seemed to suggest, the implications of the model did not basically change if one allowed for a bequest motive, as, he agreed, one certainly should.

Professor Modigliani conceded that he did regard the evidence on the macroeconomic effects of social security as somewhat surprising, but not as a "bitter disappointment". The possibility that social security might affect the length of retirement, and the length of retirement in turn might affect the aggregate saving rate, were precisely the type of implications to be derived from the life-cycle model. The tentative evidence that these effects could roughly offset the "replacement effect" was not what he would have suspected, but this did not mean that it contradicted the life-cycle model.

Finally, Professor Pasinetti appeared to have interpreted

Professor Modigliani's first lecture as an indication that he regarded the *General Theory* as a development within traditional economics rather than as a radical break with it. Professor Pasinetti's conclusion appeared to be based on Professor Modigliani's proposition that there were no longer any basic analytical differences between Keynesians and monetarists. He felt that Professor Pasinetti had misunderstood him, for by that statement he had certainly not meant that Keynesians had jettisoned (short-run) wage rigidity or liquidity preference and hence, the role of effective demand. What he had been trying to say was that the monetarists had in principle accepted those radical Keynesian innovations. Although he should perhaps have added for clarity that he did not include among monetarists the "Macro Rational Expectations" fringe, which probably accepted just about nothing of the *General Theory*.

Professor Modigliani suspected that Professor Pasinetti had in mind some other aspects of the *General Theory* which represented an even more radical departure with tradition. Unfortunately, for lack of time, he had not been able to state precisely what he had in mind and they would have to wait for some later occasion such as the one to which he had referred.

Professor Modigliani found the questions asked by Professor ONIDA – whether the natural rate of unemployment was stable over time and whether it had risen substantially in recent times – difficult to answer. Professor Onida himself had suggested that the natural rate of unemployment could have risen in response to the rapid change in the structure of the economy caused by the massive rise in the price of oil and of energy in general. As a result the available supply of unemployed labour might not have the skills required to fill the existing vacancies. In support of his hypothesis Professor Onida had suggested that there was some evidence for a simultaneous increase in both unemployment and vacancies. Professor Modigliani did not feel in a position to provide a fully substantiated answer to Professor Onida's question, but was not inclined to attach much weight to his hypothesis as an explanation for the rise in recorded unemployment, at least in the case of the United States and some European countries.

Professor Modigliani's scepticism was based in part on past experience: in the first half of the 1960s, the United States had suffered from a sustained high level of unemployment. At that time there had been a fashionable and widespread view that the rise in unemployment was the effect of a mismatch between the available labour force and the higher skills required by technological changes. This explanation had been challenged by people who maintained that the higher unemployment was simply due to the conventional problem of lack of effective demand. At the time the constraints imposed on monetary policy by the balance of payments and from the well-known difficulty of persuading Congress to pass tax cuts put serious obstacles in the way of expansionary measures. The next few years had proved the supporters of the effective demand view to be correct: by the mid-1960s unemployment had fallen sharply, even below the level that had previously been considered "natural", although the stage had been set for the inflationary period that was to follow.

In the case of Italy, however, Professor Modigliani had no doubt that the high degree of labour immobility was a significant factor in the reluctance of employers to hire more labour and thus helped to increase unemployment, especially among young people.

The other issues raised by Professor Onida related to the dangers that might arise from a policy calling for "rapid recovery now, slowing down thereafter". Professor Modigliani shared Professor Onida's concern for the problems that this could create in an open economy under a flexible exchange-rate regime. In developing his analysis Professor Modigliani had been thinking of the United States and therefore had not attached much importance to the implications for an open economy. He agreed that if an open economy with flexible exchange rates wanted to bring about an expansion at a faster rate than its trading partners while at the same time avoiding a devaluation, then it had to engineer capital inflows, from either official or private sources. However, Professor Modigliani could not help pointing out that the re-entry policy he advocated was quite the opposite of the rapid expansion followed by a slow-down suggested by Professor Onida. On the contrary, Professor Modigliani explained that in terms of his own analysis the optimal path called for an immediate restriction of output to the appropriate level followed by a reflation of demand only after the inflation rate had moved sufficiently close to its target level. It followed that an open economy with flexible exchange rates would find such a path *less* painful to follow.

Professor Modigliani concluded the debate by thanking all the participants who, with their criticisms and clarifications, had contributed to making the lectures a rewarding experience that he would remember and cherish for a long time.

BIOGRAPHY OF FRANCO MODIGLIANI

Biography of Franco Modigliani

1. *Biographical Note.* – 2. *Contributions to the Development of Economic Theory:* i) *Monetary and Macroeconomic Theory;* ii) *The Theory of Saving;* iii) *The Theory of Corporate Finance.* – 3. *Publications.* – 4. *Collected Papers.*

1. *Biographical Note*[1]

FRANCO MODIGLIANI belongs to an old Roman family of Jewish ancestry. His father, Enrico, was a distinguished paediatrician with a private practice who also lectured at the University of Rome (as "Libero Docente"). Early in his career he had made significant scientific contributions (notably in the field of scarlet fever) and his name and biographical sketch appear in the major Italian encyclopaedia.[2] Franco Modigliani's mother, Olga Flaschel, was born in Florence of a Polish father and an Italian mother. She and her family had lived in Paris and Vienna before settling in Rome at the beginning of the century. Before her marriage she attended the University of Rome (which, at the time, was rather unusual for a woman), although she completed her degree in pedagogy only in the 1930s. Franco Modigliani's parents married in 1911 and had their first son, Giorgio, two years later; Franco, their second and last son, was born in 1918 (18th June).

Franco Modigliani had a normal and happy childhood; according to some accounts he was an obstinate child, with occasional wild tantrums. His parents were loving but strict, and also very busy. He was encouraged to participate in sports and to enjoy the open air. In the summer the Modiglianis used to spend their holidays either in the Alps, where they all enjoyed long walks, or at the sea-side. Franco Modigliani still plays tennis, swims, and goes sailing and skiing. Enrico Modigliani served as

---

1. This biographical note is based on information kindly provided by Professor Modigliani.

2. See A[GOSTINO] PAL[ERINI], ad vocem *Modigliani Enrico* (Rome 19th September 1877 – 2nd April 1931), in Enciclopedia Italiana di Scienze, Lettere ed Arti. Rome: Istituto della Enciclopedia Italiana, 1934, pp. 527/b, 528/a.

a doctor in the First World War and, after his return to Rome, became passionately concerned with the plight of illegitimate children who, under the Italian law of that period, could be abandoned at birth by their mothers to be cared for by a variety of Roman Catholic institutions. The Roman Catholic Church actively encouraged abandonment as a way of hiding "the fruits of sin". Franco Modigliani's father, who had volunteered as a doctor in one of these institutions, was shocked by the enormously high mortality rate of these abandoned babies and, well ahead of his time, concluded that this could be largely explained as a "lack of love syndrome". Thus, with the help of his wife, he devoted a good part of his life to the establishment and super-vision of an organization aimed at encouraging and assisting mothers to keep their children at least through the nursing phase and possibly for longer.

When the young Franco was just under thirteen a major crisis occurred: his father died after a duodenal ulcer operation. In spite of his premature death, Enrico Modigliani exerted a great influence on his son: it was from him that the young Franco learned basic ethical principles and acquired a sense of social responsibility. An episode may illustrate this point: in 1929 (24th March) Franco's father had returned home after having cast his vote in the so-called "Plebiscite" (a referendum for or against the fascist regime) and announced, in a matter-of-fact tone, that he had voted "No", even though it was well known that ballots were not secret.

In the early years Franco Modigliani's school performance had been good, but not outstanding: for the three years following his father's death his performance was at best erratic. Eventually he decided to move to the *Liceo Visconti*, Rome's best known and most demanding high school, and the challenge proved healthy: the young Franco suddenly matured and turned into an out-standing student. Spurred by the success, he decided to sit for his high-school final exams one year early (even though he was already one year ahead of his class) and passed successfully the examinations required to enter the University of Rome at the age of seventeen (two years ahead of his fellow-students).

At the time he had no clear career preference, although his

family had come to expect that he would follow his father in the medical profession and to that end provisions had been made to put together the necessary resources. He hesitated for a while and then decided against it because of his very low tolerance level for blood and suffering. Instead he opted for Law, which in Italy provides a wide choice of career opportunities. During his second year, having a great deal of time on his hands, he entered a national competition in the area of economics, sponsored by the Italian university student organization (*Littoriali della Cultura*). The topic was the design and management of price controls that at the time were in operation in Italy because of the Ethiopian War (October 1935 – May 1936). He had happened to discuss extensively this very topic with an older cousin, who lived with Franco's family and was vice-president of the National Trade Association. Much to his surprise, Franco Modigliani was awarded first prize in the competition: his first essay may not have been a major contribution to economics (not by his present standards), but was the determinant factor that steered him towards economics. Unfortunately, the teaching of economics in the Faculty of Law at the University of Rome was at the time at a very low ebb and consisted primarily of fascist propaganda. However, he was advised by some good economists (especially Riccardo Bachi of the Faculty of Economics and Commerce), and began studying the works of the best Italian economists as well as of the British classics (Smith, Ricardo).

Winning the economics competition had put him in contact with some of the brightest and most articulate young people of his generation; in fact, although the competition itself had been organized by a fascist student organization, many of the participants were strongly anti-fascist and later played a leading role in the underground and resistance movement as well as in post-war politics. They helped open his eyes to the true and despicable nature of the fascist regime and awakened him from his hitherto scant interest in politics. His growing political awareness was also heightened both by his disgust with the fascist intervention in Spain and by the views of his fiancée, later to become his wife, Serena Calabi, and of her remarkable father, Giulio. As a result, when the racial law went into effect in the summer of 1939, the twenty-one-year-old Franco was psychologically prepared to leave the country and, following the invitation of his future in-laws, was able to emigrate promptly to France. In 1938–1939 he worked part-time in Paris and spent the rest of his day at the Sorbonne Library, for he had found the teaching of economics at the Sorbonne quite uninspiring.

In May 1939 he married Serena. Although she lived in Bologna, he had known her since childhood, because their great-grandmothers as well as their grandmothers had been intimate friends.

She has played a vital role in his life ever since, giving him valuable support in his professional activities, not only as a companion and homemaker, but also as a steadying influence in the face of his professional success.

In the spring of 1939, as dark clouds were gathering over Europe, Franco Modigliani and his in-laws made plans to visit the United States and secured immigration visas in case it became necessary to settle there. In July he went back to Rome to defend his thesis and to complete the requirements for the degree in Law. They all left Europe on the very day the German-Soviet pact was signed and arrived in New York when the war had already begun.

Among the many refugees who had already settled in New York there was Paolo Contini, a close friend of Franco Modigliani, who held a research position at the New School for Social Research. With his help the twenty-one-year-old Franco obtained a scholarship at the New School. In the autumn of 1939 he was able, for the first time, to study economics (and other social sciences) in a systematic way and under the supervision of outstanding teachers, such as Fritz Lehman, Adolph Lowe, Jacob Marschak and Kurt Wertheimer.

Although his work-load was heavy, for he had to work full-time during the day (selling European books) in order to earn a living and thus could study only at night, this was a very happy period for him because he was fascinated with the subject-matter of his studies and had found that he had an aptitude for it. He gradually came to the conclusion that economics was his vocation. In this he was greatly helped by Jacob Marschak, who not only gave him a firm grounding in economics and econometrics, but also introduced him to the great issues of the time and was a source of constant encouragement. The mixture of theory and empirical work – in the sense of testable theories and theory-guided empirical analysis – that characterizes much of Modigliani's work owes much to Jacob Marschak's influence. Marschak also contributed to Modigliani's training as an economist by inviting him to an informal seminar held in New York in 1940–1941, whose members included, among others, Abraham Wald, Tjalling Koopmans and Oskar Lange.

Modigliani's training as an economist can be said to have finished in 1941 when Marschak left the New School to join the University of Chicago and he himself obtained his first teaching job. In 1942, in fact, Modigliani gave up his job in the book business to become an Instructor in Economics and Statistics at Bard College (then a residential college of Columbia University) and thus came to appreciate the unique qualities of life in an American college campus, especially the close association with first-rate students. Of this period it is his first article in English, 'Liquidity Preference and the Theory of Interest and Money'[1] which is largely based on his doctoral dissertation and which Modigliani himself regards as one of his major contributions to economics. This article, resulting from the discussions in Marschak's Seminar and from a prolonged debate with Abba Lerner, attempts to integrate the so-called "Keynesian Revolution" into the mainstream of classical economics.

In 1944 he returned to the New School as a Lecturer and a Research Associate at the Institute of World Affairs where, together with Hans Neisser, he was responsible for a project whose results were eventually published in *National Income and International Trade*. Of the same period it is also his first contribution to the theory of saving, which has since come to be known as the Duesenberry-Modigliani hypothesis of saving.

In Autumn 1948 he left New York, having been awarded the prestigious Political Economy Fellowship of the University of

---

[1]. *Econometrica*, vol. 12(1), January 1944, pp. 45-88; reprinted in MODIGLIANI, vol. 1, pp. 23-66.

Chicago; he also joined as a Research Consultant the Cowles Commission for Research in Economics, then the leading institution in the field. Shortly after his arrival there, he accepted an attractive position at the University of Illinois, as director of a Research Project on "Expectations and Business Fluctuations".

However, for the 1948–1949 academic year he stayed in Chicago, where he benefitted greatly from his association with the Cowles Commission, which was staffed and visited by scholars such as Marschak, Koopmans, Arrow and Simon at a time when two major revolutions were being absorbed by the economic profession, namely the one initiated by von Neumann and Morgenstern on the theory of choice under uncertainty, and the other on statistical inference from non-experimental observations, inspired by Haavelmo.

His association with the University of Illinois lasted only till 1952 because of internal strife. During this brief period he befriended a young brilliant graduate student, Richard Brumberg, with whom he laid the foundations of what was to become the Life-Cycle Hypothesis of Saving. The original idea was further developed in 1953–1954 in two joint papers after both Modigliani and Brumberg had left the University of Illinois, the former to complete his Ph.D. at the Johns Hopkins University, the latter to join the Carnegie Institute of Technology (now Carnegie-Mellon University). This second paper was published as an article in Franco Modigliani's *Collected Papers* only in 1980, because the untimely death of Brumberg in 1955 had sapped Modigliani's will to undertake the revision necessary to bring the original papers up to the standard of publication required by professional journals.

Modigliani's association with Carnegie, which lasted until 1960, was very productive. In addition to completing the two basic papers setting out the foundations of the Life-Cycle Hypothesis, he collaborated with Holt, Muth and Simon on a book dealing with optimal production scheduling and wrote two essays with Merton Miller on the effects of financial structure and dividend policy on the market value of firms (see below). He also published a joint paper with Emile Grunberg on the predictability of social events which was to provide one of the pillars of the "Theory of rational expectations". To a certain extent, all these contributions can be seen as the coming to fruition of the earlier work on "Expectations and Business Fluctuations".

In 1960, Modigliani went to the Massachusetts Institute of Technology as Visiting Professor, where he returned in 1962, after a year at Northwestern University, and where he has remained ever since. Here he has been able to pursue his early interests in macroeconomic theory and applications, especially the criticism of monetarism, the generalization of the monetary mechanism and empirical tests of the Life-Cycle Hypothesis. He has also branched out into new areas and in particular international finance, the effects of, and cures for, inflation, stabilization policies in highly-indexed open economies, as well as in various fields of the theory of finance, such as credit rationing, the term structure of interest rates and the valuation of speculative assets.[1]

Franco Modigliani has participated actively to the debate on economic policies both in Italy and in the United States, concentrating more recently on the deleterious effects of large public deficits.

Franco Modigliani, who has been Institute Professor at the M.I.T. since 1970, was awarded the LL.D. (*ad honorem*) in 1967 by the University of Chicago, the Doctorate in Economics (*honoris causa*) in 1974 by the Université Catholique de Louvain (Belgium), the Doctorate in Economics and Commerce (*honoris*

---

1. *Franco Modigliani's Career*: Institute Professor, Massachusetts Institute of Technology, 1970–; Professor of Economics and Finance, M.I.T., 1962–; Professor of Economics, Northwestern University, 1960–1962; Visiting Professor of Economics, M.I.T., 1960–1961; Professor of Economics and Industrial Administration, Carnegie Institute of Technology, 1952–1960; Visiting Professor of Economics, Harvard Unisity, 1957–1958; Fullbright Lecturer, University of Rome and Palermo, Italy, 1955; Associate Professor, 1949, Professor of Economics, 1950–1952, University of Illinois; Research Consultant, Cowles Commission for Research in Economics, University of Chicago, 1949–1954; Research Associate and Chief Statistician, Institute of World Affairs, New York, 1945–1948; Lecturer, 1943–1944 and Assistant Professor of Mathematical Economics and Econometrics, 1946–1948, New School for Social Research; Instructor, Associate in Economics and Statistics, Bard College of Columbia University, 1942–1944; Instructor in Economics and Statistics, New Jersey College for Women, 1942.

causa) in 1979 by the Istituto Universitario di Bergamo (Italy) and the Doctorate in Letters in 1985 by the Bard College, New York.

In October 1985 he was awarded the Nobel Prize in Economics by the Royal Swedish Academy of Sciences in recognition of his work on "the construction and development of the life-cycle hypothesis of household saving and the formulation of the Modigliani-Miller theorems of the valuation of firms and of capital costs".

2. *Contribution to the Development of Economic Theory*

The scientific output that Franco Modigliani has produced in the last forty years is impressive not only in terms of the breadth of his research interests and the depth of his contributions, but also for the huge quantity of books and articles published in all the major professional journals. However, three main areas stand out as the fields in which his contributions have been most influential for the development of economic theory.

i) *Monetary and Macroeconomic Theory*

His research in this area has been designed to integrate Keynesian and classical monetary theory, to clarify the role of monetary and fiscal policy in the determination of aggregate output, the price level and interest rates and to assess the extent to which monetary and fiscal policies can be relied upon to stabilize the economy. Three papers can be singled out from his copious production as especially important. In chronological order these are:

'Liquidity Preference and the Theory of Interest and Money', *Econometrica*, vol. 12(1), January 1944, pp. 45–88;[1]

'The Monetary Mechanism and its Interaction with Real Phenomena', *Review of Economics and Statistics*, vol. 45(1), Part 2, Supplement, February 1963, pp. 79–107;[2]

'The Monetarist Controversy or, Should We Forsake Stabilization Policies?', *American Economic Review*, vol. 67(2), March 1977, pp. 1–19 (Presidential Address delivered at the American Economic Association, 17th September 1976).[3]

Franco Modigliani incorporated many of the views set forth in the above papers in the Econometric Model of the United

1. Reprinted in MODIGLIANI, vol. 1, pp. 23-66.
2. Reprinted in MODIGLIANI, vol. 1, pp. 69-97.
3. Reprinted in MODIGLIANI, vol. 1, pp. 3-21. Franco Modigliani was President of the American Economic Association in 1976, Vice-President in 1971 and member of the Executive Committee, 1967–1969.

States, which was developed in the late 1960s under his supervision (and with the collaboration of others, especially Albert Ando) and sponsored by the Board of Governors of the Federal Reserve System. A modified form of this model is still used as an input to policy making.[1] A brief description of the model can be found in:

'Channels of Monetary Policy in the Federal Reserve-MIT-University of Pennsylvania Econometric Model of the United States', in George A. Renton (ed.), *Modelling the Economy*. London: Heinemann Educational Books, 1975, pp. 240–67;[2]

'Monetary Policy and Consumption: Linkages via Interest Rate and Wealth Effects in the FMP Model', in *Consumer Spending and Monetary Policy: The Linkages*, Federal Reserve Bank of Boston, Conference Series No. 5, June 1971, pp. 9–84.[3]

ii) *The Theory of Saving*

In the early 1950s Franco Modigliani, in collaboration with Richard Brumberg, put forward a novel hypothesis as a guide to understanding saving behaviour. The then generally accepted view was that the proportion of income saved by a household (or a nation) was systematically related to, and therefore could be largely accounted for by, current income, even though such a view was proving increasingly inadequate to explain the available empirical evidence. Modigliani and Brumberg instead advanced the hypothesis that a household's saving in a given period was best understood as the residual difference between income earned in that period and a rate of consumption reflecting the allocation over the life cycle of the resources anticipated over

---

1. Franco Modigliani has been a member of the Social Sciences Research Council Committee on Economic Stability and Growth and co-chairman of the Advisory Sub-Committee on the MIT-Pennsylvania-SSRC Model since 1970. He was also a member of the SSRC Sub-Committee on Monetary Mechanism, 1970–1977. Since 1966 he has been an academic consultant to the Board of Governors of the Federal Reserve System.
2. Reprinted in MODIGLIANI, vol. 1, pp. 114-41.
3. Reprinted in MODIGLIANI, vol. 2, pp. 442-517.

the entire life. This hypothesis, which has since become known as the Life-Cycle Hypothesis of saving, is capable of accounting for many of the regularities regarding individual and economy-wide behaviour that did not fit the received model of saving. For instance, it helps explain why the saving ratio in the United States is now no higher than it was a century ago, even though per capita income is several times higher, or why it is considerably lower than in many other developed or developing countries with much lower incomes.

The major papers developing and testing this hypothesis are:

'Utility Analysis and the Consumption Function: An Interpretation of Cross-Section Data' (joint article with Richard Brumberg), in *Post-Keynesian Economics*, Kenneth K. Kurihara (ed.). New Brunswick, N.J.: Rutgers University Press, 1954, pp. 388–436;[1]

'The "Life Cycle" Hypothesis of Saving: Aggregate Implications and Tests' (joint article with Albert K. Ando), *American Economic Review*, vol. 53(1), Part I, March 1963, pp. 55–84;[2]

'The life cycle hypothesis of saving twenty years later', in *Contemporary Issues in Economics*, Michael Parkin and A. Robert Nobay (eds.). Manchester: Manchester University Press, 1975, pp. 2–36.[3]

iii) *The Theory of Corporate Finance*

Two issues had long been central to the theory of corporate finance, namely (i) the extent to which it is advantageous for a corporate firm to finance its assets by debt rather than by equity; and (ii) whether the value of corporate stock is determined primarily by dividends, earnings or by something else. In two joint articles with Merton H. Miller, Franco Modigliani showed that in a competitive market with rational investors (and as long as the effects of taxes were ignored): (a) the way in which firms are financed is irrelevant, in the sense that the total market value

---

1. Reprinted in MODIGLIANI, vol. 2, pp. 79-127.   2. Reprinted in MODIGLIANI, vol. 2, pp. 275-304.   3. Reprinted in MODIGLIANI, vol. 2, pp. 41-75.

of firms will be independent of their financial structure; and (b) the market value of shares will be independent of dividend policy.

The two articles listed below re-directed the whole theory of finance, not only because their main results run counter to widely accepted views, but also because they pioneered the application of economic analysis to finance:

'The Cost of Capital, Corporation Finance and the Theory of Investment', *American Economic Review*, vol. 48(3), June 1958, pp. 261–97;[1]

'Dividend Policy, Growth and the Valuation of Shares', *Journal of Business*, vol. 34(4), October 1961, pp. 411–33.[2]

Finally one further short article should be mentioned here, even though it lies outside Modigliani's main line of research, in view of its substantial impact on later developments:

'The Predictability of Social Events' (joint article with Emile Grunberg), *Journal of Political Economy*, vol. 62(6), December 1954, pp. 465–78.[3]

The purpose of this article was to disprove the previously generally accepted view that *public* economic forecasts are bound to be invalidated in so far as economic agents can systematically change their behaviour in response to the forecast. The argument developed in this article has provided an important building block for one branch of monetarism, known as the "Macro Rational Expectations" School, which has been highly influential in recent years.

1. Reprinted in MODIGLIANI, vol. 3, pp. 3-39.
2. Reprinted in MODIGLIANI, vol. 3, pp. 40-62. For this article Franco Modigliani and Merton Miller were awarded the *Journal of Business* "Award for Best Contribution of the Year" in 1961. Moreover, Franco Modigliani has been awarded the Graham and Dodd Plaque for the outstanding articles published in 1974 and 1979 in the *Financial Analysts Journal*: 'An Introduction to Risk and Return: Concepts and Evidence', joint article with Gerald A. Pogue (Part I), vol. 30 (2), March-April 1974, pp. 68-80; (Part II), vol. 30 (3), May-June 1974, pp. 69-86; 'Inflation, Rational Valuation and the Market', joint article with Richard Cohn, vol. 35 (2), March-April 1979, pp. 24-44.
3. Reprinted in MODIGLIANI, vol. 3, pp. 461-74.

3. Publications*

'Liquidity Preference and the Theory of Interest and Money', *Econometrica*, vol. 12(1), January 1944, pp. 45-88; see also 'Postscript of the paper —', in Henry HAZLITT, *The Critics of Keynesian Economics*. Princeton: D. Van Nostrand, 1960, pp. 183-4; reprinted in MODIGLIANI, vol. 1, pp. 23-68.

'L'Organizzazione e la direzione della produzione in una economia socializzata', *Giornale degli Economisti*, Anno VI (N.S.), nos. 9-10, September-October 1947, pp. 441-514.

'Fluctuations in the Saving-Income Ratio: A Problem in Economic Forecasting', in *Studies in Income and Wealth*, vol. 11. New York: National Bureau of Economic Research, 1949, pp. 371-443; Sections I-VII (pp. 371-402) and XIII (pp. 427-31) reprinted in MODIGLIANI, vol. 2, pp. 3-40.

'Liquidity and Uncertainty – Discussion', *American Economic Review*, vol. 34(3), May 1949, pp. 201-8.

'New Areas of Opinion Research: Economics', *Public Opinion Quarterly*, Winter, 1949-1950, pp. 770-3.

'The Measurement of Expectation' (abstract), *Econometrica*, vol. 20(3), July 1952, pp. 481-2.

'The Effects of Availability of Funds and the Terms Thereof, on Business Investment' (with Morton ZEMAN), in *Conference on Research in Business Finance*. New York: National Bureau of Economic Research, 1952, pp. 263-309.

National Incomes and International Trade. A Quantitative Analysis (with Hans NEISSER). Urbana, Ill.: University of Illinois Press, 1953.

'Preface' to Robert FERBER, *The Railroad Shipper's Forecasts*, Studies in Business Expectations and Planning. University of Illinois, Bureau of Economic and Business Research. Urbana, Ill.: University of Illinois Press, 1953, pp. 3-5.

'Utility Analysis and the Consumption Function: An Interpretation of Cross-Section Data' (with Richard BRUMBERG), in Kenneth K. KURIHARA (ed.), *Post-Keynesian Economics*. New Brunswick, N.J.: Rutgers University Press, 1954, pp. 388-436; reprinted in MODIGLIANI, vol. 2, pp. 79-127.

* References to *The Collected Papers of Franco Modigliani* are given in the form: MODIGLIANI, vol. 1 (etc.).

'The Predictability of Social Events' (with Emile GRUNBERG), *Journal of Political Economy*, vol. 62(6), December 1954, pp. 465-78; reprinted in MODIGLIANI, vol. 3, pp. 461-74.

Production Planning Over Time and the Nature of the Expectation and 'Planning Horizon' (with Franz E. HOHN), *Econometrica*, vol. 23(1), January 1955, pp. 46-66; reprinted in MODIGLIANI, vol. 3, pp. 347-67.

'A Linear Decision Rule for Production and Employment Scheduling' (with Charles C. HOLT and Herbert A. SIMON), *Management Science*, vol. 2(1), October 1955, pp. 1-30.

'Economic Expectations and Plans of Firms in Relation to Short-Term Forecasting' (with Owen H. SAUERLENDER), in *Short-Term Economic Forecasting*, Studies in Income and Wealth, vol. 17, National Bureau of Economic Research. Princeton: Princeton University Press, 1955, pp. 261-351.

'Derivation of a Linear Decision Rule for Production and Employment' (with Charles C. HOLT and John F. MUTH), *Management Science*, vol. 2(2), January 1956, pp. 159-177.

Ricerca Operativa (Lecture Notes, Istituto Superiore per la Direzione Aziendale) Rome: Confederazione Italiana Dirigenti d'Azienda, 1956.

Editor of: *Problems of Capital Formation: Concepts, Measurement, and Controlling Factors*, Studies in Income and Wealth, vol. 19, National Bureau of Economic Research. Princeton: Princeton University Press, 1957.

'Introduction' to above volume, pp. 3-12.

'Business Reasons for Holding Inventories and their Macro-Economic Implications', same volume as above, pp. 495-506.

'Comment' on 'Capacity, Capacity Utilization, and The Acceleration Principle' by Bert G. HICKMAN, same volume as above, pp. 450-63.

'Private Investment in the Electric Power Industry and the Acceleration Principle' (with Avram KISSELGOFF), *Review of Economics and Statistics*, vol. 39(4), November 1957, pp. 363-79.

'Tests of the Life Cycle Hypothesis of Savings' (with Albert K. ANDO), *Bulletin of the Oxford University Institute of Statistics*, vol. 19(2), May 1957, pp. 99-124.

'Forecasting Uses of Anticipatory Data on Investment and Sales' (with Herbert M. WEINGARTNER), *Quarterly Journal of Economics*, vol. 72(1), February 1958, pp. 23-54; reprinted in MODIGLIANI, vol. 3, pp. 426-57.

'—: Reply' (with Herbert M. WEINGARTNER), *Quarterly Journal of Economics*, vol. 73(1), February 1959, p. 173.

'Mathematics for Production Scheduling' (with Melvin ANSHEN, Charles C. HOLT, John F. MUTH and Herbert A. SIMON), *Harvard Business Review*, vol. 36(2), March-April 1958, pp. 51-58.

'New Developments on the Oligopoly Front', *Journal of Political Economy*, vol. 66(3), June 1958, pp. 215-33; reprinted in MODIGLIANI, vol. 1, pp. 400-18.

'—: Reply', *Journal of Political Economy*, vol. 67(4), August 1959, pp. 418-19.

'The Cost of Capital, Corporation Finance and the Theory of Investment' (with Merton H. MILLER), *American Economic Review*, vol. 48(3), June 1958, pp. 261-97; reprinted in MODIGLIANI, vol. 3, pp. 3-39.

'—: Reply' (with Merton H. MILLER), *American Economic Review*, vol. 49(4), September 1959, pp. 655-69.

'The Significance and Uses of *Ex ante* Data' (with Kalman L. COHEN), in Mary J. BOWMAN (ed.), *Expectations, Uncertainty, and Business Behavior*. New York: Social Science Research Council, 1958, pp. 151-64.

'Preface' to Robert FERBER, *Employers' Forecasts of Manpower Requirements: A Case Study*. Urbana, Ill.: University of Illinois Press, 1958, pp. 3-5.

'Growth, Fluctuations, and Stability' (with Albert K. ANDO), *American Economic Review*, vol. 49(2), May 1959, pp. 501-24.

'Economic Analysis and Forecasting: Recent Developments in Use of Panel and Other Survey Techniques' (with Frederick E. BALDERSTON), in Eugene BURDICK and Arthur J. BRODBECK (eds.), *American Voting Behavior*. Glencoe, Ill.: Free Press, 1959, pp. 372-98.

'Postscript' of 'Liquidity Preference and the Theory of Interest and Money' [see *Econometrica*, vol. 12(1), January 1944, pp. 45-88], in Henry HAZLITT (ed.), *The Critics of Keynesian Economics*. Princeton: D. Van Nostrand, 1960, pp. 183-4; reprinted in MODIGLIANI, vol. 1, pp. 66-8.

'The Source of Regressiveness in Surveys of Businessmen's Short Run Expectations' (with John BOSSONS), in *The Quality and Economic*

Significance of Anticipation Data. National Bureau of Economic Research. Princeton: Princeton University Press, 1960, pp. 239-62.

'—: Reply' (with John Bossons), same volume as above, pp. 261-2.

'Introduction' (with Albert G. Hart and Guy H. Orcutt), same volume as above, pp. 3-8.

Planning Production, Inventories, and Work Force (with Charles C. Holt, John F. Muth and Herbert S. Simon). London: Prentice-Hall, 1960.

'The "Permanent Income" and the "Life Cycle" Hypothesis of Saving Behavior: Comparison and Tests' (with Albert K. Ando), in *Consumption and Saving*, vol. 2. Philadelphia: University of Pennsylvania Press, 1960; reprinted in Modigliani, vol. 2, pp. 229-74 only Sections II, I-II (pp. 74-108) and III, 4 (pp. 138-147).

The Role of Anticipations and Plans in Economic Behavior and their Use in Economic Analysis and Forecasting (with Kalman J. Cohen). Urbana, Ill.: University of Illinois Press, 1961; reprinted in Modigliani, vol. 3, pp. 368-425 only Introduction (pp. 9-11) and Sections I, A-B (pp. 14-42), II, A (pp. 81-96); and also Bibliography (pp. 158-66).

'Dividend Policy, Growth, and the Valuation of Shares' (with Merton H. Miller), *Journal of Business*, vol. 34(4), October 1961, pp. 411-33; reprinted in Modigliani, vol. 3, pp. 40-62.

'Dividend Policy and Market Valuation: A Reply' (with Merton H. Miller), *Journal of Business*, vol. 36(1), January 1963, pp. 116-19.

'Long-Run Implications of Alternative Fiscal Policies and the Burden of the National Debt', *Economic Journal*, vol. 71(284), December 1961, pp. 730-55; reprinted in Modigliani, vol. 2, pp. 415-41.

'Firm Costs Structures and the Dynamic Responses of Inventories, Production, Work Force and Orders to Sales Fluctuations' (with Charles C. Holt), in *Inventories Fluctuations and Economic Stabilization, Part 2, Causative Factors in Movements of Business Inventories.* Joint Economic Committee, 87th Congress, Second Session. Washington: U.S. Government Printing Office, 1961, pp. 3-50.

'The Monetary Mechanism and its Interaction with Real Phenomena', *Review of Economics and Statistics*, vol. 45(1), Part 2, Supplement, February 1963, pp. 79-107; reprinted in Modigliani, vol. 1, pp. 69-97.

'The "Life Cycle" Hypothesis of Saving: Aggregate Implications and

Tests' (with Albert K. ANDO), *American Economic Review*, vol. 53(1), part I, March 1963, pp. 55-84; reprinted in MODIGLIANI, vol. 2, pp. 275-304.

'—: A Correction' (with Albert K. ANDO), *American Economic Review*, vol. 54(2), Part I, March 1964, pp. 111-13.

'Corporate Income Taxes and the Cost of Capital: A Correction' (with Merton H. MILLER), *American Economic Review*, vol. 53(3), June 1963, pp. 433-43; reprinted in MODIGLIANI, vol. 3, pp. 63-73.

'Economic Forecasting When the Subject of the Forecast is Influenced by the Forecast: Comment' (with Emile GRUNBERG), *American Economic Review*, vol. 53(4), September 1963, pp. 734-7.

'—: Correction' (with Emile GRUNBERG), *American Economic Review*, vol. 54(4), Part I, June 1964, p. 423.

'A Critique of Central Banking in the United States – Discussion', Federal Reserve Bank of Boston, *Annual Report*, April 1964, pp. 24-9.

'Some Empirical Tests of Monetary Management and of Rules versus Discretion', *Journal of Political Economy*, vol. 72(3), June 1964, pp. 211-45.

'Monetary Policy and the Rate of Economic Activity: A Project of the Committee on Economic Stability', *Items*, Social Science Research Council, vol. 18(3), September 1964, pp. 36-8.

'How to Make a Burden of the Public Debt: A Reply to Mishan', *Journal of Political Economy*, vol. 52(5), October 1964, pp. 483-5.

'Comment' on "A Survey of Some Theories of Income Distribution" by Tibor SCITOVSKY, in *The Behavior of Income Shares, Selected Theoretical and Empirical Issues*, Studies in Income and Wealth, vol. 27, National Bureau of Economic Research. Princeton: Princeton University Press, 1964, pp. 39-50.

'Comment' on "A Postwar Quarterly Model: Description and Applications" by Lawrence R. KLEIN, in *Models of Income Determination*, Studies in Income and Wealth, vol. 28, National Bureau of Economic Research. Princeton: Princeton University Press, 1964, pp. 41-53.

'Discussion: Reflexive Prediction' (with Emile GRUNBERG), *Philosophy of Science*, vol. 32(2), April 1965, pp. 173-4.

'The Relative Stability of Monetary Velocity and the Investment Multiplier' (with Albert K. ANDO), *American Economic Review*, vol. 55(4), September 1965, pp. 693-728.

'Rejoinder' (to 'Reply' by Milton FRIEDMAN and David MEISELMAN), same volume as above, pp. 786-90.

'Épargne et consommation en avenir aléatoire' (with Jacques H. DRÈZE), *Cahiers du Séminaire d'Econométrie*, no. 9, 1966, pp. 7-33 [for a shortened English version see 'Consumption Decision under Uncertainty', *Journal of Economic Theory*, vol. 5(3), December 1972.

'A suggestion for solving the International Liquidity Problem' (with Peter KENEN), *Banca Nazionale del Lavoro Quarterly Review*, no. 76. March 1966, pp. 3-17; reprinted in MODIGLIANI, vol. 3, pp. 263-77.

'Research on the Links between Monetary Policy and Economic Activity: A Progress Report of a Subcommittee of the Committee on Economic Stability', *Items*, Social Science Research Council, vol. 20(1), March 1966, pp. 7-8.

'Statistical vs Structural Explanations of Understatement and Regressivity in "Rational" Expectations' (with John BOSSONS), *Econometrica*, vol. 34(2), April 1966, pp. 347-53.

'Innovations in Interest Rate Policy' (with Richard SUTCH), *American Economic Review*, vol. 56(2), May 1966, pp. 178-97; reprinted in MODIGLIANI, vol. 1, pp. 267-86.

'The Life Cycle Hypothesis of Saving, the Demand for Wealth and the Supply of Capital', *Social Research*, vol. 33(2), Summer 1966, pp. 160-217; reprinted in MODIGLIANI, vol. 2, pp. 323-81.

'Some Estimates of the Cost of Capital to the Electric Utility Industry, 1954-57' (with Merton H. MILLER), *American Economic Review*, vol. 56(3), June 1966, pp. 333-91.

'—: A Reply' (with Merton H. MILLER), *American Economic Review*, vol. 57(5), December 1967, pp. 1288-1300.

'Su alcuni aspetti della congiuntura e della politica monetaria italiana nell'ultimo quinquennio' (with Giorgio LA MALFA), *Moneta e Credito*, vol. 19, (75), September 1966, pp. 211-57.

'The Pasinetti Paradox in Neoclassical and More General Models' (with Paul A. SAMUELSON), *The Review of Economic Studies*, vol. 33(4), October 1966, pp. 269-301.

'—: Reply to Pasinetti and Robinson' (with Paul A. SAMUELSON), same issue as above, pp. 321-30.

'Inflation, Balance of Payments Deficit and their Cure through Monetary Policy: the Italian Example' (with Giorgio LA MALFA), *Banca Nazionale del Lavoro Quarterly Review*, no. 80, March 1967, pp. 3-47; reprinted in MODIGLIANI, vol. 3, pp. 127-71.

'Debt Management and the Term Structure of Interest Rates: An Empirical Analysis of Recent Experience' (with Richard Sutch), *Journal of Political Economy*, vol. 75(4), Part 2, Supplement, August 1967, pp. 569-89; reprinted in MODIGLIANI, vol. 1, pp. 287-308.

'Estimates of the Cost of Capital Relevant for Investment Decisions under Uncertainty' (with Merton H. MILLER), in Robert FERBER (ed.), *Determinants of Investment Behavior*, National Bureau of Economic Research. New York: Columbia University Press, 1967, pp. 179-213.

'—: Reply' (with Merton H. MILLER), same volume as above, pp. 260-7.

'Testimony'. Hearings before the Joint Economic Committee, 90th Congress, Second Session, May 1968, in *Standards for Guiding Monetary Action*. Washington: U.S. Government Printing Office, 1968, pp. 8-13 and pp. 50-76.

'The Transmission of Demand Fluctuations through a Distribution Production System, the TV-Set Industry' (with Charles C. HOLT and John P. SHELTON), *The Canadian Journal of Economics*, vol. 1(4), November 1968, pp. 718-39.

'Liquidity Preference' in David L. SILLS (ed.), *International Encyclopedia of the Social Sciences*, vol. 9. New York: Crowell-Collier and Macmillan, 1968, pp. 394-409; reprinted in MODIGLIANI, vol. 1, pp. 98-113.

'The Term Structure of Interest Rates: A Re-examination of the Evidence' (with Richard SUTCH), *Journal of Money, Credit and Banking*, vol. 1(1), February 1969, pp. 112-20.

'Econometric Analysis of Stabilization Policies' (with Albert K. ANDO), *American Economic Review*, vol. 59(2), May 1969, pp. 296-314.

'Reply to Heins and Sprenkle' (with Merton H. MILLER), *American Economic Review*, vol. 59(4), Part 1, September 1969, pp. 592-95.

'A Theory and Test of Credit Rationing' (with Dwight M. JAFFEE), *American Economic Review*, vol. 59(5), December 1969, pp. 850-72; reprinted in MODIGLIANI, vol. 3, pp. 74-96.

'Central Bank Policy, the Money Supply and the Short-Term Rate of Interest' (with Robert RASCHE and J. Phillip COOPER), *Journal of Money, Credit and Banking*, vol. 2(2), May 1970, pp. 166-218; reprinted in MODIGLIANI, vol. 1, pp. 171-223.

'The Life Cycle Hypothesis of Saving and Intercountry Differences in the Saving Ratio', in Walter A. ELTIS, Maurice F. SCOTT and James N. WOLFE (eds), *Induction, Growth and Trade: Essays in Honour of Sir Roy Harrod*. Oxford: Clarendon Press, 1970, pp. 197-226; reprinted in MODIGLIANI, vol. 2, pp. 382-412.

'Monetary Policy and Consumption: Linkages via Interest Rate and Wealth Effects in the FMP Model', in *Consumer Spending and Monetary Policy: The Linkages*. Monetary Conference Series no. 5. Federal Reserve Bank of Boston, 1971, pp. 9-84; reprinted in MODIGLIANI, vol. 2, pp. 442-517.

'Testimony'. Hearings before the Joint Economic Committee, 92nd Congress, First Session, 20th July 1971, *The Midyear Review of the Economy*. Washington: U.S. Government Printing Office, 1971, pp. 111-27.

'The Reform of the International Payments System' (with Hossein ASKARI). *Essays in International Finance*, no. 89, International Finance Secion, Department of Economics. Princeton: Princeton University Press, September 1971, pp. 3-28; reprinted in MODIGLIANI, vol. 3, pp. 278-304.

'Curva di Phillips, sottosviluppo e disoccupazione strutturale' (with Ezio TARANTELLI), *Quaderni di Ricerche*, no. 9, Ente per gli Studi Monetari, Bancari e Finanziari Luigi Einaudi, October 1971.

'Some Proposals for a Reform of the Discount Window', in *Reappraisal of the Federal Reserve Discount Mechanism*, vol. 2. Board of Governors of the Federal Reserve System, December 1971, pp. 59-76.

'A More American Dollar' (with Hossein ASKARI), *Technology Review*, vol. 74, December 1971, p. 70.

'Efficiency of European Capital Markets and Comparison with the American Market' (with Gerald A. POGUE, Myron S. SCHOLES and Bruno SOLNIK), in *The Stock Exchange: How to Make it an Instrument of Economic-Social Progress in Europe and in the World*. Proceedings of the First International Conference on Stock Exchanges (Milan, 14th-16th March 1972). Milan: CISMEC, Centro Informazioni e Studi sulle Comunità Europee, 1973, vol. 1, pp. 248-72.

'Stock Market and Economy – Discussion', *American Economic Review*, vol. 62(2), May 1972, pp. 229-33.

'The International Payments System: Past, Present and Future' (with Hossein ASKARI), *Sloan Management Review*, vol. 13(3), Spring 1972, pp. 1-16.

'The Dynamics of Portfolio Adjustment and the Flow of Savings through Financial Intermediaries', in Edward M. GRAMLICH and Dwight M. JAFFEE, (eds.), *Savings Deposits, Mortgages, and Housing: Studies for the Federal Reserve – MIT – Penn Econometric Model*. Lexington, Mass.: Lexington Books, 1972, pp. 63-102; reprinted in MODIGLIANI, vol. 1, pp. 224-64.

'Consumption Decisions under Uncertainty' (with Jacques H. DRÈZE), *Journal of Economic Theory*, vol. 5(3), December 1972, pp. 308-36 (shortened English version of 'Èpargne et consummation en avenir aléatoire', *Cahiers du Séminaire d'Econométrie*, no. 9, 1966); reprinted in MODIGLIANI, vol. 2, pp. 198-226.

'International Capital Movements, Fixed Parities, and Monetary and Fiscal Policies', in Jagdish BHAGWATI and Richard S. ECKAUS (eds.), *Development and Planning: Essays in Honour of Paul Rosenstein Rodan*. London: George Allen & Unwin, 1972, pp. 239-53; reprinted in MODIGLIANI, vol. 3, pp. 305-20.

'Appendix to Part One: Equations and Definitions of Variables for the FRB–MIT–Penn Econometric Model, November 1969' (with Albert K. ANDO and Robert RASCHE), in Bert G. HICKMAN (ed.), *Econometric Models of Cyclical Behavior*, Studies in Income and Wealth, no. 36, vol. 1, National Bureau of Economic Research. New York: Columbia University Press, 1972, pp. 543-98.

'Import and Export Price Indices' (with Hossein ASKARI), *Journal of Political Economy*, vol. 81(1), January/February 1973, pp. 237-42.

'Inflation, Rational Expectations and the Term Structure of Interest Rates' (with Robert J. SHILLER), *Economica*, vol. 40(157), February 1973, pp. 12-43; reprinted in MODIGLIANI, vol. 1, pp. 309-41.

'Un'analisi empirica dei flussi finanziari e della composizione della ricchezza finanziaria dell'economia' (with Franco COTULA), *Moneta e Credito*, vol. 26 (101-102), March-June 1973, pp. 48-74 [for an English translation see: 'An Empirical Analysis of the Composition of Financial Wealth in Italy' (with Franco COTULA), *Banca Nazionale del Lavoro Quarterly Review*, no. 109, June 1974, pp. 140-66].

'A Generalization of the Phillips Curve for a Developing Country' (with Ezio TARANTELLI), *Review of Economic Studies*, vol. 40(2), no. 122, April 1973, pp. 203-23; reprinted in MODIGLIANI, vol. 1, pp. 379-99.

'The International Transfer of Capital and the Propagation of Domestic Disturbances Under Alternative Payment Systems' (with Hossein ASKARI), *Banca Nazionale del Lavoro Quarterly Review*, no. 107,

December 1973, pp. 3-19; reprinted in MODIGLIANI, vol. 3, pp. 321-37.

'Testimony'. Hearings before the Joint Economic Committee, 93rd Congress, Second Session, in *The Economic Report of the President*, Part 2, 22nd February 1974. Washington: U.S. Government Printing Office, 1974, pp. 643-76.

'An introduction to Risk and Return: Concepts and Evidence' (with Gerald A. POGUE). *Financial Analysts Journal*, (Part I), vol. 30(2), March-April 1974, pp. 68-80; (Part II), vol. 30(3), May-June 1974, pp. 69-86.

'On the Role of Expectations of Price and Technological Change in an Investment Function' (with Albert K. ANDO, Robert RASCHE and Stephen J. TURNOVSKY), *International Economic Review*, vol. 15(2), June 1974, pp. 384-414; reprinted in MODIGLIANI, vol. 1, pp. 345-75.

'The 1974 Report of the President's Council of Economic Advisors: A Critique of Past and Prospective Policies', *American Economic Review*, vol. 64(4), September 1974, pp. 544-57; reprinted in MODIGLIANI, vol. 3, pp. 172-85.

'Balance of Payments Implications of the Oil Crisis and How to Handle Them Through International Cooperation', Prepared Statement, for Hearings before the Joint Economic Committee, 93rd Congress, Second Session, 19th - 22nd February 1974, in *Economic Report of the President*. Washington: U.S. Government Printing Office, 1974, pp. 650-5; reprinted in MODIGLIANI, vol. 3, pp. 338-43.

'Targets for Monetary Policy in the Coming Year' (with Lucas D. PAPADEMOS), *Brookings Papers on Economic Activity*, 1975(1), pp. 141-63; reprinted in MODIGLIANI, vol. 1, pp. 419-41.

'Alternative Exchange-Rate Systems: A Rejoinder' (with Hossein ASKARI), *Banca Nazionale del Lavoro Quarterly Review*, no. 112, March 1975, pp. 118-9.

'Testimony'. Hearings before the Joint Economic Committee, 94th Congress, First Session, 24th April 1975, *Financial Aspects of the Budget Deficit*. Washington: U.S. Government Printing Office, 1975, pp. 27-34.

'Rediscovery of Money - Discussion', *American Economic Review*, vol. 65(2), May 1975, pp. 179-81.

'Alternative investment performance free arrangements for SEC regulatory policy' (with Gerald A. POGUE), *Bell Journal of Economics*, vol. 6(1), Spring 1975, pp. 127-60.

'The Channels of Monetary Policy in the Federal Reserve – MIT – University of Pennsylvania Econometric Model of the United States', in George A. RENTON (ed.), *Modelling the Economy*. London: Heinemann Educational Books, 1975, pp. 240-67; reprinted in MODIGLIANI, vol. 1, pp. 114-41.

'Inflation and the Housing Market: Problems and Potential Solutions' (with Donald LESSARD), *Sloan Management Review*, vol. 17(1), Fall 1975, pp. 19-35; see also Franco MODIGLIANI and Donald LESSARD (eds.), *New Mortgage Designs for Stable Housing in an Inflationary Environment*, Conference Series no. 14, Federal Reserve Bank of Boston, 1975, pp. 13-45.

'The Consumption Function in a Developing Economy and the Italian Experience' (with Ezio TARANTELLI), *American Economic Review*, vol. 65(5), December 1975, pp. 825-42; reprinted in MODIGLIANI, vol. 2, pp. 305-22.

'The life cycle hypothesis of saving twenty years later', in Michael PARKIN and A. Robert NOBAY, (eds), *Contemporary Issues in Economics*. Manchester: Manchester University Press, 1975, pp. 2-36; reprinted in MODIGLIANI, vol. 2, pp. 41-75.

'Some Reflections on Describing Structures of Finance Sectors' (with Albert K. ANDO) and 'Appendix' (with Karl SHELL), in Gary FROMM and Lawrence R. KLEIN (eds.), *The Brookings Model: Perspective and Recent Developments*. Amsterdam: North-Holland, 1975, pp. 524-63.

Mercato del Lavoro, Distribuzione del reddito e Consumi Privati, (with Ezio TARANTELLI). Bologna: Il Mulino, 1975.

'Testimony and prepared statement'. Hearings before the Subcommittee on Financial Institutions Supervision, Regulation and Insurance of the Committee on Banking, Currency and Housing, 94th Congress, First Session, in *Financial Institutions and the Nation's Economy (FINE): Discussion Principles*, part I, 3rd December 1975, pp. 186-225, part II, February 1976. Washington, U.S. Government Printing Office, 1976, pp. 506-79.

'Monetary Policy for the Coming Quarters: The Conflicting Views' (with Lucas D. PAPADEMOS), *New England Economic Review*, March/April 1976, pp. 2-35; reprinted in MODIGLIANI, vol. 3, pp. 186-219.

'Discussion' on 'Public Pension Funding and U.S. Capital Formation: A Medium-Run View' by Benjamin M. FRIEDMAN, in *Funding Pen-*

sions: Issues and Implications for Financial Markets, Conference Series no. 16. Federal Reserve Bank of Boston, 1976, pp. 201-5.

'General Discussion: What have we learned? Where are the Fundamental Conflicts of Opinion?', by Lars CALMFORS and Clas WIHLBORG (eds.), Proceedings of a Conference on 'Flexible Exchange Rates and Stabilization Policy' organized by the Institute for International Economic Studies at the University of Stockholm, Staltsjöbaden (Stockholm), 26th-27th August 1975, *Scandinavian Journal of Economics*, vol. 78(2), 1976, pp. 392-5.

'Some Economic Implications of the Indexing of Financial Assets with Special Reference to Mortgages', in Mario MONTI (ed.), *The New Inflation and Monetary Policy*. London: Macmillan, 1976, pp. 90-116; reprinted in MODIGLIANI, vol. 3, pp. 97-123.

'Statement and Discussion', *Third Meeting on the Conduct of Monetary Policy*, 94th Congress, Second Session, 5th May 1976. Washington: U.S. Government Printing Office, 1976, pp. 84-120.

'Impacts of Fiscal Actions on Aggregate Income and the Monetarist Controversy: Theory and Evidence' (with Albert K. ANDO, and with the assistance of J. GIANGRANDE), in Jerome L. STEIN (ed.), *Monetarism*, vol. 1. Amsterdam: North-Holland, 1976, pp. 17-42; reprinted in MODIGLIANI, vol. 1, pp. 142-67.

'Some Currently Suggested Explanations and Cures for Inflation: A Comment', in Karl BRUNNER and Allan H. MELTZER (eds.), *Institutional Arrangements and the Inflation Problem*, Carnegie-Rochester Conference Series on Public Policy, vol. 3. Amsterdam: North-Holland, 1976, pp. 179-84.

'A Theory and Test of Credit Rationing: A Reply' (with Dwight M. JAFFEE), *American Economic Review*, vol. 66(5), December 1976, pp. 918-20.

'Comment', in *Crisi economica e condizionamenti internazionali dell'Italia*. Proceedings of a Conference organized by the CESPE, Centro Studi di Politica Economica, Rome 15th-17th March 1976; *Quaderni di Politica ed Economia*, nos. 1-2. Rome: Editori Riuniti, 1976, pp. 223-30.

'Comment' on 'Eurocurrencies and the Evolution of the International Monetary System' by John H. MAKIN, in C. H. STEM, John H. MAKIN and Dennis E. LOGUE (eds.), *Eurocurrencies and the International Monetary System*. Washington: American Enterprise Institute for Public Policy Research, 1976, pp. 60-70.

'Models of the Economy and Optimal Stabilization Policies', in Sydney SCHULMAN (ed.), *Mathematic Models in Economics*. Proceedings of a US-USSR Seminar in Moscow, 16th-18th June 1976. New York: National Bureau of Economic Research, 1976, pp. 211-44.

'Forze di mercato, azione sindacale e la Curva di Phillips in Italia' (with Ezio TARANTELLI), *Moneta e Credito*, vol. 29 (114); June 1976, pp. 3-35 [for an English translation see: 'Market Forces, Trade Union Action, and the Phillips Curve in Italy', *Banca Nazionale del Lavoro Quarterly Review*, no. 120, March 1977, pp. 3-36].

'Is a Tax Rebate an Effective Tool for Stabilization Policy?' (with Charles STEIDEL), *Brookings Papers on Economic Activity*, 1977(1), pp. 175-209.

'Comment' on 'Investment, Interest Rates, and the Effects of Stabilization Policies' by Robert E. HALL, same issue as above, pp. 107-12.

'A Note on Capital Movements and the Relation of Spread in Spot and Forward Rates to Variations in the Short-Term Interest Differential' (with Hossein ASKARI), *Kyklos*, vol. 30(1), January 1977, pp. 38-50.

'Statement and Discussion', *The Economic Report of the President*, Part 2, 95th Congress, First Session, 7th February 1977. Washington: U.S. Government Printing Office, pp. 140-77.

'The Monetarist Controversy or, Should We Forsake Stabilization Policies?', Presidential Address delivered at the American Economic Association, 17th September 1976, *American Economic Review*, vol. 67(2), March 1977, pp. 1-19; reprinted in MODIGLIANI, vol. 1, pp. 3-22.

'The Monetarist Controversy', Federal Reserve Bank of San Francisco, *Economic Review Supplement*, Spring 1977, pp. 5-26.

'La politica economica in una economia aperta con salari indicizzati al 100% o più' (with Tommaso PADOA-SCHIOPPA), *Moneta e Credito*, vol. 30(117), March 1977, pp. 3-53 [for an English translation see: 'The Management of an Open Economy with "100% Plus" Wage Indexation', *Essays in International Finance*, no. 130, International Finance Section, Department of Economics. Princeton: Princeton University Press, December 1978; reprinted in MODIGLIANI, vol. 3, pp. 220-59.

'Disoccupazione, inflazione e svalutazione nell'economia italiana: diagnosi e cure' (with Tommaso PADOA-SCHIOPPA), *Bancaria*, March 1977, no. 3, pp. 219-31.

'Should Control Theory be Used for Economic Stabilization?: A Comment', in Karl BRUNNER and Allan H. MELTZER, *Optimal Policies, Control Theory and Technology Exports*, Carnegie-Rochester Conference Series on Public Policy, vol. 7. Amsterdam: North-Holland, 1977, pp. 85-91.

'Implications for Policy: A Symposium', *Brookings Papers on Economic Activity*, 1978(2), pp. 514-8.

'Comment' on 'Efficient-Market Theory: Implications for Monetary Policy' by Frederic S. MISHKIN, *Brookings Papers on Economic Activity*, 1978(3), pp. 757-62.

'Discussion' on 'Inflation and Unemployment in a Macro-econometric Model' by Ray C. FAIR, in *After the Phillips Curve: Persistence of High Inflation and High Unemployment*, Conference Series no. 19. Federal Reserve Bank of Boston, 1978, pp. 194-200.

'Optimal Demand Policies against Stagflation' (with Lucas D. PAPADEMOS), *Weltwirtschaftliches Archiv*, vol. 114(4), 1978, pp. 736-81.

'Towards an Understanding of the Real Effects and Costs of Inflation' (with Stanley FISCHER), same volume as above, pp. 810-32.

'Statement'. Hearings before the Subcommittee on International Economics of the Joint Economic Committee, 95th Congress, Second Session, *The Dollar Rescue Operations and their Domestic Implications*, 14th and 15th December 1978. Washington: U.S. Government Printing Office, 1979, pp. 2017-215.

'Has the Economist Lost Control of the Economy?', *Bulletin of the American Academy of Arts and Sciences*, vol. 32(6), March 1979, pp. 38-49.

'Inflation, Rational Valuation and the Market' (with Richard A. COHN), *Financial Analysts Journal*, vol. 35(2), March-April 1979, pp. 24-44.

'—: A Reply' (with Richard A. COHN), *Financial Analysts Journal*, vol. 37(3), May-June 1981, pp.72-3.

'The Financial Goal of the Firm in a Market Economy', *Bulletin of the European Federation of Financial Analysts Societies*, no. 13, May 1979, pp. 100-2.

'Structural and Transitory Determinants of Labour Mobility: "Holt's Conjecture" and Italian Experience' (with Ezio TARANTELLI), *Banca Nazionale del Lavoro Quarterly Review*, no. 130, September 1979, pp. 205-26.

'Effetti dell'inflazione sui mercati finanziari', *Associazione per lo Sviluppo degli Studi di Banca e Borsa*, Quaderno no. 19, September 1979, pp. 3-16.

'Comment' on 'Modeling the Economic Linkages Among Countries' by Ray C. FAIR, in Rudiger DORNBUSCH and Jacob A. FRENKEL (eds.), *International Economic Policy. Theory and Evidence*. Baltimore: Johns Hopkins University Press, 1979, pp. 239-42.

'Problems and Prospects for the World Economy: Round Table', same volume as above, pp. 329-31.

'Discussion' of 'Costs of Economic Growth' by Edmond MALINVAUD, in Edmond MALINVAUD (ed.), *Economic Growth and Resources. Volume One: The Major Issues*. London: Macmillan, pp. 217-23.

'Coupon and tax effects on new and seasoned bond yields and the measurement of the cost of debt capital' (with Robert J. SHILLER), *Journal of Financial Economics*, vol. 7(3), September 1979, pp. 297-318.

'Comment' on 'The Central Role of Credit Crunches in Recent Financial History' by Albert M. WOJNILOWER, *Brookings Papers on Economic Activity*, 1980(2), pp. 332-37.

'Comment' on 'The Determination of Long-Term Interest Rates: Implications for Fiscal and Monetary Policies' by Benjamin M. FRIEDMAN, *Journal of Money, Credit and Banking*, vol. 12(2), May 1980, Special Issue, pp. 370-3.

'Utility Analysis and Aggregate Consumption Functions: An Attempt at Integration' (with Richard BRUMBERG); in MODIGLIANI, vol. 2, pp. 128-97.

'The Structure of Financial Markets and the Monetary Mechanism' (with Lucas D. PAPADEMOS), in *Controlling Monetary Aggregates*, vol. III, Conference Series no. 23. Federal Reserve Bank of Boston, 1980, pp. 111-155.

The Collected Papers of Franco Modigliani: vol. 1, *Essays in Macroeconomics*; vol. 2, *The Life Cycle Hypothesis of Saving*; vol. 3, *The Theory of Finance and Other Essays* (edited by Andrew ABEL). Cambridge, Mass.: M.I.T. Press, 1980.

'The Trade-Off Between Real Wages and Employment in an Open Economy (Belgium)' (with Jacques H. DRÈZE), *European Economic Review*, vol. 15(1), January 1981, pp. 1-40.

'A New Look at the Monetary Mechanism', *Queen's University Discussion Paper*, no. 447, Kingston, Ontario, 1981.

'Comment' on 'Scale of Macro-Econometric Models and Accuracy of Forecasting' by Gary FROMM and Lawrence R. KLEIN, in Jan KMENTA and James B. RAMSEY (eds.), *Large-Scale Macro-Econometric Models*. Amsterdam: North-Holland, 1981, pp. 393-4.

'Comment' on 'Where Have All the Flowers Gone? Economic Growth in the 1960s' by Robert M. SOLOW, in Joseph A. PECHMAN and Norman J. SIMLER (eds.), *Economics in the Public Service. Papers in Honor of Walter W. Heller*. New York: W. W. Norton, 1981, pp. 75-83.

'Inflation and the Stock Market' (with Richard A. COHN), in J. Anthony BOECKH and Richard T. COGHLAN (eds.), *The Stock Market and Inflation*. Homewood, Ill.: Dow Jones-Irwin, 1982, pp. 97-118.

'Statement'. Hearings before the Subcommittee on Housing and Community Development of the Committee on Banking, Finance and Urban Affairs, 97th Congress, Second Session, *To Expand and Reorganize the Federal Home Loan Mortgage Corporation*, 21st April, 1982. Washington: U.S. Government Printing Office, 1982, pp. 319-29.

'Debt, Dividend Policy, Taxes, Inflation and Market Valuation', *Journal of Finance*, vol. 37(2), May 1982, pp. 255-73; see also '—: Erratum', *Journal of Finance*, vol. 38(3), June 1983, pp. 1041-2.

'Inflation-Induced Errors in Stock Market Values – United States' in Patrick GRADY (ed.), *Peering Under the Inflationary Veil*. Toronto: Economic Council of Canada, 1982, pp. 17-9.

'Comment' on 'The Non-adjustment of Nominal Interest Rates: A Study of the Fisher Effect' by Lawrence H. SUMMERS, in James TOBIN (ed.), *Macroeconomics, Prices and Quantities. Essays in Memory of Arthur M. Okun*. Washington: The Brookings Institution, 1983, pp. 241-4.

Joint Editor (with Richard HEMMING), *The Determinants of National Saving and Wealth*. Proceedings of a Conference held by the International Economic Association at Bergamo, Italy, 9th-14th June 1980. London: Macmillan Press Ltd., 1983.

'Introduction', same volume as above, pp. xi-xv.

'Determinants of Private Saving with Special Reference to the Role of Social Security – Cross-country Tests' (with Arlie STERLING), same volume as above, pp. 24-55.

'Inflation, financial and fiscal structure, and the monetary mechanism' (with Lucas D. PAPADEMOS), *European Economic Review*, vol. 21, nos. 1-2, March/April 1983, pp. 203-50.

'Discussion' of 'Investment versus Savings Incentives: The Size of the Bang for the Buck and the Potential for Self-Financing Business Tax Cuts' by Alan J. AUERBACH and Laurence J. KOTLIKOFF, in Laurence H. MAYER (ed.), *The Economic Consequences of Governement Deficits*. Boston: Kluwer-Nijhoff, 1983, pp. 151-4.

'Sviluppi e prospettive del sistema finanziario italiano. Il ruolo delle istituzioni, l'inflazione e il deficit pubblico', in *Borsa Valori, Impieghi Finanziari e Risparmio*. Milan: Borsa Valori, 1983, pp. 49-58.

'Government Deficits, Inflation and Future Generations', in David W. CONKLIN and Thomas J. COURCHENE (eds.), *Deficits: How Big and How Bad?*, Ontario Economic Council Special Report. Toronto: Ontario Economic Council, 1983, pp. 55-77.

'—: Erratum', *Journal of Finance*, vol. 38(3), June 1983, pp. 1041-2; correction to 'Debt, Dividend Policy, Taxes Inflation, and Market Valuation', *Journal of Finance*, vol. 37(2), May 1982, pp. 255-73.

'Reply' (with Richard A. COHN) to 'Interesse reale e interesse finanziario' by Augusto GRAZIANI, *Studi Economici*, vol. 20, 1983, pp. 121-3.

'Comment' of 'Retirement Annuity Design in an Inflationary Climate' by Zvi BODIE and James E. PESANDO, in Zvi BODIE and John B. SHOVEN (eds.), *Financial Aspects of the United States Pension System*. Chicago: The University of Chicago Press, 1983, pp. 316-22.

'Comment' on 'Opportunities and Implications of a Return to Fixed Exchange Rates: Is the Gold Standard an Answer?' by Professors YEAGER and SCHWARTZ, in Tamir AGMON, Robert G. HAWKINS and Richard M. LEVICH (eds.), *The Future of the International Monetary System*. Lexington, Mass.: Lexington Books, 1984.

'I problemi di indicizzazione nel finanziamento dell'edilizia abitativa: Il progetto MIT di mutuo ipotecario per i giovani', *Bancaria*, no. 8, July 1984, pp. 607-17.

'Comment' on 'Changes in the Balance Sheet of the U.S. Manufacturing Sector' by John H. CICCOLO JR. and C. F. BAUM, in BENJAMIN M. FRIEDMAN (ed.), *Corporate Capital Structures in the United States*. Chicago: The University of Chicago Press, 1985, pp. 109-15.

'The Public Spending Deficit and the Over-Valued Dollar', in Gianni ZANDANO (ed.), *Thema: The International Monetary System and Economic Recovery*. Torino: Istituto Bancario San Paolo, 1985, pp. 99-102.

'Inflation and Corporate Finance Management' (with Richard A. COHN), in Edward I. ALTMAN and Marti G. SUBRAHMANYAM (eds.), *Recent Advances in Corporate Finance.* Chicago: Richard D. Irwing, 1985, pp. 341-70.

'Past Experience with Deindexation. Italy', in John WILLIAMSON (ed.), *Inflation and Indexation: Argentina, Brazil, and Israel.* Cambridge, Mass.: MIT Press, 1985, Chapter 5, pp. 118-21.

'The Impact of Fiscal Policy and Inflation on National Saving: the Italian Case' (with Tullio JAPPELLI and Marco PAGANO), *Banca Nazionale del Lavoro Quarterly Review*, no. 153, June 1985, pp. 91-126.

4. Collected Papers

Published in 1980 by The MIT Press, Cambridge, Mass. and London, England

Editor of the Series: Andrew Abel

VOLUME 1. ESSAYS IN MACROECONOMICS

Part I. The Monetary Mechanism

1. pp. 3-22 'The Monetarist Controversy or, Should We Forsake Stabilization Policies?', *American Economic Review* 6, vol. 67(2), March 1977, pp. 1-19.

2. pp. 23-68 'Liquidity Preference and the Theory of Interest and Money', *Econometrica*, vol. 12(1), January 1944, pp. 45-88. Plus "Postscript" of the paper in *The Critics of Keynesian Economics*, edited by Henry HAZLITT. Princeton: D. Van Nostrand, 1960, pp. 183-4.

3. pp. 69-97 'The Monetary Mechanism and its Interaction with Real Phenomena', *Review of Economics and Statistics*, vol. 45(1), Part II, Supplement, February 1963, pp. 79-107.

4. pp. 98-113 'Liquidity Preference', *International Encyclopedia of the Social Sciences*, edited by David L. SILLS, vol. 9. New York: Crowell-Collier and Macmillan, 1968, pp. 394-409.

5. pp. 114-41 'The Channels of Monetary Policy in the Federal Reserve-MIT-University of Pennsylvania Econometric Model of the United States', in George A. RENTON (ed.), *Modelling the Economy*, based on papers presented at the Social Science Research Council's Conference on Econometric Modelling, July 1972. London: Heinemann Educational Books, 1975, pp. 240-67.

6. pp. 142-67 'Impacts of Fiscal Actions on Aggregate Income and the Monetarist Controversy: Theory and Evidence' (with Albert K. ANDO, and with the assistance of J. GIANGRANDE), in Jerome L. STEIN (ed.), *Monetarism*, vol. 1. Amsterdam: North-Holland 1976, pp. 17-42.

Part II. The Demand and Supply of Money and Other Deposits

7. pp. 171-223 'Central Bank Policy, the Money Supply, and the Short-Term Rate of Interest' (with Robert RASCHE and J. Phillip COOPER), *Journal of Money, Credit and Banking*, vol. 2(2), May 1970, pp. 166-218.

8. pp. 224-64 'The Dynamics of Portfolio Adjustment and the Flow

of Savings through Financial Intermediaries', in Edward M. GRAM-LICH and Dwight M. JAFFEE (eds.), *Savings Deposits, Mortgages, and Housing: Studies for the Federal Reserve-MIT-Penn Econometric Model*. Lexington, Mass.: Lexington Books, 1972, pp. 63-102.

Part III. The Term Structure of Interest Rates

9. pp. 267-86 'Innovations in Interest Rate Policy' (with Richard SUTCH), *American Economic Review*, vol. 56(2), May 1966, pp. 178-97. Paper presented at the 78th annual Meeting of the American Economic Association, 28th-30th, December 1965.

10. pp. 287-308 'Debt Management and the Term Structure of Interest Rates: An Empirical Analysis of Recent Experience' (with Richard SUTCH), *Journal of Political Economy*, vol. 75(4), Part 2, Supplement, August 1967, pp. 569-89. Paper presented at the Conference of University Professors, The American Bankers Association, 19th September 1966.

11. pp. 309-41 'Inflation, Rational Expectations and the Term Structure of Interest Rates' (with Robert J. SHILLER), *Economica*, vol. 40 (157), February 1973, pp. 12-43.

Part IV. The Determinants of Investment

12. pp. 345-75 'On the Role of Expectations of Price and Technological Change in an Investment Function (with Albert K. ANDO, Robert RASCHE, and Stephen J. TURNOVSKY), *International Economic Review*, vol. 15(2), June 1974, pp. 384-414.

Part V. The Determinants of Wages and Prices

13. pp. 379-99 'A Generalization of the Phillips Curve for a Developing Country' (with Ezio TARANTELLI), *Review of Economic Studies*, vol. 40(2), April 1973, no. 122, pp. 203-23.

14. pp. 400-18 'New Developments on the Oligopoly Front', *Journal of Political Economy*, vol. 66(3), June 1958, pp. 215-33.

15. pp. 419-41 'Targets for Monetary Policy in the Coming Year' (with Lucas D. PAPADEMOS), *Brookings Papers on Economic Activity* 1975(1), pp. 141-63.

VOLUME 2. THE LIFE CYCLE HYPOTHESIS OF SAVING

Part I. Antecedent and Overview

1. pp. 3-40 'Fluctuations in the Saving-Income Ratio: A Problem in Economic Forecasting', *Studies in Income and Wealth*, vol. 11. New

York: National Bureau of Economic Research, 1949. Paper presented at the Conference on Research in Income and Wealth; reprinted only Sections I-VII (pp. 371-402) and XIII (pp. 427-31).

2. pp. 41-75 'The life cycle hypothesis of saving twenty years later', in Michael PARKIN and A. Robert NOBAY (eds.) *Contemporary Issues in Economics*. Manchester: Manchester University Press, 1975, pp. 2-36.

Part II. The Theory

3. pp. 79-127 'Utility Analysis and the Consumption Function: An Interpretation of Cross-Section Data' (with Richard BRUMBERG), in Kenneth K. KURIHARA (ed.), *Post-Keynesian Economics*. New Brunswick, N.J.: Rutgers University Press, 1954, pp. 388-436.

4. pp. 128-97 'Utility Analysis and Aggregate Consumption Functions: An Attempt at Integration' (with Richard BRUMBERG).

5. pp. 198-226 'Consumption Decisions under Uncertainty' (with Jacques H. DRÈZE), *Journal of Economic Theory*, vol. 5(8), December 1972, pp. 308-35.

Part III. Empirical Verifications

6. pp. 229-74 'The "Permanent Income" and the "Life Cycle" Hypothesis of Saving Behavior: Comparison and Tests' (with Albert K. ANDO), *Consumption and Saving*, vol. 2, Wharton School of Finance and Commerce. Philadelphia: University of Pennsylvania Press, 1960; reprinted only Sections II, 1-11 (pp. 74-108) and III, 4 (pp. 138-47).

7. pp. 275-304 'The "Life Cycle" Hypothesis of Saving: Aggregate Implications and Tests' (with Albert K. ANDO), *American Economic Review*, vol. 53(1), Part 1, March 1963, pp. 55-84.

8. pp. 305-22 'The Consumption Function in a Developing Economy and the Italian Experience' (with Ezio TARANTELLI), *American Economic Review*, vol. 65(5), December 1975, pp. 825-42.

9. pp. 323-81 'The Life Cycle Hypothesis of Saving, the Demand for Wealth and the Supply of Capital', *Social Research*, vol. 33(2), Summer 1966, pp. 160-217.

10. pp. 382-412 'The Life Cycle Hypothesis of Saving and Inter-country Differences in the Saving Ratio', in Walter A. ELTIS, Maurice FG. SCOTT and James N. WOLFE (eds.), *Induction, Growth and Trade: Essays in Honour of Sir Roy Harrod*. Oxford: Clarendon Press, 1970, pp. 197-225.

Part IV. Policy Applications

11. pp. 415-41 'Long-Run Implications of Alternative Fiscal Policies and the Burden of the National Debt', *Economic Journal*, vol. 71(284), December 1961, pp. 730-56.

12. pp. 442-517 'Monetary Policy and Consumption: Linkages via Interest Rate and Wealth Effects in the FMP Model', in *Consumer Spending and Monetary Policy: The Linkages*, Monetary Conference Series no. 5. Federal Reserve Bank of Boston, 1971, pp. 9-84.

VOLUME 3. THE THEORY OF FINANCE AND OTHER ESSAYS

Part I. Essays in the Theory of Finance

1. pp. 3-39 'The Cost of Capital, Corporation Finance and the Theory of Investment' (with Merton H. MILLER), *American Economic Review*, vol. 48(3), June 1958, pp. 261-97.

2. pp. 40-62 'Dividend Policy, Growth and the Valuation of Shares,' (with Merton H. MILLER), *Journal of Business*, vol. 34(4), October 1961, pp. 411-33.

3. pp. 63-73 'Corporate Income Taxes and the Cost of Capital: A Correction' (with Merton H. MILLER), *American Economic Review*, vol. 53(3), June 1963, pp. 433-43.

4. pp. 74-96 'A Theory and Test of Credit Rationing' (with Dwight M. JAFFEE), *American Economic Review*, vol. 59(5), December 1969, pp. 850-72.

5. pp. 97-123 'Some Economic Implications of the Indexing of Financial Assets with Special Reference to Mortgages', in Mario MONTI (ed.), *The New Inflation and Monetary Policy*. London: Macmillan, 1976 pp. 90-116.

Part II. Stabilization Policies

6. pp. 127-71 'Inflation, Balance of Payments Deficit and their Cure through Monetary Policy: The Italian Example' (with Giorgio LA MALFA), *Banca Nazionale del Lavoro Quarterly Review*, no. 80, March 1967, pp. 3-47.

7. pp. 172-85 'The 1974 Report of the President's Council of Economic Advisers: A Critique of Past and Prospective Policies', *American Economic Review*, vol. 64(4), September 1974, pp. 544-57.

8. pp. 186-219 'Monetary Policy for the Coming Quarters: The Conflicting Views' (with Lucas D. PAPADEMOS), *New England Economic Review*, March/April 1976, pp. 2-35.

9. pp. 220-59 'The Management of an Open Economy with "100% Plus" Wage Indexation (with Tommaso PADOA-SCHIOPPA), *Essays in International Finance*, no. 130. International Finance Section, Department of Economics. Princeton: Princeton University Press, December 1978, pp. 1-39.

Part III. Essays in International Finance

10. pp. 263-77 'A Suggestion for Solving the International Liquidity Problem' (with Peter KENEN), *Banca Nazionale del Lavoro Quarterly Review*, no. 76, March 1966, pp. 3-17.

11. pp. 278-304 'The Reform of the International Payments System' (with Hossein ASKARI), *Essays in International Finance*, no. 89. International Finance Section, Department of Economics. Princeton: Princeton University Press, September 1971, pp. 3-28.

12. pp. 305-20 'International Capital Movements, Fixed Parities, and Monetary and Fiscal Policies', in Jagdish BHAGWATI and Richard S. ECKAUS (eds.), *Development and Planning: Essays in Honor of Paul Rosenstein-Rodan*. London: George Allen & Unwin, Ltd., 1972, pp. 239-53.

13. pp. 321-37 'The International Transfer of Capital and the Propagation of Domestic Disturbances under Alternative Payment Systems' (with Hossein ASKARI), *Banca Nazionale del Lavoro Quarterly Review*, no. 107, December 1973, pp. 3-19.

14. pp. 338-43 'Balance of Payments Implications of the Oil Crisis and How to Handle Them through International Cooperation', in *Economic Report of the President*. Prepared statement for Hearings before the Joint Economic Committee, 93rd Congress, Second Session, 19th-22nd February 1974. Washington: U.S. Government Printing Office, 1974, pp. 650-5.

Part IV. The Role of Expectations and Plans in Economic Behavior

15. pp. 347-67 'Production Planning over Time and the Nature of the Expectation and Planning Horizon' (with Franz E. HOHN), *Econometrica*, vol. 23(1), January 1955, pp. 46-66.

16. pp. 368-425 *The Role of Anticipations and Plans in Economic Behavior and Their Use in Economic Analysis and Forecasting* (with Kalman J. COHEN), Studies in Business Expectations and Planning, no. 4. Bureau of Economic and Business Research. Urbana, Ill.: University of Illinois Press, January 1961; reprinted only Introduction (pp. 9-11) and Sections I, A-B (pp. 14-42), II, A (pp. 81-96); and also Bibliography (pp. 158-66).

17. pp. 426-57 'Forecasting Uses of Anticipatory Data on Investment and Sales' (with Herbert M. WEINGARTNER), *Quarterly Journal of Economics*, vol. 72(1), February 1958, pp. 23-54.

Part V. Miscellaneus

18. pp. 461-74 'The Predictability of Social Events' (with Emile GRUNBERG), *Journal of Political Economy*, vol. 62(6), December 1954, pp. 465-78.

REFERENCES

Ando Albert K., 'Some Aspects of Stabilization Policies, the Monetarist Controversy and the MPS Model', *International Economic Review*, vol. 15(3), October 1974, pp. 541-71.

Ando Albert K. and Modigliani Franco, 'The "Life Cycle" Hypothesis of Saving: Aggregate Implications and Tests', *American Economic Review*, vol. 53(1), Part 1, March 1963, pp. 55-84; reprinted in Modigliani, vol. 2, pp. 275-304.

Ando Albert K. and Modigliani Franco, 'Some Reflections on Describing Structures of Financial Sectors', (Appendix with Shell Karl), in Fromm Gary and Klein Lawrence R. (eds.), *The Brookings Model: Perspective and Recent Developments*, pp. 524-63.

Bach George L. and Stephenson James B., 'Inflation and the Redistribution of Wealth', *Review of Economics and Statistics*, vol. 56(1), February 1974, pp. 1-14.

Bain Joe S., *Barriers to New Competition*. Cambridge, Mass.: Harvard University Press, 1956.

Barro Robert J., 'Are Government Bonds Net Wealth?', *Journal of Political Economy*, vol. 82(6), November-December 1974, pp. 1095-1118.

Barro Robert J., *The Impact of Social Security and Private Saving. Evidence from the U.S. Time Series*. Washington: American Enterprise Institute, 1978.

Barro Robert J. and Macdonald Glenn M. T., 'Social Security and Consumer Spending in an International Cross Section, *Journal Public Economics*, vol. 11(3), June 1979, pp. 275-90.

Baumol William L., 'The Transactions Demand for Cash: An Inventory Theoretic Approach', *Quarterly Journal of Economics*, vol. 66(4), November 1952, pp. 545-56.

Boskin Michael J., 'Social Security and Retirement Decisions', *Economic Inquiry*, vol. 15(1), January 1977, pp. 1-25.

Boskin Michael J. and Hurd Michael D., 'The Effect of Social Security on Early Retirement', *Journal of Public Economics*, vol. 10(3), December 1978, pp. 361-378.

Brady Dorothy S. and Friedman Rose D., 'Savings and the Income Distribution', in *Studies in Income and Wealth*, vol. 10, pp. 250-97.

Brainard William C., 'Financial Intermediaries and a Theory of Monetary Control', *Yale Economic Essais*, vol. 4(1), Fall 1964, pp. 431-82; reprinted in Hester Donald D. and Tobin James (eds.),

Financial Markets and Economic Activity, Cowles Foundation Monograph 21, pp. 94-141.

BRONFENBRENNER Martin R., *Is the Business Cycle Obsolete?*. New York: Wiley-Interscience, 1969.

BRUNNER Karl and MELTZER Allan H., 'The Meaning of Monetary Indicators', in HORWICH George (ed.), *Monetary Process and Policy: A Symposium*, pp. 187-217.

BURNS Arthur F., 'Progress Towards Economic Stability', *American Economic Review*, vol. 50(1), March 1960, pp. 1-19.

CAGAN Phillip D., 'Financial Developments and the Erosion of Monetary Controls', in FELLNER William (ed.), *Contemporary Economic Problems*, pp. 117-51.

CARSON Deane (ed.), *Banking and Monetary Studies*. Homewood, Ill.: Richard Irwin, 1963.

Consumer Spending and Monetary Policy: The Linkages. Proceedings of a Monetary Conference held at Nantucket Island, Mass., June 1971. Conference Series no. 5. Federal Reserve Bank of Boston, 1971.

DEATON Angus, 'Involuntary Saving through Unanticipated Inflation', *American Economic Review*, vol. 67(5), December 1977, pp. 899-910.

DIAMOND Peter and HAUSMAN Jerry, 'Individual Savings Behavior', Paper prepared for the U.S. National Commission on Social Security, May 1980.

DOLDE Walter C. Jr. and TOBIN James, 'Mandatory Retirement Saving and Capital Formation', in MODIGLIANI Franco and HEMMING Richard (eds.), *The Determinants of National Saving and Wealth*, pp. 56-88.

DRÈZE Jacques H. and MODIGLIANI Franco, 'Consumption Decisions under Uncertainty', *Journal of Economic Theory*, vol. 5(3), December 1972, pp. 308-36; reprinted in MODIGLIANI, vol. 2, pp. 198-226.

DUESENBERRY James S., *Income, Saving, and the Theory of Consumer Behavior*. Cambridge, Mass.: Harvard University Press, 1949.

ELTIS Walter A., SCOTT Maurice Fg. and WOLFE James N. (eds.), *Induction, Growth and Trade: Essays in Honour of Sir Roy Harrod*. Oxford: Clarendon Press, 1970.

FELDSTEIN Martin, 'Social Security, Induced Retirement, and Aggregate Capital Accumulation, *Journal of Political Economy*, vol. 82(5), September-October 1974, pp. 905-26.

FELDSTEIN Martin, 'Social Security and Private Savings: International Evidence in an Extended Life-Cycle Model', in FELDSTEIN Martin and INMAN Robert (eds.), *The Economics of Public Services*, pp. 174-205.

FELDSTEIN Martin and INMAN Robert (eds.), *The Economics of Public Services*. London: Macmillan, 1977.

FELDSTEIN Martin and PELLECHIO Anthony J., 'Social Security and Household Wealth Accumulation: New Microeconometric Evidence, *Review of Economics and Statistics*, vol. 61(3), August 1979, pp. 261-368.

FELLNER William (ed.), *Contemporary Economic Problems*. Washington: American Enterprise Institute, 1979.

FISCHER Stanley, 'Long-Term Contracts, Rational Expectations and the Optimal Money Supply Rule, *Journal of Political Economy*, vol. 85(1), February 1977, pp. 191-206.

FISCHER Stanley and HUIZINGA John, 'Inflation, Unemployment, and Public Opinion Polls', *Journal of Money, Credit and Banking*, vol. 14(1), February 1982, pp. 1-19.

FISHER Irving, 'Stabilizing the Dollar in Purchasing Power', in FRIEDMAN Elisha (ed.), *American Problems of Reconstruction*, pp. 361-90.

FISHER Irving, *Stabilizing the Dollar*. New York: Macmillan, 1920.

FISHER Irving, *The Money Illusion*. New York: Adelphy Company, 1928 (also London: Allen & Unwin, 1928).

FRIEDMAN Benjamin M. 'Targets, Instruments and Indicators of Monetary Policy', *Journal of Monetary Economics*, vol. 1(4), October 1975, pp. 443-74.

FRIEDMAN Benjamin M. 'The Inefficiency of Short-Run Monetary Aggregates for Monetary Policy', *Brookings Papers on Economic Activity*, 1977 (2), pp. 293-335.

FRIEDMAN Elisha (ed.), *American Problems of Reconstruction*. New York: E. P. Dutton & Co., 1918.

FRIEDMAN Milton, 'The Quantity Theory of Money: A Restatement', in FRIEDMAN Milton (ed.), *Studies in the Quantity Theory of Money*, 1956, pp. 3-21.

FRIEDMAN Milton (ed.), *Studies in the Quantity Theory of Money*. Chicago: University of Chicago Press, 1956.

FRIEDMAN Milton, *A Theory of the Consumption Function*. Princeton: Princeton University Press, 1957.

FRIEDMAN Milton, 'The Demand for Money: Some Theoretical and Empirical Results', *Journal of Political Economy*, vol. 67(4), August 1959, pp. 327-51.

FRIEDMAN Milton, 'The Role of Monetary Policy', *American Economic Review*, vol. 58(1), March 1968, pp. 1-17.

FRIEDMAN Milton, 'The Optimum Quantity of Money', in FRIEDMAN Milton, *The Optimum Quantity of Money and Other Essays*, pp. 1-50.

FRIEDMAN Milton B., *The Optimum Quantity of Money and Other Essays*. Chicago: Aldine Press, 1969 (also London: Macmillan, 1969).

FRIEDMAN Milton 'A Theoretical Framework for Monetary Analysis', *Journal of Political Economy*, vol. 78(2), March-April 1970, pp. 193-238; reprinted in GORDON Robert J. (ed.), *Milton Friedman's Monetary Framework: A Debate with His Critics*, pp. 1-62.

FRIEDMAN Milton and SCHWARTZ Anna J., *A Monetary History of the United States 1867-1960*. Princeton: Princeton University Press, 1963.

FROMM Gary and KLEIN Lawrence R. (eds.), *The Brookings Model: Perspective and Recent Developments*. Amsterdam: North Holland, 1975.

FURSTENBERG George M. von (ed.), *Social Security versus Private Saving*. Cambridge, Mass.: Ballinger Press, 1979.

GORDON Robert J. (ed.), *Milton Friedman's Monetary Framework: A Debate with His Critics*. Chicago: University of Chicago Press, 1974.

GORDON Roger H., WISE Donald E. and BLINDER Alan S., *An Empirical Study of the Effects of Pensions on the Saving and Labor Supply Decisions of Older Men*, Study prepared for the U.S. Labor Department, May 1980.

GRUNBERG Emile and MODIGLIANI Franco, 'The Predictability of Social Events', *Journal of Political Economy*, vol. 62(6), December 1954, pp. 465-78; reprinted in MODIGLIANI, vol. 3, pp. 461-74.

GURLEY John G. and SHAW Edward S., *Money in a Theory of Finance* (with a mathematical Appendix by ENTHOVEN Alan C.). Washington: The Brookings Institution, 1960.

HAANES-OLSEN Leif, 'Earnings-Replacement Rate of Old Age Benefits, 1965-75, Selected Countries', *Social Security Bulletin*, vol. 41(1), January 1978, pp. 3-14.

HESTER Donald D. and TOBIN James (eds.), *Financial Markets and Economic Activity*, Cowles Foundation Monograph 21. New York: John Wiley and Sons, 1967.

HICKS John R., 'Mr. Keynes and the "Classics"; A Suggested Interpretation', *Econometrica*, vol. 5(2), April 1937, pp. 147-59; reprinted in HICKS John R., *Critical Essays in Monetary Theory*, pp. 126-42.

HICKS John R., *Critical Essays on Monetary Theory*. Oxford: Clarendon Press, 1967.

HORWICH George (ed.), *Monetary Process and Policy: A Symposium*. Homewood, Ill.: Richard Irwing, 1967.

KAHN Richard F., *The Making of Keynes' General Theory*, Raffaele Mattioli Lectures. Cambridge: Cambridge University Press, 1984.

KALDOR Nicholas, *Essays on Value and Distribution*. Collected Economic Essays, vol. 1. London: Duckworth, 1960.

KATONA George, *Essays on Behavioral Economics* (with a contribution by MORGAN James N.). Institute for Social Research, University of Michigan. Ann Arbor, Mich.: Survey Research Center, 1980.

KEYNES John Maynard, *The General Theory of Employment, Interest and Money*. London: Macmillan, 1936.

KOPITS George F. and GOTUR Padma C., 'The Influence of Social Security on Household Savings: A Cross-Country Investigation', *International Monetary Fund*, Staff Paper no. 27, March 1980, pp. 161-90.

KOTLIKOFF Laurence J., 'Testing the Theory of Social Security and Life Cycle Accumulation', *American Economic Review*, vol. 69(3), June 1979, pp. 396-410.

KOTLIKOFF Laurence J. and SUMMERS Lawrence H., *The Role of Intergenerational Transfers in Aggregate Capital Accumulation*, Working Paper No. 445. New York: National Bureau of Economic Research, February 1980; reprinted in *Journal of Political Economy*, vol. 89(4), August 1981, pp. 706-31.

KURIHARA Kenneth K. (ed.), *Post Keynesian Economics*. New Brunswick, N.J.: Rutgers University Press, 1954.

KUZNETS Simon S., *National Income: A Summary of Findings*. New York: National Bureau of Economic Research, 1946.

LEFF Nathaniel H., 'Dependency Rates and Savings Rates', *American Economic Review*, vol 59(5). December 1969, pp. 886-96.

LEIMER Dean R. and LESNOY Selig D., 'Social Security and Private Saving: A Re-examination of the Time Series Evidence Using Alternative Social Security Wealth Variables', Paper presented at the 1980 American Economic Association Meeting, Denver, Col., 6th September 1980; see also 'Social Security and Private Saving: New Time – Series Evidence', *Journal of Political Economy*, June 1982, vol. 90(4), pp. 605-29.

LESSARD Donald and MODIGLIANI Franco, 'Inflation and the Housing Market: Problems and Potential Solutions, in Modigliani Franco and Lessard Donald *New Mortgage Designs for Stable Housing in an Inflationary Environment*, pp. 13-45.

LIPSEY Richard G., 'The Relation between Unemployment and the Rate of Change of Money Wage Rates in the United Kingdom, 1861-1957: A Further Analysis', *Economica*, vol. 27(105), February 1960, pp. 1-31.

LUCAS Robert E. Jr., 'Expectations and the Neutrality of Money', *Journal of Economic Theory*, vol. 4(2), April 1972, pp. 103-24.

MAYER Thomas, 'The Structure of Monetarism', *Kredit und Kapital*, vol. 8(2), 1975, pp. 191-215 and vol. 8(3), 1975, pp. 293-313; reprinted in Thomas MAYER, *The Structure of Monetarism*. New York-London: W. W. Norton and Company, 1978, pp. 1-46.

MIKESSEL Raymond M. and ZINSER James E., 'The Nature of the Savings Function in Developing Countries: A Survey of the Theoretical and Empirical Literature, *Journal of Economic Literature*, vol. 11(1), March 1973, pp. 1-26.

MILLER Merton H. and MODIGLIANI Franco, 'Dividend Policy, Growth and the Valuation of Shares', *Journal of Business*', vol. 34(4), October 1961, pp. 411-33; reprinted in MODIGLIANI, vol. 3, pp. 40-62.

MILLER Merton H. and ORR Daniel, 'A Model of the Demand for Money by Firms', *Quarterly Journal of Economics*, vol. 80(3), August 1966, pp. 413-35.

MODIGLIANI Franco, 'Liquidity Preference and the Theory of Interest and Money', *Econometrica*, vol. 12(1), January 1944, pp. 45-88; reprinted in MODIGLIANI, vol. 1, pp. 23-66.

MODIGLIANI Franco, 'Fluctuations in the Saving-Income Ratio: A Problem in Economic Forecasting', Paper prepared in connection with a Research Project of the Institute of World Affairs and presented at the Conference on Research in Income and Wealth; in *Studies in Income and Wealth*, vol. 11, pp. 371-443; Sections I-VII (pp. 371-402) and XIII (pp. 427-31) reprinted in MODIGLIANI, vol. 2, pp. 3-40.

REFERENCES

Modigliani Franco, 'New Developments on the Oligopoly Front', *Journal of Political Economy*, vol. 66(3), June 1958, pp. 215-33; reprinted in Modigliani, vol. 1, pp. 400-18.

Modigliani Franco, 'Long-Run Implications of Alternative Fiscal Policies and the Burden of National Debt', *Economic Journal*, vol. 71 (284), December 1961, pp. 730-56; reprinted in Modigliani, vol. 2, pp. 415-41.

Modigliani Franco, 'The Monetary Mechanism and its Interaction with Real Phenomena', *Review of Economics and Statistics*, vol. 45(1), Part 2, Supplement, February 1963, pp. 79-107; reprinted in Modigliani, vol. 1, pp. 69-97.

Modigliani Franco, 'The Life Cycle Hypothesis of Saving and Inter-country Differences in the Saving Ratio', in Eltis Walter A., Scott Maurice Fg. and Wolfe James N. (eds.), *Induction, Growth and Trade: Essays in Honour of Sir Roy Harrod*, pp. 197-226; reprinted in Modigliani, vol. 2, pp. 382-412.

Modigliani Franco, 'Monetary Policy and Consumption: Linkages via Interest Rate and Wealth Effects in the FMP Model', in *Consumer Spending and Monetary Policy: The Linkages*, pp. 9-84; reprinted in Modigliani, vol. 2, pp. 442-517.

Modigliani Franco, 'Channels of Monetary Policy in the Federal Reserve – MIT – University of Pennsylvania Econometric Model of the United States', based on Papers presented at the Social Science Research Council's Conference on Economic Modelling, July 1972, in Renton George A. (ed.), *Modelling the Economy*, pp. 240-67; reprinted in Modigliani, vol. 1, pp. 114-41.

Modigliani Franco, 'The life cycle hypothesis of saving twenty years later', in Parkin Michael and Nobay Robert A. (eds.), *Contemporary Issues in Economics*, 1975, pp. 2-36; reprinted in Modigliani, vol. 2, pp. 41-75.

Modigliani Franco, 'The Monetarist Controversy or, Should We Forsake Stabilization Policies?', Presidential Address delivered at the American Economic Association, 17th September 1976, *American Economic Review*, vol. 67(2), March 1977, pp. 1-19; reprinted in Modigliani, vol. 1, pp. 3-21.

Modigliani Franco, *The Life Cycle Hypothesis of Saving*, in Modigliani, vol. 2, edited by Andrew Abel. Cambridge, Mass.: MIT Press, 1980.

Modigliani Franco and Ando Albert K., 'The Relative Stability of Monetary Velocity and the Investment Multiplier', *American Economic Review*, vol. 55(4), September 1965, pp. 693-728.

MODIGLIANI Franco and BRUMBERG Richard, 'Utility Analysis and the Consumption Function: An Interpretation of Cross-Section Data', in KURIHARA Kenneth K. (ed.), *Post Keynesian Economics*, pp. 388-436; reprinted in MODIGLIANI, vol. 2, pp. 79-127.

MODIGLIANI Franco and BRUMBERG Richard, 'Utility Analysis and Aggregate Consumption Functions: An Attempt at Integration', in MODIGLIANI, vol. 2, pp. 128-97.

MODIGLIANI Franco and COHN Richard A., 'Inflation, Rational Valuation and the Market', *Financial Analysts Journal*, vol. 35(2), March-April 1979, pp. 24-44.

MODIGLIANI Franco and HEMMING Richard (eds.), *The Determinants of National Saving and Wealth*, Proceedings of a Conference held by the International Economic Association at Bergamo, Italy, 9th-14th June, 1980. London: Macmillan, 1983.

MODIGLIANI Franco and LESSARD Donald (eds.), *New Mortgage Designs for an Inflationary Environment*, Conference Series no. 14. Federal Reserve Bank of Boston, 1975.

MODIGLIANI Franco and MILLER Merton H., 'The Cost of Capital, Corporation Finance and the Theory of Investment', *American Economic Review*, vol. 48(3), June 1958, pp. 261-97; reprinted in MODIGLIANI, vol. 3, pp. 3-39.

MODIGLIANI Franco and PADOA-SCHIOPPA Tommaso, 'La politica economica in una economia con salari indicizzati al 100 o più', *Moneta e Credito*, vol. 30(117), March 1977, pp. 3-53; translated in 'The Management of an Open Economy with "100% Plus' Wage Indexation"', *Essays in International Finance*, no. 130, Princeton: Princeton University Press, December 1978, pp. 1-39; reprinted in MODIGLIANI, vol. 3, pp. 220-59.

MODIGLIANI Franco and PAPADEMOS Lucas D., 'Targets for Monetary Policy in the Coming Year', *Brookings Papers on Economic Activity*, 1975 (1), pp. 141-63; reprinted in MODIGLIANI, vol. 1, pp. 419-41.

MODIGLIANI Franco and PAPADEMOS Lucas D., 'Optimal Demand Policies against Stagflation'. *Weltwirtschaftliches Archiv*, vol. 114(4), December 1978, pp. 736-81.

MODIGLIANI Franco and POGUE Gerald A., 'An Introduction to Risk and Return: Concepts and Evidence', *Financial Analysts Journal* (Part I), vol. 30(2), March-April 1974, pp. 68-80; (Part II), vol. 30(3), May-June 1974, pp. 69-86.

MODIGLIANI Franco and STERLING Arlie, 'Determinants of Private Saving with Special Reference to the Role of Social Security –

REFERENCES

Cross-country Tests' in MODIGLIANI Franco and HEMMING Richard (eds.), *The Determinants of National Saving and Wealth*, pp. 24-55.

MODIGLIANI Franco and TARANTELLI Ezio, 'The Consumption Function in a Developing Economy and the Italian Experience', *American Economic Review*, vol. 65(5), December 1975, pp. 825-842; reprinted in MODIGLIANI, vol. 2, pp. 305-322.

MUTH John F., 'Rational Expectations and the Theory of Price Movements', *Econometrica*, vol. 29(3), July 1961, pp. 315-35.

New Mortgage Designs for an Inflationary Environment. Proceedings of a Conference held at Cambridge, Mass., January 1975. Conference Series no. 14. Federal Reserve Bank of Boston, 1975.

OKUN Arthur M., 'Efficient Disinflationary Policies', *American Economic Review*, vol. 68(2), May 1978, pp. 348-52.

ORGANISATION FOR ECONOMIC CO-OPERATION AND DEVELOPMENT (OECD), *Towards Full Employment and Price Stability.* A report to the OECD by a Group of independent experts (Paul McCracken, Guido Carli, Herbert Giersch, Attila Karaosmanoglu, Ryutaro Komiya, Assar Lindbeck, Robert Marjolin, Robin Matthews). Paris: OECD, June 1977.

PARKIN Michael and NOBAY A. Robert (eds.), *Contemporary Issues in Economics.* Manchester: Manchester University Press, 1975.

PASINETTI Luigi L., 'Rate of Profit and Income Distribution in Relation to the Rate of Economic Growth', *Review of Economic Studies*, vol. 29(81), October 1962, p. 267-79.

PECHMAN Joseph A., AARON Henry J. and TAUSSIG Michael K., *Social Security: Perspectives for Reform.* Washington: The Brookings Institution, 1968.

PHELPS Edmund S., 'Money-Wage Dynamics and Labor-Market Equilibrium', *Journal of Political Economy*, vol. 76(4, Part II), July/August 1968, pp. 678-711.

PHILLIPS Alban W., 'The Relation between Unemployment and the Rate of Change of Money Wage Rates in the United Kingdom, 1861-1957, *Economica*, vol. 25(100), November 1958, pp. 283-99.

POOLE William, 'Optimal Choice of Monetary Policy Instruments in a Simple Stochastic Macro Model', *Quarterly Journal of Economics*, vol. 84(2), May 1970, pp. 197-216.

RENTON George A. (ed.), *Modelling the Economy.* London: Heinemann Educational Books, 1975.

SARGENT Thomas J., 'A Classical Macroeconometric Model for the United States, *Journal of Political Economy*, vol. 84(2), April 1976, pp. 207-38.

SARGENT Thomas J., *Macroeconomic Theory*, New York: Academic Press, 1979.

SARGENT Thomas J. and WALLACE Neil, '"Rational" Expectations, the Optimal Monetary Instrument, and the Optimal Money Supply Rule', *Journal of Political Economy*, vol. 83(2), April 1975, pp. 241-54.

SILBER William L., 'Monetary Policy Effectiveness: The Case of a Positively Sloped IS Curve', *Journal of Finance*, vol. 26(5), December 1971, pp. 1077-82.

Studies in Income and Wealth, vol. 10. New York: National Bureau of Economic Research, 1947.

Studies in Income and Wealth, vol. 11. New York: National Bureau of Economic Research, 1949.

SUMMERS Robert, KRAVIS Irving B. and HESTON Alan, 'International Comparisons of Real Product and its Composition: 1950-1977', *Review of Income and Wealth*, Series 26(1), March 1980, pp. 19-66.

SYLOS LABINI Paolo, *Oligopolio e Progresso Tecnico*. Milan: Giuffrè, 1957; revised edition: *Oligopoly and Technical Progress*. Cambridge, Mass.: Harvard University Press, 1969.

TOBIN James, 'Commercial Banks as Creators of "Money"', in CARSON Deane (ed.), *Banking and Monetary Studies*, pp. 408-19; reprinted in HESTER Donald D. and TOBIN James (eds.), *Financial Markets and Economic Activity*, Cowles Foundation Monograph 21, pp. 1-11.

TOBIN James, 'A General Equilibrium Approach to Monetary Theory', *Journal of Money, Credit and Banking*, vol. 1(1), February 1969, pp. 15-29.

TOBIN James, *Essays in Economics, Volume 1, Macroeconomics*. Amsterdam: North-Holland, 1971.

TOBIN James and BRAINARD William C., 'Financial Intermediaries and the Effectiveness of Monetary Controls', *American Economic Review*, vol. 53(2), May 1963, pp. 383-400; reprinted in HESTER Donald D. and TOBIN James (eds.), *Financial Markets and Economic Activity*, Cowles Foundation Monograph 21, pp. 55-93.

VARIAN Hal R., 'Non-Walrasian Equilibria', *Econometrica*, vol. 45(3), April 1977, pp. 573-90.

INDEX

INDEX

RAFFAELE MATTIOLI LECTURES

SCIENTIFIC COMMITTEE (October 1977): Innocenzo Gasparini, Chairman; Paolo Baffi, Innocenzo Monti, Adalberto Predetti, Gaetano Stammati, Sergio Steve, Franco Venturi; Enrico Resti, Secretary.

ORGANIZATION: Banca Commerciale Italiana-Università Commerciale Luigi Bocconi · Milano.

ADMINISTRATION: Banca Commerciale Italiana · Milano.

RAFFAELE MATTIOLI FOUNDATION
Fondazione Raffaele Mattioli
per la Storia del Pensiero Economico

Published

RICHARD F. KAHN, *The Making of Keynes' General Theory* (1st Edition, May 1984).

To be published

CHARLES P. KINDLEBERGER, *Economic Laws and Economic History*.

PETER MATHIAS, *The Industrial Revolution in England*.

ERIK F. LUNDBERG, *The Development of Swedish and Keynesian Macroeconomic Theory and its Impact on Economic Policy*.

NICHOLAS KALDOR, *Causes of Growth and Stagnation in the World Economy*.

SHIGETO TSURU, *Institutional Economics Revisited*.

PUBLISHER: Cambridge University Press · Cambridge.

THE MONETARY MECHANISM*

Part A – Conventional Model

(1)	$M = k(r)\Upsilon$	Demand for money	M	$=$ Money demand
			r	$=$ Interest rate
			Υ	$=$ Nominal income
(2)	$\frac{S}{P} = S\left(\frac{\Upsilon}{P}\right)$	Saving function	S	$=$ Nominal saving
			P	$=$ Price level
(3)	$\frac{I}{P} = I(r)$	Investment function	I	$=$ Nominal rate of investment
(4)	$I = S$	Commodity market clearing		
(5)	$\Phi(P,\Upsilon) = 0$	"Price" equation		
(5a)	$\frac{\Upsilon}{P} = \bar{X}$	Perfect price flexibility	$\bar{X}$	$=$ "Full-employment" output
(5b)	$P = \bar{P}$	Absolute price rigidity	$\bar{P}$	$=$ "Received" price level
(6)	$M = M^s$	Money market clearing	M^s	$=$ Money supply
(P.1)	$M = \bar{M}$	Monetary policy equation	$\bar{M}$	$=$ Exogenously set money supply

Part B – Financial Structure

(1a)	$m = k(r)\Upsilon - M(-1)$		$m = M - M(-1)$ increment in money holdings	
(7)	$I = E + B$	Source and use of funds for firms' sector	E	$=$ Equity sources
			B	$=$ Credit sources
(8)	$B = \beta(r, \Upsilon)$ $\beta_r < 0$ $\beta_\Upsilon < 0$	Determinants of borrowing		
(9)	$S = m + da + E$	Source-and-use statement for household sector	da	$=$ Increase in deposit accounts balances
(10)	$m + da = L^b$	Source-and-use statement for banking sector	L^b	$=$ Flow of bank credit
(11)	$B = L^b$	Loan market clearing		
(P.2)	$L^b = \frac{\bar{M}\,\bar{B}^b}{\lambda} = \bar{L}^b$			

* Reproduced from p. 92.

THE MONETARY MECHANISM